AF541152

GWADAR

A Chinese Gibraltar

GWADAR

A CHINESE GIBRALTAR

Alok Bansal

PENTAGON PRESS LLP

First published in 2024 by
PENTAGON PRESS LLP
206, Peacock Lane, Shahpur Jat
New Delhi-110049, India
Contact: 011-26491568 • 011-26490600

Typeset in Adobe Garamond, 11.5 Point
Printed by Aegean Offset Printers, Greater Noida, U.P.

ISBN 978-81-951894-8-9

www.pentagonpress.in

Dedicated to my wife, Neema, for standing by me through all the ups and downs of life

Contents

Acknowledgement

This book is a logical outcome of my 18 yearlong research into the subject, which started with my quest for a doctoral degree and would not have fructified without the encouragement, cooperation and support of many well-wishers. I would like to express my deep gratitude to Vice Admiral Pradeep Chauhan, AVSM & Bar, VSM, Director, National Maritime Foundation (NMF) and the NMF for agreeing to honour a time barred commitment and facilitate publication of this book. They have backed me up completely, without in any way interfering with my way of thinking or choices. It would not be out of place to record the enormous support that I received from my publisher, Mr Rajan Arya of Pentagon Press LLP, who as always, went an extra mile to facilitate my last minute requests and delivered the book in record time.

As someone, who did not have his moorings in research, I needed lot of support from my colleagues, who had come up in this field over years. I would like to express my sincere gratitude to Professor Sanjay Bhardwaj, Prof. Uma Singh and Late Prof Savita Pandey of the JNU for encouraging me and helping me to understand the subtle nuances of research. I was fortunate in getting the unstinted support of my colleagues at Institute for Defence Studies and Analyses (IDSA), NMF, Jamia Millia Islamia, Centre for Land Warfare Studies (CLAWS) and India Foundation. It would not be out of the place to name a few of them. Dr Shristi Pukhrem, went through my drafts and gave valuable advice, whereas Siddharth Singh helped me in getting articles and other material online from JNU library. Dr Meena Singh Roy readily provided valuable maps from her own research to add gravitas to the book. I also need to acknowledge the help that I received from my other colleagues from time to time, Dr Rushda Siddiqui, Dr Sreeradha Datta, Dr Ashok Behuria, Dr Smruti Pattanaik, Prof. Srikanth Kondapalli, and Gp Capt Ajey Lele are some of the names that immediately come to mind, but there are many others, who were always willing to help, whenever I approached them.

Any book on a project within Pakistan creates its own problems for an author in India, especially during tensions between the two countries, as has been the case during last few years. Consequently, I have not been able to visit the project site, although I could visit, Afghanistan, China, Iran, UAE and even Pakistan, while I was working on the subject. However, to get valuable insights, I had to depend on various experts from Pakistan, who graciously answered the questionnaire sent to them and even answered queries sent to them from time to time. I was specifically helped by an old friend, well known academic and author Dr Ayesha Siddiqa, who has valuable insights into the thinking of Pakistan's military, especially the Navy. Former Pakistani Ambassador to the United States, Hussain Haqqani, not only gave me his views, but also provided a presentation on Gwadar by Mahmud Ali Durrani, his predecessor and subsequently the National Security Advisor of Pakistan. An old friend and well known Baloch journalist Malik Siraj Akbar provided me the Baloch perspective on this vexed issue. Finally, well known author and former director of the South Asia Centre at The Atlantic Council, Shuja Nawaz, gave me valuable inputs on the thinking of the Pakistan Army. He was also instrumental in facilitating my visit to Pakistan.

Last but not the least, a long drawn process of more than a decade like this, takes its toll on family relations. I would like to express my deep gratitude to my parents, my wife Neema and my son Vikalp and daughter Vidushi for their total support, during these troubled times and putting up with my unearthly hours. My mother, wife and daughter kept pushing me even in those times, when I had given up in despair. Vidushi, in fact also helped me to copy edit the text. Without the complete and unstinted support of my family, this work would not have seen the light of the day.

Alok Bansal

List of Abbreviations

A2/AD	Anti Access/Area Denial
ADB	Asian Development Bank
APTTA	Afghanistan Pakistan Transit Trade Agreement
ATTA	Afghanistan Transit Trade Agreement
BDM	Balochistan Dehi Muhafiz
BLA	Baloch Liberation Army
BLF	Balochistan Liberation Front
BPLF	Baloch People's Liberation Front
BRAS	Baloch Raaji Aajoi Sangar
BRI	Belt and Road Initiative
BSO	Baloch Students Organisation
CAR	Central Asian Republics
CPC	Communist Party of China
CFPD	China Foundation for Peace and Development
CHEC	China Harbour Engineering Company Ltd
CMF	Combined Maritime Forces
CM Ports	China Merchants Port Holding Company Ltd
CNOOC	China National Offshore Oil Corporation
COPHC	China Overseas Port Holding Company
COPHCL	China Overseas Port Holding Company Pakistan (Pvt.) Ltd

COSCO	China Ocean Shipping Company
CPC	Communist Party of China
CPEC	China Pakistan Economic Corridor
CTF	Combined Task Force
CWS	Coastal Watch Station
DSC	Digital Selective Calling
DWT	Dead Weight Tonnage
ECNEC	Executive Committee of National Economic Council (of Pakistan)
EEZ	Exclusive Economic Zone
ETIM	East Turkmenistan Islamic Movement
EU	European Union
FATA	Federally Administered Tribal Areas (of Pakistan)
FBR	Federal Board of Revenue (of Pakistan)
FDI	Foreign Direct Investment
FOCAC	The Forum on China Africa Cooperation
FTZ	Free Trade Zone
FWO	Frontier Works Organisation
GB	Gilgit-Baltistan
GCC	Gulf Coordination Council
GDP	Gross Domestic Product
GPA	Gwadar Port Authority
IGPL	India Global Ports Limited
IMSC	International Maritime Security Construct
INMARSAT	International Maritime Satellite
INSTC	International North South Transport Corridor
IOR	Indian Ocean Region
JCC	Joint Cooperation Committee (of CPEC)
JMCC	Joint Military Consultative Committee

JMICC	Joint Maritime Information and Coordination Centre
JUI	Jamiat Ulema-e-Islam
KKH	Karakoram Highway
LAC	Line of Actual Control
LNG	Liquefied Natural Gas
MCC	Metallurgical Corporation of China
MGD	Million Gallons per Day
mmcfd	Million Cubic Feet Daily
MNC	Multinational Corporation
MoU	Memorandum of Understanding
MSRI	Maritime Silk Road Initiative
NAP	National Awami Party
NGIA	New Gwadar International Airport
NLC	National Logistics Cell (of Pakistan)
NRA	New Regionalism Approach
OBOR	One Belt One Road
PFAR	Popular Front for Armed Resistance
PHE	Public Health Engineering
PLA	Peoples Liberation Army (of China)
PLAN	People's Liberation Army Navy
PNS	Pakistan Naval Ship
POJK	Pakistan occupied Jammu and Kashmir
PSA	Port of Singapore Authority
PSDP	Public Sector Development Programme
QICT	Qasim International Container Terminal
RMSP	Regional Maritime Security Patrols
RORO	Roll On Roll Out
RSCT	Regional Security Complex Theory

RTGS	Rubber Tyred Gantry Cranes
SAARC	South Asian Association for Regional Cooperation
SAFTA	South Asian Free Trade Area
SAIL	Steel Authority of India Limited
SEZ	Special Economic Zone
SLOC	Sea Lines of Communication
SOE	State Owned Enterprise
SPM	Single Point Mooring
SREB	Silk Road Economic Belt
STFA	Sezai Turkes Ferzi Akkaya (of Turkey)
STM	Savunma Teknolojileri Mühendislik ve Ticaret A.S.
TDAP	Trade Development Authority of Pakistan
TEU	Twenty foot Equivalent Unit
UAE	United Arab Emirates
UC	Union Council
UK	United Kingdom
UNGA	United Nations General Assembly
US	United States
USA	United States of America
USGS	United States Geological Survey
USSR	Union of Soviet Socialist Republics
VHF	Very High Frequency
XUAR	Xinjiang Uyghur Autonomous Region

Introduction

Right from its inception in 1947, Pakistan has been beset with problems of perceived as well as genuine security threats. These problems have had internal as well as external dimensions. The Indo-Pak War of 1971 and the Indian Navy's attack on Karachi exposed Pakistan to a critical vulnerability, which stemmed from its overwhelming dependence on the port of Karachi for its maritime trade as well as the security of its coastline. The war also brought home the catastrophic consequences of aggressive sub-nationalism to Pakistan, as it culminated in its break-up and the liberation of Bangladesh. At the moment, the most powerful ethno-linguistic movement in Pakistan is Baloch nationalism, which is driven by real, as well as imaginary, grievances of an ethnic minority against the state. Islamabad has been trying to use developmental projects in the region as economic sops to placate the restive population in Balochistan.

Any major infrastructural project, especially on the peripheries of a state, in a region inhabited by an aggrieved ethnic minority, is bound to disturb the regional equilibrium. The problem is further accentuated when the project is being undertaken by an external power, the People's Republic of China, and is perceived as the external power's gateway to a geopolitically sensitive region. The Gwadar Deep Sea Port project is not only a mega project being built and operated by the Chinese in a rather impoverished region on Pakistan's periphery, but more significantly, the region is inhabited by the Baloch, who have long-standing grievances against the Pakistani state.

Balochistan, the largest province in Pakistan,[1] also happens to be the most backward of its provinces.[2] During the seven and half decades of Pakistan's existence there has been negligible development in the region, which appears to be frozen in time. The Baloch, right from the very beginning, were reluctant to join Pakistan and over a period of time this reluctance has given rise to a strong ethno-nationalist movement, which often results in violence. Despite being endowed with vast natural resources, its hostile and extremely arid climate along with frequent bouts of violence has prevented economic development in this region. Of all its regions, Makran, the coastal region along the Arabian Sea, offers the best avenues for economic development. Pakistan has planned numerous mega developmental projects in Makran, some of them like the Gwadar Deep Sea Port, Makran Coastal Highway, Saindak Copper Mines and Mirani Dam are in various stages of completion. These projects, if successfully implemented, have the potential to revive the sinking economy of Pakistan.

Of these 'developmental' projects, the Gwadar Deep Sea Port project is the largest and the most controversial. It is the largest infrastructural project being undertaken in Pakistan since its inception. The project aims at creating a deep sea port at Gwadar in Pakistan and forms the crux of the China Pakistan Economic Corridor (CPEC), which is one of the most significant components of China's Belt and Road Initiative (BRI). The BRI, launched in 2013 by President Xi, is a key component of his foreign policy and has been joined by over 150 countries of the world. President Xi has invested his personal reputation behind this project, which is Beijing's most significant economic initiative and incorporates one of the most ambitious infrastructure projects ever conceived on the planet. Originally conceived to connect Europe with East Asia by physical infrastructure, its scope has expanded with the rising stature of China. Today it incorporates Africa, Latin America and Oceania as well.[3] On account of its massive scope and scale, it has often been called China's version of the Marshall Plan, albeit much bigger and bolder.[4]

Gwadar Port besides being a key component of the CPEC and BRI with enormous economic potential is also a strategically significant project, which provides China a strong foothold in the Arabian Sea at the mouth of the Persian Gulf, which is an extremely turbulent and volatile region with enormous geopolitical and geo-economic significance. The port could further bolster China's growing influence in the region and eclipse the historical dominance of the Persian Gulf by the West led by the USA. It has the potential to adversely affect India's long-term economic and maritime interests. Although conceived as purely an economic project, the port could potentially provide China with a strong military outpost in the Indian Ocean just outside the Strait of Hormuz at the mouth of the Persian Gulf. The manner in which Islamabad suddenly changed the operator of the port from Port of Singapore Authority (PSA) Ltd. to the Chinese Government-owned China Overseas Port Holding Company (COPHC) on 18 February 2013[5] indicates that there are other factors that are influencing the decisions regarding the port, besides economics.

The Chinese presence at the mouth of the Persian Gulf threatens not only Western interests and the interests of the Persian Gulf littorals, but also of India, which is dependent on the region for the bulk of its energy imports. China has already emerged as an economic power house and has become the largest investor in the region. China has followed up its economic outreach with huge diplomatic initiatives. In one of the biggest diplomatic coups, Beijing successfully managed to bring Saudi Arabia and Iran, two traditional foes, together. It has also volunteered to mediate between the Israelis and Palestinians to solve one of the most intractable disputes in the region. These diplomatic initiatives have vastly endeared China to the masses in the Persian Gulf region. It has emerged as a much more popular country than the USA amongst the Arab masses and the population across the region views it quite favourably. It is therefore in a position to upstage the dominant influence of the USA in the region.

The Chinese presence at Gwadar Port, just outside the Gulf, allows it to provide military back-up to its economic and diplomatic initiatives in the GCC countries and the entire Middle East. China has already indicated that military ties are the key to its relationship with Pakistan and it is looking for new vistas of defence cooperation. The US Department of Defence has already identified Gwadar as a possible location of a Chinese military base in the future.[6] The Washington-based US Institute for Peace perceives that China could use the port to project power. According to its analysis China might deploy PLA Navy Marine Corps units at Gwadar, which would eventually provide it with significant capability to project power in the Indian Ocean,[7] in conjunction with its base in Djibouti.

For Pakistan, the Gwadar Deep Sea Port project has huge economic and security potential. It is the first major commercial port outside the Karachi

Port Bin Qasim complex. It therefore removes Pakistan's critical dependence on these ports by providing Islamabad with an alternative to unload vital supplies in case of non-availability of the Karachi-Bin Qasim complex, due to natural disasters, accidents or a naval blockade. The consequences of the non-availability of these two contiguous ports was painfully realised by Islamabad during the Kargil conflict, when the Indian Navy had aggressively positioned itself in the Northern Arabian Sea. More significantly for Pakistan, the Gwadar Port also embeds an external actor, namely, the People's Republic of China, in the security dynamics of South Asia by making it a stakeholder in ensuring the safety and operational availability of Gwadar Port in Pakistan. Consequently, Gwadar Port solves Islamabad's internal and external security problems, while providing Beijing a vital outpost in the Indian Ocean Region.

The project has the potential to emerge as an ideal Gateway to Central Asia and change the landscape of the Makran coast, in the process transforming the demography of Balochistan, while delivering avenues of livelihood to discontented Baloch youth. It has the potential to provide the shortest access to the warm waters of the Arabian Sea and the vast untapped resources of Central Asia. Islamabad's objective is to make Gwadar a major transhipment hub so that it enables Pakistan to be at the centre of Asian growth. Pakistan's ambition is to become Asia's trade, energy and transport corridor, connecting China, Central Asia, Iran and the Middle East through Gwadar. General Pervez Musharraf, the president of Pakistan during the ground-breaking ceremony of the port on 22 September 2002 had stated that the Port of Gwadar, on account of its location, would have strategic advantages and once the rail and road infrastructure was fully developed, it would become a regional hub for trade and commercial activity. It would serve as the mother port at the junction of traditional trade routes opposite the Strait of Hormuz at the mouth of the Persian Gulf and would provide an alternative access to the sea for export and import of cargo from and to the northern areas of Pakistan.[8] The statement highlights Pakistan's expectations from Gwadar. The port, if it eventually becomes a success, could pay Islamabad huge economic dividends and provide a fillip to its tottering economy. It also has the potential to enhance Pakistan's maritime capabilities, as well as provide much-needed strategic depth to its maritime forces against India.

The Gwadar project not only encompasses the establishment of a deep sea port, but also the creation of an industrial behemoth with its entire associated infrastructure. A new international airport, which will be the largest in Pakistan is being established with Chinese assistance and is expected to be complete by the end of 2023.[9] An oil refinery has been planned by the Kingdom of Saudi Arabia,[10] and China has started building another.[11] On 18 May 2023, the Polan-Gabd electricity transmission line, which will provide 100 MW power to Gwadar daily was inaugurated jointly by Shehbaz Sharif, the Prime Minister of Pakistan, and Seyed Ebrahim Raisi, the President of Iran.[12] In addition, a coal-fired power plant is being set up to meet the growing demand. A desalination plant set up with Chinese assistance to desalinate 1.2 million gallons of sea water daily is in the final stages of completion and should be commissioned by the end of 2023.[13] In addition, a reverse osmosis plant is also being set up to meet the requirements of fresh water.

As part of the CPEC, Chinese companies are also looking at constructing a liquefied natural gas (LNG) terminal at the port and gas pipelines to bring gas to the terminal at a cost of $ 2.5 billion. The proposed terminal will have a floating storage gasification unit and a capacity to handle 500 mcfd (million cubic feet daily) of LNG. Chinese are also looking at completing the Pakistan portion of the Iran-Pakistan gas pipeline to bring gas from Iran to the terminal at Gwadar.[14] The port is being connected to the Baloch hinterland as well as to neighbouring Afghanistan and Iran by a network of roads and railways. A feasibility report commissioned by the Chinese government to assess the cost of a railway line to connect Gwadar to Kashgar in Xinjiang as part of the BRI has estimated it to be $ 58 billion. Despite this humongous price tag, the feasibility study has recommended the railway connectivity to be worth it, on account of its strategic significance.[15]

A special economic zone (SEZ) modelled on Chinese SEZs as a free trade area has been created with manufacturing zones, logistics hubs, warehouses, and display centres. In order to attract investments from across the globe Islamabad has provided large-scale tax incentives not only to the companies involved in the construction of the port infrastructure, but also to all those who invest in the Gwadar special economic zone. The special economic zone is a free trade area comprising 2,282 acres, of which over 2,000 acres have been leased to a Chinese company for 43 years.[16] All businesses in the Gwadar free zone have been granted complete exemption from income tax, sales tax and federal excise duty for 23 years. All contractors and sub-contractors of COPHCL have been given tax exemption for 20 years. Custom duty has been exempted for 40 years on material imports for the construction of Gwadar port and the free zone, which includes plants, machinery, equipment, appliances, accessories and even ship bunker oils to supply fuels and lubricants to ships in the port and its terminals.[17] It is quite evident that the government of Pakistan is leaving no stone unturned to create a megacity at Gwadar, which could emerge as a major trading and industrial hub and eventually grow to be another Karachi or Islamabad.

This creates an apprehension in the minds of local residents, who fear being converted into a minority within their own land. More significantly, all decisions pertaining to Gwadar are being taken by bureaucrats and generals in Islamabad and Rawalpindi, respectively, whereas the provincial government in Quetta has been completely cut off from all aspects of the project. Consequently, local residents perceive that Gwadar is nothing, but an instrument created by Punjabi land sharks to colonise their home land. Baloch nationalists have often complained that Punjabi settlers have been grabbing prime land and property in and around Gwadar in stark violation of local land laws and have vehemently opposed it.[18] This has provided fuel to the existing Baloch insurgency and has aggravated the security situation in Balochistan. Consequently, the Baloch have been attacking various infrastructural projects associated with the port and personnel working in them. They have also targeted the Pakistani security personnel guarding these infrastructural projects.

As a result, although the first phase of the port was commissioned in 2007 and the first cargo vessel 'Pos Glory' berthed alongside on 15 March 2008, the port has not been able to generate adequate traffic to make it commercially viable. In fact, in its first 14 months of operation, it handled just one commercial ship and that too after it had offloaded part of its cargo at anchorage to reduce the draught.[19] Despite its enormous potential, Gwadar has many such dubious records to its credit and is still not fully functional or commercially viable, although the government claimed in March 2019 that in the last three years, gross revenue generated from the port was Rs, 358.151 million, of which the share of the Gwadar Port Authority at nine per cent was just Rs. 32.324 million.[20] The government has been able to persuade the Pak-Afghan Chamber of Commerce & Industry (PACCI) and the Gwadar Chamber of Commerce & Industry (GCCI), to use the port for Afghan transit trade after the Taliban came to power;[21] however, it has not increased the port calls in any significant way.

Historically, Gwadar was part of the Sultanate of Oman for centuries and a large number of people from the entire region still serve in the armed forces of Oman, as part of the treaty signed while handing over Gwadar. This trained manpower has provided Baloch nationalist groups ready recruits for taking up arms against the government, whereas the overseas Diaspora has been in the forefront of providing funds for the Baloch cause. Chinese paranoia coupled with Pakistan's desperation has resulted in some kneejerk reactions from the authorities, wherein locals have been completely prohibited from entering key localities where Chinese are residing or working, especially in the port and free zone. This has resulted in greater alienation of the population and establishment of the Haq Do Tehreek (HDT), an outfit led by Maulana Hidayatur Rehman to espouse the rights of local fishermen in Gwadar. The outfit has been peacefully protesting against numerous security check posts that have been set up in the region and the trawlers from outside that are depriving the local fishermen of their catch.[22] On the other hand, more militant Baloch organisations have declared all Chinese personnel and investments in Balochistan as valid targets. They have been targeting works and personnel associated with the port from time to time.

Chinese involvement in the construction of the port and subsequently in its operations, has led many strategic analysts to perceive Gwadar as a Chinese outpost in South Asia. China's promotion of the CPEC has given further credence to this belief. As brought out, the port does provide China with an important strategic outpost at the mouth of the Persian Gulf, which may disturb the geopolitical balance in the region by providing China a military base to bolster its growing influence not only in West Asia and North Africa, but in the entire Indian Ocean Region. China has already gained a groundswell of support in the region by facilitating rapprochement between Iran and Saudi Arabia. The deal clearly shows that the regional powers are more than keen to engage with China, an emerging global power to the detriment of the Western powers, who have traditionally wielded influence in the region.[23] The port provides Pakistan and China access to the Persian Gulf and enables them to monitor their energy shipments from the Gulf, while providing them the capacity to interdict energy shipments to hostile powers, including India, Japan and other European nations.

Consequently, one sees that there are numerous dimensions to the Gwadar Deep Sea Port project, which is being touted as purely an economic one that will have an impact on both the traditional and non-traditional dimensions of security in the region. This book looks at the historical background of Balochistan, Makran Coast and Gwadar, and its evolution through the ages. It highlights the facilities being set up within the port and in its vicinity, as well as the significance of the port for the CPEC and BRI and for the wider Chinese interests in the region. It also covers its potential impact on Pakistan's maritime security as well as internal security. It also makes an effort to analyse its impact on Pakistan's economy as well as on the economically significant Persian Gulf region and South Asia, especially on India.

This book approaches the subject primarily from India's point of view. It attempts to provide a comprehensive in-depth understanding of the impact that the port will have on Indo-Pakistan strategic balance and the possibility of it threatening India's energy security. It also aims to provide an assessment of China's potential increase in influence in the region as a direct consequence of the port's construction. Significantly, India's pre-eminence in the maritime sphere in the region can be threatened as its direct consequence. The port's construction may further enhance China's engagement with India's neighbours and undermine India's security. It is also critical from the Indian perspective to develop a clear understanding of Baloch nationalism and the fragility of the Pakistani State. Such an analysis has the potential to shape Indian policies towards Pakistan.

This book analyses the significance of the Gwadar Deep Sea Port project for the State of Pakistan in general and for the province of Balochistan in particular and analyse its impact on regional security, without getting into the theoretical realm of defining regional security. It aims to study how Gwadar port and Makran coast have evolved over the ages. It also attempts to delineate the domestic and regional politics in Pakistan for building the port and the extent of the Chinese political connection. The proposed study will also assess the potential strategic significance of the Gwadar ort to the security interests of Pakistan and what specific needs are met by the development of this port.

It analyses its economic implications: how this port has the potential to change the economic landscape of a region that has traditionally been the most backward in Pakistan.

It attempts to evaluate the impact of the Gwadar port project on Pakistan's security (maritime security, energy security as well as economic security) and finally analyses the impact of the Gwadar port on the maritime and energy security of India.

NOTES

1. Balochistan is the largest province of Pakistan in terms of area, but smallest in terms of population.
2. It is the poorest province of Pakistan in terms of GDP per capita and its sub-national Human Development Index is the lowest in Pakistan (the HDI of FATA was marginally lower than Balochistan in 2021, but with the merger of FATA with Khyber Pakhtunkhwa, Balochistan is at the bottom).
3. James McBride, Noah Berman, and Andrew Chatzky, "China's Massive Belt and Road Initiative", Council on Foreign Relations, 2 February 2023, from https://www.cfr.org/backgrounder/chinas-massive-belt-and-road-initiative (7 July 2023).
4. Christina Lu, "China's Belt and Road to Nowhere", *Foreign Policy*, 13 February 2023.
5. "Pakistan hands over Gwadar Port operation to China", *The Nation*, Lahore, 25 February 2013.
6. "China may be looking at setting up a military base in Pakistan", *The Times of India*, New Delhi, 12 May 2023.
7. "China could project military power from Pakistan's Gwadar port", *The Economic Times*, 28 March 2023.
8. "President at Ground Breaking Ceremony of Gwadar Deep-Sea Port", 22 March 2002 from https://presidentmusharraf.wordpress.com/2005/01/24/musharraf-ground-breaking-gwadar/ (accessed on 10 July 2023).
9. "12 MW approved for New Gwadar International Airport", *Daily Times*, 7 June 2023.
10. Zafar Bhutta, "Riyadh renews $10b refinery project", *The Express Tribune*, 25 October 2022.
11. "China starts Oil Refinery Construction in Gwadar", *Dunya News* 17 January 2023, from https://dunyanews.tv/en/Business/690634- (Accessed on 30 June 2023).
12. "Border projects: Pakistan, Iran inaugurate Polan-Gabd electricity transmission line", *Business Recorder*, 18 May 2023.
13. "Desalination plant in Gwadar to be inaugurated on June 30", *Pakistan Today*, 4 June 2023.
14. "China to build $2.5 billion worth LNG terminal, gas pipeline in Pakistan", *Deccan Chronicle*, 1 October 2015.
15. Umair Jalal, "China-Pakistan Ties Steam Ahead With Proposed Rail Project", *The Diplomat*, 3 May 2023.
16. "Pakistan hands over 2000 acres to China in Gwadar port city", *Indian Express*, 12 November 2015.

17. Shahbaz Rana, "Pakistan approves massive tax exemptions for Gwadar port operators", *The Express Tribune*, 24 May 2016.
18. Urmila Phadnis, "Ethnic Movements in Pakistan" in Pandav Nayak (ed.), *Pakistan: Society and Politics* – South Asian Studies Series, 6. New Delhi: South Asian Publishers Pvt. Ltd., 1984, p. 195.
19. "Gwadar port: 'history-making milestones'," *Dawn*, 14 April 2008.
20. M. Faizan, "Gwadar Port generates Rs358.151m revenue during last three years: Ali Haider Zaidi", 20 March 2019 from https://customstoday.media/gwadar-port-generates-rs358-151m-revenue-during-last-three-years-ali-haider-zaidi/ (Accessed on 10 July 2023).
21. Bahram Baloch, "Gwadar Port to be utilised for Afghan transit trade", *Dawn*, 19 March 2022.
22. Behram Baloch and Muhammad Akbar Notezai, "Gwadar's Haq Do Tehreek – genuine movement or political ambition", *Dawn*, 26 December 2022.
23. Zakiyeh Yazdanshenas and Alam Saleh, "Iranian-Saudi détente and 'Asianisation' of the Persian Gulf: China fills the gap", Middle East Institute Website https://www.mei.edu/publications/iranian-saudi-detente-and-asianization-persian-gulf-china-fills-gap (Accessed on 1 July 2023).

1

Gwadar, Makran Coast, and Balochistan: Historical Evolution

Gwadar Port is the third major port of Pakistan after Karachi and Port Bin Qasim. It is located in the south-western part of Balochistan province at a distance of approximately 120 km from Pakistan's border with Iran. It is relatively far from Pakistan's other two ports and is located at a distance of 533 km from the city of Karachi. It has been conceived as a gateway for the land-locked countries of Central Asia and Afghanistan. It probably provides the shortest access to open oceans for the Eurasian heartland. Consequently, it is also the most significant component of the China-Pakistan Economic Corridor (CPEC), as it has been projected as the link between China's Belt and Road Initiative (BRI), earlier known as One Belt One Road (OBOR) project and its 21st Century Maritime Silk project. Consequently, all economic activities associated with the CPEC converge at this port and a large number of projects costing billions of dollars are being implemented or have been implemented in the port city or its vicinity.[1]

Gwadar has an excellent geostrategic location just outside the mouth of the oil-rich Persian Gulf, close to the Strait of Hormuz, in the vicinity of major shipping routes to Africa, Asia, and Europe; which makes it an ideal transhipment port. It also gives it enormous geopolitical and commercial significance.[2] The port along with communication links is expected to boost economic development all along the Makran coast, a region that has historically been amongst the most backward in Pakistan. The Makran coast is predominantly inhabited by Baloch, who are the largest ethnic group in Balochistan province of Pakistan. Balochistan has an extremely chequered history and has been part of various regimes at different times in history. The Baloch identity as such is a relatively recent phenomenon and has evolved over the last few centuries. It is therefore essential to understand the geography and history of this enormous stretch of land as well as its historical evolution from ancient times, before understanding the present problems that the plague Gwadar port project.

History of Gwadar

The initial history of Gwadar and the surrounding region of the Makran coast begin with the settlement of unknown Bronze Age people in the few oases that existed within this predominantly dry and parched region. It is reported that at the time of Prophet Dawood (David), people of the region entombed themselves in the small cairns (known locally as *dambi*) to avoid famine. It was subsequently conquered by Cyrus the Great, who founded the Achaemenid Empire and incorporated it as Gedrosia region of the Persian Empire. Pura was the capital of Gedrosia and is believed to have been located near Bampur in Sistan and Balochistan[3] province of Iran. Firdousi in his *Shahnama* has described it as the battleground between the Iranian and Turanian kings. It formed part of the kingdom of Iran during the reign of King Kaus, who travelled from Makran to other parts of his dominion by boat. Both Makran and Gwadar have also been mentioned by great travellers like Ibn Batuta, Marco Polo, and Turkish admiral Sidi Ali. They have all mentioned the inhospitable nature of the weather and the terrain, which discouraged invaders from residing permanently there.[4]

During the retreat of Alexander's army from Indus, his admiral, Nearchus, led a fleet, which passed through this region. He has described the region as extremely dry and mountainous, which is inhabited by Ichthyophagi or 'fish eaters', a Greek translation of the ancient Persian phrase 'mahikhoran', which has over the years evolved as Makran. After the collapse of Alexander's empire, the region came under the rule of Seleucus Nicator, who was a general of Alexander and controlled his eastern territories after Alexander's death.

Subsequently, the region became part of the Mauryan Empire, after Chandragupta Maurya defeated Seleucus around 305 BC.[5]

After the weakening of the Mauryan Empire, the region came under the rule of local chieftains and remained on the side lines of history till it was conquered by an Arab army led by Muhamad Bin Qasim in 711. For the next few centuries, the ownership of the region was contested between rulers from India and Persia, which also included the Mughal Empire of India and the Safavid Empire of Persia.[6] In between, whenever the control of these far-flung empires weakened, the region was also controlled by various Baloch tribes. The Ottoman admiral, Sidi Ali Reis, visited the city in the 1550s and described his visit to Gwadar in his book *Miratul Memalik* (The Mirror of Countries), which was published in 1557. According to his accounts, the Baloch inhabited the city and were led by Malik Jelaleddin, who was the son of Malik Dinar.[7]

During the 16th century, the Portuguese launched several attacks on this area from the sea, but failed to comprehensively defeat Mir Hamal Baloch, the local ruler. They did, however, manage to capture Gwadar and Pasni once, but had to abandon them eventually and burnt them before retreating from these towns. This was followed by centuries of local rule by various Baloch tribes. In 1716, Mir Abdullah Jan Qahar attacked Gwadar after capturing Panjgur and Kech. Subsequently, in 1756-57, Mir Muhammed Nasir Khan, the Khan of Kalat, attacked this area and came very close to Gwadar, but could not capture it. He attacked the area again with the support of Ahmed Shah Abdali and defeated the local ruler, Umar Khan Gichki, thereby bringing the area under his control. Later, he appointed Umer Gichki as his governor on the assurance that half the revenues from this area would be given to him.[8]

Subsequently, when Nasir Khan got his daughter married to Jam Ghulam Shah of Las Bela, he awarded the income of Gwadar to his son-in-law but after the death of Jam, the Gichkis of Kech started many uprisings against Kalat's control. The Khan of Kalat had to eventually negotiate with them and bring down his share of the revenue to seven hundred rupees per annum. In 1783, the Khan of Kalat appointed Prince Sultan Saeed Bin Ahmed of Oman, who had taken shelter, as his deputy in Gwadar, but after the death of Nasir Khan, the prince refused to accept the supremacy of the Khan of Kalat. However, Jam Mir Khan, brother of the late Jam Ghulam Shah ousted him from Gwadar. The prince was however, not willing to part with the area.

Consequently, after he became the ruler of Oman by capturing supreme power in Muscat in 1792, he despatched a naval force to attack Gwadar. His attack forced Mir Khan to flee to Somiani, in Lasbela area.[9]

Sultan Saeed Bin Ahmed of Oman thereafter went on to complete the annexation of Gwadar with Oman and made it an integral part of his sultanate. He ruled the city though his *wali* or governor, who was also directed to capture Chabahar, another town in the vicinity, which is presently part of Iran. Omani rulers got the Gwadar fort built, whereas the British, who had established their presence in South Asia by then, extended their telegraph network into Gwadar by connecting Iran, India, and Oman.[10] Throughout history, Gwadar existed as a small fishing port, whose population depended on fishing for its economic sustenance. The port on the Makran coast of Balochistan remained an isolated outpost of Oman till the advent of the British in the subcontinent changed its significance. The people who inhabit Gwadar and its surrounding region as well as most of Balochistan, call themselves Baloch; and have common aspirations. It is, therefore, important to understand Balochistan and its resources, which have contributed to make Gwadar both a remote as well as geo-strategically an important port of the region.

Balochistan and its Resources

With 147,000 square miles, the province of Balochistan has almost half the landmass of the Islamic Republic of Pakistan. Its location is significant as it sits astride the oil lanes of the Persian Gulf. Squeezed into the triangle where Pakistan, Iran, and Afghanistan meet, it is geopolitically and strategically the most significant part of Pakistan. With over 750 kilometres of coastal strip along the Arabian Sea, it virtually commands almost the entire sea coast of Pakistan.[11]

The province has enormous geographical diversity. It has snow-capped mountains, as well as lush green valleys and barren deserts. Geologists trace its origin to the Tertiary period, when the Himalayas rose from the Tethys Sea. During this period, the Himalayas rose along with an expanse of region, which subsequently, turned into this tract of land due to continual stratification of crusts upon crusts through the centuries. Balochistan is therefore geographically an extension of the Himalayan mountain range, even though a junior offspring in a purely geological sense. The sedimentary nature of the rocks in Balochistan points towards their maritime origin. However, volcanic traces on many of these rocks indicate volcanic activity in the past. Consequently, the region abounds with numerous craters of extinct volcanoes called *Darya-e-Chashm* along its vast coastline.[12]

The traditional Baloch territory is presently divided politically amongst Pakistan, Afghanistan, and Iran; however, its exact borders are undetermined. It is generally believed that it occupies the south eastern part of the Iranian plateau from Kirman desert till the western borders of Sindh and Punjab. According to the *Encyclopaedia Britannica*, it includes the south-eastern part of Iran and its extremities touch the Sulaiman Mountains and the Kirthar Hills in the East and Iran and Afghanistan in the West. Its borders stretch all the way from the Gomal river in the north-east to the Arabian Sea in the south. Lord Curzon had termed Balochistan as the territory between the Helmand and the Arabian Sea, and between Kirman and Sindh. During the colonial period, it was generally considered to encompass the region bound by the kingdom of Afghanistan in the north, the Persian state on the west, the British provinces of Sindh on the east and the Arabian Sea in the south. Besides British Balochistan, it comprised Persian Balochistan, the Khanate of Kalat and the British district of Dera Ghazi Khan, Jacobabad, and Shikarpur up to the Indus. During the latter part of the Mughal era, the Chenab River marked the boundary between Balochistan and Mughal India.[13]

Physically, Balochistan is a part of the Central Asian plateau, rather than the Indian subcontinent. Phenomenal natural barriers prevent easy access to Baloch territory.[14] Western Balochistan, which comprises the Iranian province of Sistan and Balochistan, is geographically a southward continuation of the Iranian plateau. The topography is similar to that of Iran and the sedimentary rocks contain layers of soft stone, sand stone and shells, indicating their formation between the Mesozoic and Tertiary periods. The mountain ranges running north to south parallel the 66°15′ east longitude are believed to have evolved from underground. The western mountains are believed to have been formed during the Permian period, but bear the characteristics of the carboniferous period. On the other hand, the eastern mountains are of much recent origin and have large parts of calcium carbonate. The rocks are Triassic, Jurassic and Cretaceous and have layers of shale and big fossils of the Tertiary period.[15]

The vast desert in the western part of Balochistan has its origins in the Oligocenic and Milocenic ages and contains sandstone, earth and shale. The sedimentary rocks on the Makran range are of Triassic age and have an intermediate interference of the volcanic age. There is a vast bed of sulphur in the Sultan, Toftan and Bazman hills. The hills and ground in the Marri-Bugti region are of much more recent origin. On the hills and below them are rock some 2,000 feet thick, "covered with a layer of conglomerates reaching a depth of about 5,000 feet below ground level." As a result of this thick layer of rock, it becomes extremely difficult to obtain water in this dry parched region.[16]

Topographically, the Pakistani province of Balochistan can be divided into four main regions:

(a) Mountain ranges of middle and mid-eastern Balochistan.
(b) Hilly regions comprising the Pab Range in the east and Chagai, Kharan and Makran in the west.
(c) Plains consisting of Kachhi, Western Lasbela, and Dasht regions.
(d) Desert region comprising numerous sand hills and a rocky region in the north-west.[17]

Climatically Balochistan lies in the temperate zone and the average rainfall ranges from three to 12 inches. There are regions which get no rain for years in succession. As a result, agriculture is followed only in regions where irrigation facilities exist, which include mountain springs, rivers and underground water sources.[18] Almost all the rivers, with the exception of the Indus and Helmand, are seasonal. Due to scarcity of water, more than three-quarters of the area consist of barren deserts and rugged mountains.[19] Consequently, only about 4.5 million acres out of 47 million acres of plain land is cultivated. Fruits are grown in higher altitudes and limited quantities of wheat, jowar, barley, rice, potatoes and onions are cultivated. Tobacco and cotton are the cash crops grown in the province.[20]

It rains in October and March in the mountains and in July and August in the plains. It is extremely hot in summer and cold in winter. In the hills, the summers are pleasant and the winters are extremely cold. Scarcity of water and variations in temperature has led to a semi-nomadic life of the people.[21] Cattle rearing is the primary source of livelihood for the majority of the population and 90 per cent of Balochistan's area is used as pasture. Sheep is the most common animal that is reared, although cows, bullocks, and chickens are also reared in some regions. The Makran coast is rich in marine life and a large quantity of fish, prawns and lobsters are harvested.[22]

Though, there is not much vegetation in the province, it is quite rich in natural resources and apart from natural gas has large reserves of minerals. The province has plenty of marble and limestone reserves and contains 95 per cent of the world's asbestos. It also has significant reserves of barites, chromites, silica, gypsum, magnesite, antimony, manganese, graphite, sulphur, fluorite and iron ore. The region is also believed to have large petroleum deposits underground,[23] but their exploration has not been possible due to fierce opposition from Baloch tribes. The Pakistani government often tends to project Balochistan as a 'wasteland of deserts and mountains' and an economic liability but nothing could be further from the truth. Balochistan is not only self-sufficient but also supports the Federal Government with its resources. Above and below the surface; in the sea; on the mountains; and even over and beneath the deserts, the province has been endowed with layers upon layers of immense natural wealth.[24]

Makran Coast and the Surrounding Region

Balochistan has a coastline of 471 miles along the Arabian Sea which is referred to as the Makran Coast. The desert region of Makran is part of the 800-mile long and 100-mile wide strip of desert called Badia-e-Iran that cuts through fertile tracts and stretches from the Al-burz Mountains near the Caspian Sea to the dry hills in Makran. This strip separates Kirman from Sistan and broadens to 200 miles at its northern and southern extremes. This desert, which is currently called 'Lut' or Dasht-e-Lut, is interspersed with saltwater bodies called *murdabi*.[25]

There are two mountain ranges in the region: The central Makran range, in the hinterland and the Makran coast range right on the coast of the Arabian Sea. Both the ranges run up to a length of approximately 280 miles and have sedimentary rocks that have been split by water. There are many mountain springs, called 'rivers' by the locals that traverse the region and merge with the Arabian Sea. Many of these 'rivers' disappear in stretches and dry up at times. Some of the important 'rivers' that traverse the region are Mula, Hab, Purali, Hingol and Dasht.[26]

Climatically, the region is extremely dry and the summers are very hot, but the winters are pleasant.[27] Being dry, there is limited vegetation; *pesh mazri*; a kind of small palm with fan-shaped leaves is found in abundance in parts of Makran.[28] Agriculture is also quite limited in the region. Rice is grown in Makran in the shadow of date trees in groves of the latter where perennial means of irrigation exist. Makran rice is quite distinct and has a smaller grain, but is considered delicious and believed to have an appetizing aroma. The paddy plant is also short and unlike other rice plantations across the world, is not transplanted. Besides rice, bajra is also grown as a staple food for the poorer sections of population in the region. Cotton is grown in the Dasht valley, but its production is totally dependent on rain. The region is virtually an oasis of dates, which is also a staple food of its people.[29]

In terms of mineral wealth, Makran has rich deposits of graphite and limestone. In terms of wildlife, there are numerous wild boars that damage the crops. Cattle rearing is the predominant occupation in the rural areas and according to the 1960 Census there were over one lakh sheep in the region. However, the 'Baluchi' sheep found in the region do not produce high quality wool and are reared primarily for their meat. The Makran coast is rich in various species of fish, the most common being *galoo* and *kir*. Unlike the rest of Balochistan, fish is a staple diet in Makran. The Makran coast is also rich in other types of marine life. Prawns, lobsters, and sharks from the region are exported widely.[30]

There is considerable divergence about the ethnic origins of the people of the Makran coast. It would be reasonable to assume that the people of the Makran region are a mixture of Iranian, Assyrian and Negro stock with a considerable mixture of Dravidian, Rajput and Afghan blood.[31] As brought out earlier, the region includes Gwadar, a natural port, which along with the surrounding region was given to an exiled Omani prince from the Sultanate of Oman as a gesture of hospitality by Nasir Khan, the ruler of Kalat. In 1938, the then Khan of Kalat raised objections about its constitutional status, but the region continued to be a part of Oman till it was transferred to Pakistan in a deal.[32]

Baloch History

The province borders Iran on the west, and during the Soviet occupation of Afghanistan, apart from Peshawar, Balochistan's northern frontier was the main launching pad for the American-sponsored *jihad* in Afghanistan. It is a vast territory that has been the fiefdom of various autocratic feudal tribal chiefs. In the distant past, it was a loose confederation of various tribes, which over a period of time transformed into four princely states, whose allegiance from time to time shifted to the rulers in Afghanistan or the Persian empire.[33]

Ethnically, the Baloch are quite distinct from the other races inhabiting the Gangetic plains of the Indian sub-continent.[34] Although a significant section of people speak Brahui, a language of Dravidian origin similar to the Gondi spoken by tribal inhabitants in parts of Central India, most Baloch speak different dialects of Balochi, a language which belong to Iranian language family. The Baloch consider themselves to be Arabic in origin and trace their lineage to Prophet Abraham. Interestingly, a majority of the Baloch live outside Balochistan,[35] mostly in Sindh and Punjab.[36] On account of its severe weather and scarcity of fertile land, the social mode of Balochistan has predominantly been nomadic pastoralism, complemented by patches of settled agriculture. It was around these patches that tribal life was organised. The social organisation of the province continues to be based on tribalism to this day.

According to historians, Balochistan was part of Darius I's Persian empire as far back as 521 BC. However, when Alexander trounced Darius III in 331 BC, it came under Greek control. After Alexander's death, his former general, Selucus Nicator, captured large parts of West and Central Asia and marched towards India through Makran. He was, however, defeated by Chandragupta Maurya in 305 BC and had to cede Makran and other territories to the Mauryan Empire. After being a part of the Mauryan empire, Balochistan became a part of the Bactrian Empire, which was overthrown by the Sakas from Central Asia in 130 BC.[37]

There are no historical records available about Balochistan for the intervening period, till the reign of the great Sassanid Naushervan from 529 to 577. Naushervan is considered the first conqueror of Balochistan. His grandson Khusrau-I stayed in Makran for over a year and improved agriculture there. He appointed General Ashkash as the governor of the region before leaving Makran. Over the next two centuries, Sassanid rule continued over Makran. Subsequently the region came under the control of the Rai dynasty of Sindh, with their capital at Alor. After the Rai Dynasty, when Chach ascended the throne and founded the Brahman dynasty, the region came under his control. He is believed to have marched towards Kirman to determine the western extent of his dominion. After conquering the territory of Arambel, he reached the western limit of Makran, where he planted numerous date trees all along a stream and designated it as the boundary of 'Hind'.[38]

During the caliphate of Hazrat Omar, the Arab army after the conquest of Persia in 643 marched towards Makran. The Arab army was led by Abdullah bin Abdullah, who was confronted by Malik Saad, the local chief. Malik Saad had reinforced his army with troops from Sindh and put up a fierce fight, but was eventually defeated. Subsequently, after a gap of 20 years, in 664 during the caliphate of the first Umayyad Caliph, Muawiyah, 44 towns in Makran including Khuzdar were captured by the invading Arab army. Thereafter, during the reign of Caliph Abdul Malik, his governor in Iraq, Hajjaj, appointed Said bin Aslam as the commander in charge of Makran, but he was killed in a raid by Alafis from Sind in 704.[39]

As mentioned earlier, before the advent of British colonial rule, the region was an extremely fragmented society, where state authority was almost absent in the localised social structures of various Baloch tribes. The concept of state authority did not figure very prominently in the tribal mode of localised social life. Some centres of power and control did evolve, but whenever and wherever they emerged, they were premised on the internal dynamics, customs, and traditions of various tribes. Although many conquering armies like the Persians, Afghans, Sindhis and Sikhs frequently overran the region, they avoided permanent control of the tribes. The Baloch identity has slowly evolved over a period of over 2000 years. The common myths and legends and the common historical experiences of the last millennium had a great impact on the emergence of the Baloch nation.[40]

Not much is known about the early political history of the Baloch. They are mentioned only in the historical accounts, when the region started attempting to rid itself from the centralised control of the caliphate. Consequently, in the early part of the 11th century, independent Baloch power centres started emerging in the Makran region. Earlier, in 707, Mohammad bin Qasim, a general of the Umayyad Caliphate, had captured Makran. Thereafter, Arab governors ruled the country till the central rule of the Abbasid caliphs began to decline by the late 10th century and local rulers and tribal chieftains began, once again, to reassert their authority. During this period, Muslim chroniclers took note of the Baloch in connection with their conflicts with the Turks and Iranians in Kirman, Khurasan and Sistan. They are reported to have been badly mauled by the Dailami rulers in the second half of the 10th century and by the Ghaznavid Sultan Mahmud and his son Masud in the beginning of the 11th century.[41]

It is widely accepted that politically the Baloch power started emerging as a powerful entity during the 12th century, when various Baloch tribes came together to form powerful unions. A confederacy of 44 Baloch tribes was established in the 12th century under Mir Jalal Khan, which was followed by the Rind-Lashkari confederacy in the 15th century. Subsequently, various political power centres like the Maliks, the Dodais, the Boleidais and the Gichkis of Makkoran (Makran) attempted to unite and merge all Baloch tribes at different point of time. However, it was eventually that the Khanate of Kalat in the 17th century, managed to bring most of the tribes under one political rule.[42]

These internal attempts at political unity and establishment of the state were not wholly successful and eventually it was Nasir Khan, the sixth Khan of Kalat in the 18th century who established a unified Baloch army and brought all the major Baloch tribes under a mutually agreed common military and administrative system, which claimed sovereignty over all land where the Baloch lived. This included Karachi and most of western Balochistan.[43] The state structure created by Nasir Khan, however, had a major lacuna; it did not have an organic bureaucracy that could provide the framework for the state to bind together various tribes in the region. The tribal chiefs only contributed troops to the state for fighting wars and in lieu were awarded land grants to maintain troops and were responsible for the establishment of law and order in their regions. Despite some semblance of political unity, there existed a considerable degree of tension between the Khan and the tribal chiefs,[44] who continued to exercise considerable autonomy.

The advent of the British in the region sounded the death knell for the unified Baloch state that had incorporated the regions, which are part of Iran and Afghanistan today.[45] The British needed a safe and secure passage for their goods and personnel traversing to Afghanistan from Sindh through the territory of Balochistan. The Khan of Kalat under pressure from the British agreed to facilitate their safe passage, but could not prevent Bugti and Marri tribesmen from attacking them. The British used this as a pretext to conquer Kalat claiming that the attacks were a breach of the treaty between them and killed the Khan of Kalat when he refused to surrender. The state of Kalat was subsequently dismembered. The Goldsmid Line gave almost one-fourth of Baloch territory to Iran in 1871 and the Durand Line assigned a narrow strip to Afghanistan in 1893.[46]

The British not only partitioned the Baloch-inhabited areas amongst Iran, Afghanistan and British India, but even the Baloch areas within the British influence were divided into three parts: British Balochistan; Balochistan states that included the state of Kalat and its vassals, Lasbela, Kharan and Makran; and the tribal areas.[47] Its strategic location and abundant mineral wealth made it a target of external manipulations and the province was sought by both the British as well as the Russians during the 'Great Game'. Russian interest in the region continued during the Cold War and the Soviet Union sought an opening to the Indian Ocean through the Baloch areas and was keen to establish its presence in the region.

The colonial rule impacted Balochistan significantly and changed the landscape considerably. British economic policies contributed towards the general economic deterioration and pauperisation of the province. Within the first decade of the 20th century, the settled population in Balochistan increased from less than five per cent to over 50 per cent. Heavy taxation imposed by the British resulted in a number of peasants selling their land; as a result in a state where there were few tenants and hardly any agricultural labour, their number increased considerably. "The development of commodity-money relations converted Balochistan into an agrarian appendage of the metropolis, as the imports of factory-made articles coupled with high taxation led to the bankruptcy of the local artisans".[48] Their numbers accordingly dropped significantly. The British also beefed up the authority of the tribal chiefs as they depended on them to ensure safe passage for British troops and trade transiting from Sindh to Afghanistan. As a result, Baloch society which was fairly egalitarian turned feudal and this feudal orientation increased with the passage of time.

Gwadar during Colonial Rule

After the emergence of the British as the paramount power in the Indian subcontinent, the Khan of Kalat in 1863 tried to re-establish his authority over this Omani enclave of Gwadar, which was a geo-political anomaly. However, his efforts did not get support from the all-powerful British, who had established subsidiary relations with Kalat as well as Oman. Subsequently, from 1895 to 1904, there were many proposals, both by the Khan of Kalat as well as by the British Indian authorities to purchase Gwadar from Oman, but these could never be finalised, although even the Sultan of Oman at times expressed a desire to sell it.[49]

The contestation continued in subsequent years and assumed a greater salience in 1914, both for the British authorities in New Delhi as well as the Khan of Kalat, after the Burmah Oil Company began oil exploration at Gwadar. This immediately enhanced the economic significance of this region for all three – British India, Kalat as well as Oman. British administrative files in the archives contain numerous documents, as well as notings pertaining to Gwadar and the question of sovereignty over it. The initial British perception was that the Sultan of Oman, Taymur bin Faycal, would be firmly opposed to the idea of relinquishing sovereignty over Gwadar, but subsequently it emerged from the communication received from the British political agent at Muscat, that the Sultan was willing to 'give the British Government Gwadar or Dhurfai (Dhofar)' in lieu of British military assistance against the rebels.[50]

In 1939, the question of cessation of Gwadar by the Sultan of Oman to British India reappeared during a discussion between the then Sultan, Sa'id bin Taymur, and Captain Tom Hickinbotham, the British Political Agent, resident in Muscat. At that time the interior of Oman was autonomously governed by an elected imam based at Nizwa and there were frequent tensions between the imamate and the sultanate. The sultan wanted to regain complete control over the imamate and wanted to develop the region, for which he lacked funds. He therefore suggested ceding his control over Gwadar, in return for British financial assistance.[51]

Your letter No.209 C July 31st. GWADUR.

It is presumed that on receipt of subsidy etc. in return for his aid in war Sultan will drop or postpone proposal for sale of Gwadur which must be most distasteful to him. When former question has been decided please take up question with Sultan on above lines. I do not want to send on his proposal to Government until I have had opportunity of discussion with you.

Telegram from the Political Resident in the Persian Gulf to the Political Agent, Muscat, dated 17 September 1939 concerning the proposed sale of Gwadar. IOR/R/15/1/380, f. 10

Hickinbotham, in his report to his immediate superior the British political resident based at Bushire in Iran, suggested three options. The first was to make significant financial contribution to the sultan in lieu of Gwadar being handed over to the British. The second option was to completely deny any financial assistance and the third was to completely take over the entire territory of Muscat and Oman. He opined that the first option would result in paying the sultan a large sum for a small piece of territory and would not usher in long-term peace or order in Oman.[52]

In Hickinbotham's considered view, the third option of taking over Oman completely was the best. He suggested positioning a British garrison there and leaving the sultan as merely a nominal ruler. The resident in his reply expressed his suspicion that the sultan would not go ahead with the sale, even after financial assistance was provided to him because he felt that ceding control over Gwadar would be an extremely bitter pill for him to swallow. Subsequently, throughout the year, discussions continued on the subject. The archival documents present a good picture of how the Sultan sought to gain political and financial benefits by establishing diplomatic links with the British representatives. On the other hand, they also give a good insight into British machinations and calculations as to whether it was in their interest to establish direct control over further territory or to rule through a proxy.[53]

After the Second World War, the question of returning Gwadar to Kalat again came up and the British appeared quite keen to resolve the issue, but the political resident from Bushire stated in a letter that although possession of Gwadar by Sultan of Oman Sultan Sa'id bin Taymur was quite anachronistic, the sultan was a ruler who would like to hold on to every inch of his territory. Hence he felt he would be unwilling to let Gwadar go without adequate financial compensation. However, discussions on the subject came to an abrupt end, as with Indian independence in 1947, Britain ceased to have any overt role in the issue.[54]

Please refer to Dixon's demi official letter No. F.57(2)-BPG/46, dated the 14th January, 1947.

2. The Sultan's retention of Gwadur is somewhat of an anachronism and from the purely practical point of view there is much to be said in favour of its retrocession by sale to Kalat.

Letter from the Persian Gulf Residency, Bahrain to the Secretary to the Government of India, dated 1 February 1947 concerning the possible sale of Gwadar to Kalat. IOR/R/15/1/381, f. 4

In 1954, Pakistan wanted to get its entire coastline surveyed and entrusted the job to the United States Geological Survey (USGS) that entrusted Worth Condrick, a surveyor, to undertake the task. In the course of his survey, Condrick found Gwadar with its hammerhead-shaped peninsula to be an ideal location for a new deep sea port. Based on the survey report, Pakistan formally approached Sultan Said bin Taimur, the ruler of Muscat and Oman to transfer Gwadar to Pakistan, in return for monetary compensation. The initial negotiations started when Malik Ghulam Muhammad was the governor-general of Pakistan and Chaudhry Muhammad Ali was entrusted the responsibility of representing Pakistan. After four years of negotiations, a British adjudicator decided that Pakistan should pay (Pakistani) Rs. 55 crore (three million dollars) to Oman, which were paid. Consequently, on 7 September 1958, Gwadar became a part of Pakistan after 174 years of Omani control.[55]

It is believed that the British government pressurised the Sultan to transfer Gwadar and subsequently, when Sultan Qaboos bin Said was the ruler of Oman, he wanted to return the sale proceeds of Gwadar and wanted it back. The agreement signed with Oman for Gwadar's return had some significant clauses:

(a) In case of oil being found in commercial quantities in the former Omani territory of Gwadar, Pakistan was under an obligation to pay a share of the revenues to the Sultan.
(b) The residents of Gwadar could retain the citizenship of Muscat, without in any way prejudicing any right enjoyed by Pakistani citizens.
(c) The entire Balochistan would form a catchment area for Omani forces. Consequently, Baloch still have a large number of personnel in the armed forces of Oman.
(d) Provision of training facilities for Omani military personnel in Pakistan's technical institutions.
(e) Extradition of deserters from the armed forces of Oman to Muscat.
(f) Complete freedom on export of rice to Muscat at normal prevailing rates, without additional tariffs.
(g) Resources of Gwadar would be further developed.[56]

By 1955, the state of Makran was completely amalgamated into Pakistan and made a district of West Pakistan province. Gwadar, being a part of Oman, was naturally not included in it. However, when in 1958, Gwadar and the territory around it was sold to Pakistan by the Sultan, it was administratively made a tehsil of Makran district of West Pakistan. In 1970, when West Pakistan was split in to four provinces, Makran district along with Gwadar became part of Balochistan province. Subsequently, on 1 July 1977, the district was upgraded to a division and split into three districts, namely, Turbat,[57] Gwadar and Panjgur.[58]

It is quite evident from various historical accounts that Gwadar was the main port of Balochistan on the Makran coast, which handled all the trade that was generated in the hinterland. Being the only functional port on the entire Makran coast and due to its strategic location at the mouth of the Persian Gulf, Gwadar attracted the attention of the British in the middle of the nineteenth century. Consequently, it became a regular fortnightly port of call for British steamers that brought mail and goods for the adjoining areas. As brought out earlier, the first Indo-European telegraph line was laid along the Makran coast and in 1863 Karachi was linked with Gwadar, where a combined posts and telegraph office was established.[59]

After Gwadar was acquired by Pakistan, its enormous potential was realised by the government, which wanted to create an air and naval base that could function as a substitute for Karachi. However, lack of financial, technical, and institutional resources ensured that vision of making Gwadar an alternative to Karachi remained a dream.[60]

NOTES

1. Parvez Jabri, "Gwadar, a challenge to develop a new economic city", *Business Recorder*, Karachi, 15 August 2018.
2. Gwadar Port home page from http://www.gwadarport.gov.pk/Home.aspx (Accessed on 5 May 2012).
3. The province is officially called *Ostân-e Sîstân vä Bälûèýstân* in Persian and is predominantly inhabited by Baloch.
4. Azhar Ahmad, Gwadar: Hope alive", *Opinion Maker*, 5 August 2012, from http://www.opinion-maker.org/2012/08/gwadar-hope-alive/ (Accessed on 3 November 2012).
5. "History of Gwadar" from http://gwadarcity.info/history-of-gwadar/ (Accessed on 3 November 2012).
6. Ibid.
7. Fordham University (2012), "Medieval Sourcebook: Sidi Ali Reis (16th Century CE): Miratul Memalik (The Mirror of Countries), 1557 CE" Fordham University Website https://sourcebooks.fordham.edu/source/16csidi1.asp (Accessed on 10 December 2012).
8. Azhar Ahmad, "Unraveling Gwadar Town", *The Frontier Post*, Peshawar, 4 May 2013.
9. Note 5 ibid., also the Imperial Gazetteer of India 1908, volume XII, "EINME to GWALIOR", Oxford: The Clarendon Press, p. 415.
10. Note 5 ibid.
11. Mary Ann Weaver. *Pakistan in the Shadow of Jihad and Afghanistan.* New York: Farrar, Straus and Giroux, 2002, p. 93.
12. Mir Ahmad Yar Khan Baluch, *Inside Balochistan–A Political Autobiography of His Highness Baiglar Bagi: Khan-e-Azam XIII*, Karachi: Royal Book Company, 1975, pp. 1-2.
13. Inayat Ulla Baloch. *The Problems of Greater Balochistan,* Stuttgart: Steiner Verlag Wiesbaden Gmbh, 1987, pp. 19-20.
14. Ibid., pp. 20-21.
15. Mir Ahmad Yar Khan Baluch, op. cit., pp. 2-3.
16. Ibid., pp. 3-4.
17. Ibid., p. 5.
18. Ibid., pp. 21-22.
19. Inayat Ulla Baloch, op.cit., p. 23.
20. Mir Ahmad Yar Khan Baluch, op,cit., pp. 22-23.
21. Inayat Ulla Baloch, op. cit., p. 24.
22. Mir Ahmad Yar Khan Baluch, op.cit., pp. 44-46.
23. Ibid., pp. 19-42.
24. Ibid., p. 48.
25. Ibid., p. 5.
26. Ibid., pp. 11-17.
27. Ibid., p. 18.
28. Ibid., p. 21.

29. Ibid., pp. 25-29.
30. Ibid., pp. 39-47.
31. Inayat Ulla Baloch, op.cit., pp. 36-41.
32. Ibid., p. 34.
33. Weaver, op. cit., p. 93.
34. Mani Shankar Iyer. "Pakistan Papers". New Delhi, UBS Publishers Distributors Ltd, 1994, pp. 123-128.
35. This statement does not take into account the numbers of Brahui speakers, which are ethnolinguistically a different group. As brought out earlier, Brahui is a Dravidian language; however, Brahui speakers broadly consider themselves as Baloch.
36. Adeel Khan, op. cit,, p.110.
37. Mir Ahmad Yar Khan Baluch, op. cit., pp. 52-53.
38. Ibid., pp. 53-55.
39. Ibid., pp. 55-57.
40. Taj Mohammad Breseeg, *Baloch Nationalism: Its Origin and Development*, Karachi: Royal Book Company, 2004, pp. 136 -138.
41. Ibid.
42. Ibid., p. 22.
43. Ibid., p. 150.
44. Adeel Khan, op. cit, pp. 110 - 111.
45. Baloch nationalists nostalgically tend to recall this era as the glorious period of Baloch history.
46. Adeel Khan, op. cit., pp. 111 - 112.
47. Tahir Amin, "*Ethno National Movements of Pakistan*". Islamabad: Institute of Policy Studies, 1988, p. 64.
48. Adeel Khan, op. cit., pp. 113 -114.
49. Martin Woodward, "Gwadar: the Sultan's Possession" from Qatar Digital Library, 18 May 2017, Website https://www.qdl.qa/en/gwadar-sultan%E2%80%99s-possession (Accessed on 10 December 2019).
50. Ibid., Primary source, British Library, London, "File 22/16 I (A 41) GWADUR, Oil, Proposed Cession and Ownership" IOR/R/15/1/378.
51. Ibid.
52. Ibid.
53. Ibid.
54. Ibid.
55. Sabahat Ali, "Gwadar-the Gateway of CPEC" *Centreline*, 13 December 2016. Also see Rafaqat Hussain, "Gwadar in Historical Perspective" from Muslim Institute Website https://www.muslim-institute.org/newsletter-op-gwadar.pdf (Accessed on 10 March 2020).
56. Azhar Ahmad (2012), op. cit.
57. Turbat is called Kech since 1994.
58. *Countries and Territories of the World, Volume II – the Middle East & the Caucasus*, Wikipedians, 2008, p. 303.
59. Rafaqat Hussain, op. cit.
60. D. Kaplan "Pakistan's Fatal Shore" *The Atlantic*, May 2009.

2

Gwadar Deep Sea Port Project: Pakistani Dream and the Present Status

Exactly one month after taking over Gwadar, Pakistan faced a military coup and, within two months, Ayub Khan was at the helm of affairs as a military dictator. As a military man, it was his regime that realised Gwadar's enormous potential and visualised it as an alternative to Karachi, which could function both as an air and naval hub. It was felt that along with Pasni in the east, Gwadar could make Pakistan a great Indian Ocean power. The absence of adequate economic, institutional, and technical resources prevented Pakistan from implementing its vision. In the 1980s, the Soviet Union eyed Gwadar during its presence in Afghanistan in support of the communist regime there. It was their ultimate objective, a warm water port that was possibly the strategic basis for their Afghan intervention itself. It was felt that Gwadar would assist them in exporting the huge hydrocarbon resources of Central Asia. However, the Afghan quagmire ensured that Soviet aspirations remained a pipedream, while Gwadar remained a congregation of few fishermen's stone houses and an inconspicuous point along the Makran coast on the map.[1]

The story continued, as successive democratic governments in the 1990s were tied down in expanding social and economic turmoil. Intense bouts of violence were prevalent in Karachi and other cities, which focussed Pakistan's policy makers' attention inward. Yet, despite its preoccupation with internal disorders, Islamabad's obsession with Afghanistan and seeking energy routes to Central Asia remained. The turbulence in Afghanistan and Central Asia after the Soviet withdrawal and its subsequent disintegration prevented Pakistan from establishing a network of roads and pipelines to Central Asia though Afghan territory. This prevented it from fulfilling its cherished desire of establishing a Muslim strategic depth to contain India.[2]

It was this obsession of bringing order in Afghanistan that prompted Benazir Bhutto's government and her interior minister General Naseerullah Babar to create a radical outfit like the Taliban to establish order and provide access to Central Asia. However, it soon realised that this Frankenstein's monster was certainly not a harbinger of peace and stability. Western energy firms also learnt this bitter lesson after burning millions of dollars in trying to build pipelines from the Caspian Sea and Central Asia through Afghanistan to Indian Ocean ports like Gwadar.

Way back even before Gwadar was 'purchased' by Pakistan from Oman, in 1954, the United States Geological Survey (USGS) made a survey of Pakistan's coast line, which identified Gwadar as the most suitable site for building a sea port. Accordingly, Pakistan after acquiring Gwadar from the Sultanate of Oman in 1958 decided as early as in 1964 to build a mega port there.[3]

The Asian Development Bank (ADB)'s Ports Master Plan studies also considered Gwadar to be the most suitable alternative to the Persian Gulf ports in terms of location, which could accommodate large super tankers as well as mother ships, to capture the transit trade of the Central Asian Republics as well as the trans-shipment trade of the region.[4] In order to reduce Pakistan's overwhelming dependence on Karachi, both for naval and economic activities, it was also decided to develop two sea ports at Port Qasim and Gwadar. Subsequently, in 1993, Pakistan initiated a study to understand the technical and financial requirements for the construction of the Gwadar Deep Sea Port. The study reinforced the belief that Gwadar was geo-strategically the ideal location to emerge as the hub for regional trade.[5] Although, the government had decided to set up a deep sea port at Gwadar as early as in 1991, work on the project could not commence till 2001, as Pakistan faced political instability and acute financial crisis.[6]

The project built with Chinese assistance is one of the largest infrastructural projects being executed in Pakistan since its independence in 1947. The port is almost complete, but various associated projects are still in phases of development. The ground-breaking ceremony was presided over by the then President of Pakistan, General Pervez Musharraf, and the Chinese Vice-Premier on 22 March 2002. A Chinese company was given the contract to build the port. The first part of the project was completed and the port was scheduled to have been formally handed over to the Pakistani government by the Chinese firm on 18 April 2005. However, the formal inauguration had to be postponed due to the prevailing security environment in Balochistan. It was stated by the Pakistani government that the port would be linked with the countries of Central Asia and Afghanistan by a network of railways and roads.[7]

During the ground-breaking ceremony of the port, General Musharraf had stated that the port of Gwadar, on account of its location, would have tremendous strategic advantages. He articulated that after the development of the rail and road infrastructure, the port would emerge as the regional hub for trade and commercial activity. He also stated that it would serve as a hub port near the junction of various trade routes around the Strait of Hormuz, just outside the mouth of the Persian Gulf. He further added that it could provide an alternative access to the sea for trade originating or bound for the northern parts of Pakistan.[8] The importance being accorded to the project is evident from the fact that the first phase of the project was initially planned to be inaugurated jointly by the Pakistani President and the Chinese Prime Minister. Eventually, President Gen Pervez Musharraf, along with Chinese Minister of Communications Li Shenglin formally inaugurated the first phase of Gwadar port on 20 March 2007.

Even before the inauguration, the operations of the port were handed over to the Port of Singapore Authority (PSA) International, which was also entrusted the responsibility to develop it, so as to make it a thriving port. However, due to government policies, prevailing political volatility in Pakistan and above all a grave sense of insecurity prevailing in Balochistan, none of the major components of the master plan could reach fructification. Consequently, in February 2013, Islamabad unilaterally transferred the leasing rights of the port from PSA International to a Chinese state owned enterprise China Overseas Port Holding Company (COPHC). As a result, Gwadar deep sea port became an extremely, significant component of the CPEC, which aims to connect Gwadar to Xinjiang through a network of roads and pipelines transiting through Gilgit-Baltistan, a territory of the former princely state of Jammu and Kashmir, currently under Pakistan's occupation.[9]

Significance of the Port

Gwadar has been a long-gestating idea in Pakistan. It is the first major port outside the Karachi-Port Bin Qasim complex and to a great extent has removed the factor of critical vulnerability for Pakistan, as the port will provide it with another option to unload vital supplies in case of non-availability of the Karachi-Bin Qasim complex either due to natural disasters, accidents or naval blockade. It provides Pakistan an alternative port, both geo-politically as well as economically and becomes extremely significant in case of any war with India.[10]

Pakistan like most other countries of the world is predominantly dependent on the sea for its trade and more than 90 per cent of its trade transits through this medium. Pakistan (the West Pakistan till 1971), since its creation in 1947 has been solely dependent on Karachi Port for its maritime trade and subsequently on the Karachi-Bin Qasim complex, after Port Muhammad bin Qasim became operational. Unfortunately for Pakistan, both these ports are part of the same complex and are fairly close to Indian waters. This makes them extremely susceptible to both attacks and blockades by the Indian Navy. This harsh reality was clearly brought out both in 1971 and subsequently during the Kargil conflict in 1999. This has impacted the thinking of both Pakistan's military as well as the civilian leadership. Gwadar port being much farther to the west and away from India is considerably less vulnerable to these threats.[11]

Most of Pakistan's trade and its entire hydrocarbon imports come from its west. Consequently, ships, especially those coming from the Red Sea or the Persian Gulf, need to hug the coast to unlade their cargo on Pakistan's eastern extremity, where both Karachi port and Port Bin Qasim are located. These ships are extremely vulnerable in their passage and may need to be protected by Pakistan's limited naval assets during war. As most of Pakistan's cargo is carried in foreign bottoms, the likelihood of their refusal to undertake such a hazardous passage in times of hostilities cannot be ruled out. Even when they agree to call on these ports, they will in all probability demand an extremely high insurance premium to cover their risks. With Gwadar, the period of their presence in Pakistan's waters reduces considerably, thereby making their interdiction quite difficult. Thus, Gwadar can not only ensure faster and more reliable supplies in times of war; it could also result in considerable savings to the exchequer.[12]

In addition, this allows the Pakistani Navy to keep its assets dispersed rather than bottled them up in the Karachi-Bin Qasim complex. It also allows it greater flexibility and better ability to monitor its maritime zones, besides giving it the crucial strategic advantage that it can now virtually monitor the entire traffic to and from the Persian Gulf, including the presence of regional and extra-regional navies. This ability creates serious problems for India and other countries dependent on the Persian Gulf for their energy needs and trade. Consequently, despite being touted as a commercial port only, it bolsters Pakistan's maritime security considerably.[13]

The port due to its location at the entrance of the Persian Gulf has immense geo-strategic significance. It has the potential to provide the shortest and consequently, the fastest and most cost-effective access to landlocked Central Asia and Afghanistan.[14] The emergence of the new Central Asian states coupled with the continued unstable regional environment in the Persian Gulf has contributed to the importance of the port. The emerging geo-political rift between Iran and the USA, and rising tensions amongst the Gulf Coordination Council (GCC) countries; as well as the presence of global terror outfits like the al-Qaeda and the Islamic State in the vicinity, further enhance the significance of Gwadar. Islamabad has always been interested in Gwadar port as it provides Pakistan strategic depth to the west away from Karachi, its major naval base.[15]

As brought out earlier, Karachi for long has been extremely vulnerable to a blockade by the Indian Navy. In order to diversify the positioning of its naval assets, Pakistan has built the Jinnah Naval Base at Ormara, which has been operational since June 2000. The base can accommodate about a dozen naval ships, submarines and other yard craft. However, the Gwadar port project is much bigger than Ormara and has enormous potential. It has been touted as an asset that would enable the Pakistan Navy to emerge as a force that can compete with other regional navies. Accordingly, the government of Pakistan has designated the area around the port as a 'sensitive defence zone'.[16]

The port is connected by the newly constructed Makran coastal highway (653 km long) from Sheikh Raj, approximately 105 km north of Karachi to Gabd, which is near Pakistan's border with Iran. The highway links Karachi to the ports on the Makran coast, namely, Ormara, Pasni, Gwadar, and Jiwani. The highway therefore has the potential to boost trade between Pakistan and Iran. Another road link on which work is in progress is the Gwadar-Ratodero (M-8) motorway which would pass through Turbat, Awaran, and Khuzdar to eventually join the Indus highway at Ratodero. It is also planned to connect Gwadar port to the provincial capital, Quetta, and to Zahidan in Iran.[17] Pakistan's railway minister has claimed that the railway link between Gwadar and Quetta would be extremely beneficial to the CPEC and would boost further economic activity in Gwadar.[18] A new rail link from Gwadar to Mastung is also envisaged, whose construction will commence in 2025.[19]

Apart from its geostrategic importance, the project is the cornerstone for the economic development of Pakistan and Balochistan and it could change the landscape of the region and the fortune of its people. The major economic benefits that the authorities perceive from the project include opportunities for trade with Afghanistan and the Central Asian Republics, promotion of movement and commerce with the states of the Persian Gulf and evolution of the port as a trans-shipment hub for computerised cargo.[20] It is planned to link the port with Pakistan's hinterland, as well as Afghanistan and the Central Asian Republics through transportation networks of railways and roads. At the same time, the Gwadar Development Authority has started the development of Gwadar town and surrounding areas in accordance with a master plan.[21]

According to *Khaleej Times*, the port, when fully completed, is expected to become one of the busiest harbours in the region, and would provide transhipment, warehousing and industrial facilities for trade and commerce with more than 20 countries including the Central Asian Republics, China, East Africa, India, Iran and countries of the Persian Gulf.[22]

The Government of Pakistan, with the avowed objective of attracting foreign investment in the region, has already granted a 15-year tax holiday in the export processing zone being developed near the port. In addition, it has also permitted China and South Korea to establish tax-free special industrial development zones near Gwadar Port.[23] Pakistan has also sought investment from Kuwait and other West Asian states. It has succeeded in persuading Oman to invest $ 80 million in Gwadar, besides the $ 20 million already invested in the project. As brought out earlier, Gwadar was part of Oman till 1958, when Oman was cajoled into selling 2,400 square miles of territory including Gwadar to Pakistan for just $ 8.4 million, by the UK.[24] The present investment by Oman in Gwadar is not only governed by nostalgia for its historical possession, but also by a realistic assessment of the enormous economic potential of the Gwadar port. It realises that Gwadar is the deepest port in Pakistan and can berth much larger tankers than either the port of Karachi or Port Bin Qasim.

The Project

The Gwadar project started on 22 March 2002 and the first phase was completed in April 2005. The first phase included construction of three multipurpose berths with a total length of 602 metres (three berths of 200 m each), one Roll-on-Roll-out (RORO) facility, a 4.7-kilometre approach channel with a width of 206 metres reducing to 155 metres, channel and berths dredged to a depth of 14.5 metres expected to increase to 20 metres after Phase II, with a turning basin of 595 metres in diameter, as well as one 100-metre long service berth as well as associated port infrastructure and handling equipment including pilot boats, tugs, survey vessels, etc.[25]

The first phase enabled the jetty to handle container carriers of up to 50,000 dead weight tonnage (DWT). The designed annual turnover of the three berths is 100,000 TEU[26] of containers, 270,000 tons of general cargo and 150,000 tons of bulk cargo.[27] The designed annual Phase-I has been constructed at a cost of Rs. (Pakistani) 14.9 billion ($ 248 million).[28] Of this, China has paid $ 198 million while Pakistan has contributed $ 50 million. China has also offered expertise in the form of technical staff and has provided the bulk of the equipment.

Phase II of the port commenced in May 2005 and was expected to be completed by 2015. It II included three terminals for handling containers (total quay length of 2,010 metres), one terminal for handling bulk cargo (length 305 metres), one terminal for handling grain (length 305 metres), one oil terminal with two piers (total length 688 metres), 600-metre long breakwater and deepening of the approach channel to 20 metres. Phase II also includes necessary back-up areas, buildings, craft and equipment, as required to berth container ships up to 50,000 DWT, dry bulk carriers of 100,000 DWT and oil tankers up to 200,000 DWT.[29]

Unfortunately for Pakistan, Phase II, which is a much bigger and ambitious project, has not been progressing as per schedule and is still underway, adjacent to Phase I and is now a part of the CPEC. The total project cost of the phase is estimated to be $ 1.02 billion. On 16 January 2019, Pakistan's Senate Standing Committee on Maritime Affairs in a meeting held at Gwadar had communicated its serious concerns about the slow pace of ongoing work on the project and had expressed dissatisfaction with the steps initiated to complete the project.[30]

Merchant ships have been calling at the port since January 2003 and have been offloading hundreds of tonnes of cargo imported for the project even before Phase I was completed. Pakistan Petroleum, which is exploring offshore gas, has also started using the port for loading and offloading equipment fairly regularly.[31] The government is also setting up special economic zones near the port to make Gwadar the hub of economic and industrial activities.[32]

While the basic purpose of Phase I was fairly modest to establish Gwadar as just a functioning port, as indicated earlier, Phase II strives to establish Gwadar as a major hub port. This phase includes plans to build nine additional berths, which will include one terminal for Roll-on-Roll-out ships and two oil terminals to berth tankers up to 200,000 DWT. The deepening of the approach channel had commenced in January 2005 and was initially estimated to be completed by June 2006. President Musharraf had asked all the agencies associated with the project to complete all the required infrastructure facilities at Gwadar port before June 2006.[33] The fact that the project has still not been completed indicates the slow progress of work. The slow pace could be deliberate, or a case of improper assessment of work.

Terminal Expansion Plan 2018-19

As the completion of the second phase has been inordinately delayed a terminal expansion plan was approved for the financial year 2018-19 to enhance the cargo handling capacity of the port. The plan envisages enhancement of the cargo handling capacity of the four berths in the port, namely, oil handling berth, dry bulk cargo berth, general cargo berth, and mineral ore berth.[34]

The expansion plans included building a 322-m long dry bulk cargo berth, with facilities to berth 150,000-ton ships and an annual handling capacity of 1,000,000 tons. The berth would have a provision for 22 hectares of land beside it for handling cargo. It also incorporates constructing a 515-metre long oil terminal with a capacity to berth 250,000-ton tankers and an annual handling capacity of 17,000,000 tons of crude oil. The terminal will encompass 14 hectares of land besides the berth for pumping facilities and other necessary infrastructure required for crude handling. The expansion also envisages a 368-metre long mineral berth with 21 hectares of land besides it for handling cargo. The berth will be able to accommodate 200,000-ton ships and will have the capacity to handle 13,000,000 tons of various ores every year. In addition, a 285-metre long general cargo berth is envisaged to be built to handle ships of up to 70,000 tons capacity and an annual handling capacity of 20,000,000 tons of general cargo. In addition, provision has made for 21 hectares of land beside the berth for cargo handling and warehousing.[35]

Despite these ambitious projections, the terminal expansion plan 2018-19 is moving slowly, whereas Phase II is virtually crawling. The existing port infrastructure at the Gwadar port, including berthing facilities, port facilities and communication set up, is as follows:

Berthing Facilities

Three multipurpose berths of 200 metres length each. One roll-on-roll-off facility. One service berth of 100 metres length.An approach channel 4.7 km long with depth of 14.4 metres maintained in the outer channel, a 13.8-metre deep inner channel/turning basin with dredged depths of 14.5 metre alongside the berth. Outer channel, which is 206 metres wide and an inner channel with a width of 155 metres. Turning basin, with a diameter of 595 metres. At present, the port has the capacity to handle bulk carriers up to 50,000 DWT with a maximum draft of 12.5 metres.

Port Facilities

Port area	64,000m^2
Container stacking area	48,278m^2
Reefer cargo space	(400 points) 367 m^2
Empty container stacking area	6,875m^2

Storage yard	28,669m^2
Transit shed	3,750m^2
Hazardous cargo storage yard	1,800m^2
Control tower (foot print only)	1,536m^2
Buoy yard	1,500m^2
Generator building	593m^2
Maintenance workshop (general)	1,440m^2
Vehicle servicing garage	450m^2
Security building	65m^2
Common offices for GPA, ustoms, Immigration	Several floors, 4,144m^2 on each floor
Mosque	324m^2
Operations office and canteen	1,742m^2 per floor
Parking for cars and lorries	1,125 m^2
Area earmarked for future development	118,575 m^2
Oil recovery system	1 complete set

Communications

VHF/DSC including INMARSAT-B

In addition, the various equipment, vessels, and craft available at the port as on 31 December 2019 are as follows:

Yard Craft and Vessels

Two tug boats of 2,400 horse power each
One survey boat
One working boat
One mooring boat
Two pilot boats

Cranes and Yard Equipment

Five rail-mounted cranes
Two 40-ton cranes with 40m spans
One 16-ton crane with 33m span
Two 10-ton cranes with 33m spans
Two 40-tons rubber tyred gantry cranes (RTGS)

Two 10-ton mobile cranes
400 refrigeration container sockets
Three power house main generators of 1.5 MW each
A 116-kW power house emergency generator
12 fork lift trucks with rated lifting capacity of 5 tons each
Two container reach stackers of 40 tons capacity
Six container tractors of 100 kN capacity
Four container semi-trailers, with carrying capacity of one 40-foot container or two 20-foot containers
Four 25-ton flat trucks
Four 10-ton flat trucks
Eight hoppers of 6 m x 6 m
Eight mobile bagging plants with capacity of 50 tons per hour each
12 fork lift trucks with five ton capacity
Two weighing bridges of 80-ton capacity
Two fire tenders for fire fighting
One vehicle for sweeping the roads
One garbage collection truck
Oil tanker[37]

In addition, considering the severe water scarcity in Gwadar, a desalination plant with a capacity of 100,000 gallons per day has been established to supply fresh water to the ships calling at the port.[38]

On completion of the project, the Gwadar deep-sea port is expected to be one of the most strategically located ports in the region and will not only emerge as the nearest port in the Arabian Sea for the landlocked countries of Central Asia, but will also start attracting traffic from other Gulf ports, mainly Dubai. If successful, the port could generate enough revenues to change the landscape of the Makran coast and its hinterland. Phase II accordingly has envisaged a much higher outlay and incorporates plans to build additional berths on a Build-Operate-Transfer basis.[39] At the moment, the commitment of funds for Phase II of the project depends entirely on the progress of CPEC projects and the ongoing operations of the port.

Unlike the Chinese, Pakistan does not visualise Gwadar as a gateway to Xinjiang only, but as an ideal point of entry for the large amount of merchandise bound for and originating from Central Asia. It plans to set up an export processing zone in Gwadar with a 15-year tax holiday to attract foreign investors. It hopes that the deep-sea port would open up "new opportunities for trade, import and export as well as transit trade facilities for Afghanistan and beyond". Gwadar provides the shortest access to the sea for the former Soviet republics of Central Asia and provides Pakistan with a lucrative option to import energy from these resource-rich countries through Afghanistan. The process of providing avenues for international trade through Gwadar port could lead to the creation of new stakeholders in Afghanistan who will benefit from the transit trade to the Central Asian Republics.[40] According to Pakistani policy makers, this could not only lead to a normalisation of the situation in Afghanistan but could also contribute to improvement of relations between Pakistan and Afghanistan. "Gwadar thus provides an avenue for improving relations between Pakistan and the region to its immediate northwest".[41] However, the trans-Karakoram pipeline gives another option of exploiting Gwadar port in case Afghanistan continues to simmer for some time.

Development of the Hinterland

The project also includes development of a number of facilities in Gwadar town that include setting up of a desalination plant to provide water in this arid region. The plant will also generate up to three megawatts of electricity. According to the authorities, Gwadar city is planned to be developed to half the size of Islamabad city in three to four years. A 350-bed hospital will be built in Gwadar, besides a fishermen town, a fishing jetty, a modern sports complex, and a few five-star hotels. The master plan for Gwadar includes development of approximately 18,600 hectares of land for the entire project. This includes two phases of port development on 400 hectares of land and the establishment of an export processing zone on 74 hectares next to the port in the East Bay. It also incorporates setting up of a special industrial zone on around 4,000 hectares of land north of Gwadar town and construction of an oil refinery northeast of Gwadar town on approximately 1,000 hectares of land. The oil refinery is planned to be connected to the proposed oil terminal in the port through an undersea pipeline passing across the East Bay. In addition, an area of 400 hectares north of the existing Gwadar town along the West Bay has been earmarked for development as a residential township in future to cater to the expanding population of the town.[42]

In order to connect Gwadar to the rest of the country, a 529-km long coastal highway has been built at a cost of 10 billion Pakistani rupees.[43] A feasibility report on connecting Gwadar port with rail tracks is being completed. The proposed 550-km track would start from Gwadar and pass via Turbat and Panjgur before terminating at Dalbandin, which is close to the border with Afghanistan and far from Iran. This would not only facilitate the movement of goods from Central Asian States and Afghanistan to Gwadar but would also enable the export of copper from the Saindak project and the Reko Diq copper gold project to various destinations abroad from this port. Rail connectivity with Gwadar port could herald a new era of prosperity in the region and would approximately cost Rs. (Pakistani) 8,500 million.[44] There were plans to upgrade the existing length of the runway at Gwadar airport from 5,000 to 15,000 feet for operation of wide-bodied jet aircraft but the growing Chinese interests have ensured that a completely new airport is being constructed.[45]

Accordingly, Prime Minister Imran Khan did the ground-breaking ceremony for the New Gwadar International Airport (NGIA) on 29 March 2019, and laid the foundation of the new airport, which is being funded by the Chinese. Work commenced on 31 October 2019.[46] Imran Khan was accompanied by General Qamar Javed Bajwa, the all-powerful Chief of the Army Staff of the Pakistan Army and Yao Jing, the Chinese Ambassador to Pakistan. The new airport with an area of 4,300 acres and located at Gurandani at a distance of 26 kilometres from Gwadar port, when completed, is going to be the largest airport in Pakistan. It will also be the second airport in Pakistan after Islamabad, which will be able to operate big aircraft like the Airbus A380 and the Boeing 777. The airport will provide air connectivity to the hub of Chinese investment under the CPEC.[47]

The economics of the airport at the moment does not appear sound, as Gwadar has a population of less than 100,000 people and the total air traffic in Gwadar in 2017-18 was 33,984. This traffic could easily have been serviced from the existing airport. With a projected passenger growth of 2.82 per cent, it will be many years before the airport will be able to reach its optimum capacity. As of now, even domestic flights to Gwadar are usually empty. Consequently, many analysts see the new airport meeting the fate of another Chinese-built airport in Hambantota.[48]

The airport project, quite unlike other projects of the CPEC, is planned to be completed in three years under a Chinese grant. This greenfield project with all modern facilities for safe operation, envisages an ultra-modern terminal building along with a large cargo terminal, which would initially have an annual capacity to handle 30,000 tons of cargo. It is envisaged by the policy makers in Islamabad that with the commissioning of a new international airport, Gwadar will become the hub of the aviation industry. The total estimated cost of the project is envisaged to be $ 256 million. The Chinese have given a grant of $ 230 million for it, which was earlier termed as a loan. It is one of several projects being financed by the Chinese government in Gwadar worth $ 690 million as part of its Belt and Road Initiative.[49]

On 29 March 2019, a memorandum of understanding (MoU) was also signed for construction of a Pak-China Friendship Hospital to provide much needed health care facilities to local residents. Another MoU was signed to set up the Pakistan and China Vocational Training Institute, to provide training to the local population. This is expected to enhance their employment opportunities. Gwadar is also being connected to the national power grid of Pakistan, while at the moment, its power needs are being met by importing power from Iran. A desalination plant for the city, as well as a solid waste management system is also envisaged. A water recycling plant and a rail link to Quetta (distinct from the earlier proposal of linking it to Dalbandin) is also being planned. Although a new airport is being built, the capacity of the existing one is also being enhanced as an interim measure. According to Imran Khan, Gwadar's ideal location and excellent connectivity will ensure that its development will result in the development of Pakistan in its entirety.[50]

In addition, a 19-km long Gwadar Eastbay Expressway to connect Gwadar port to the Makran coastal highway is being planned and a framework agreement has been signed with the government. A feasibility study on setting up of wastewater treatment plants in order to augment fresh water supply for Gwadar City and surrounding areas has been commissioned. Contract negotiations are also going on for the Gwadar Smart Port City Master Plan. Similarly, the first phase of the Gwadar Free Zone has been completed by the China Overseas Ports Holding Company Ltd (COPHC).[51] The company had taken control of the free trade zone on 11 November 2015 on a 43-year lease.[52]

In 2013, an agreement was signed between Gwadar Port Authority (GPA), COPHC and Singapore Port Authority, and the operation and future development of Gwadar free zone was entrusted to COPHC. The total area of Gwadar free zone at present is 923 hectares; of which 898 is located in the northern part of Gwadar, around seven kilometres from the existing port, whereas the initial area of 25 hectares is located west of the existing port. The initial area includes some construction for infrastructure, trade exhibition hall, business centre, warehouses, cold storage, facilities for processing fish, etc. The development period of the Free Trade Zone extends from 2015 to 2030 and has been divided into four phases. The development of the free zone is a key component of the CPEC and indicates the overall Chinese thinking of trade and commerce. It aims at the integration of the port with the free zone to link industries between China and Pakistan. The Chinese-run free zone is being projected as the economic development engine of Gwadar and a centre for international trade logistics under the CPEC.[53]

The first phase of the Gwadar Free Zone was inaugurated by the then Pakistani Prime Minister, Shahid Khaqan Abbasi, on 29 January 2018. According to the COPHC, 30 odd companies in various fields such as banking, fish processing, logistics and hotels are already in the free trade zone (FTZ) with an investment of approximately $ 474.3 million; the output is expected to touch an annual value of $ 790.5 million after full operation of the trade zone.[54]

As of March 2018, the progress on various projects in the hinterland was mixed. Of the two separate zones of the Gwadar free zone, the southern part, which was where the pilot free zone was initiated, was more or less complete at an approximate cost of $ 160 million. The zone expects additional investment of around $ 250 million from five big investors. On the other hand, the main free zone, also called the northern zone, was yet to start functioning optimally, although four industrial units were expected to start functioning soon. Similarly, the project for construction of the Eastbay Expressway was approved in 2016 by Pakistan's Executive Committee of the National Economic Council (ECNEC). It was scheduled to be completed by 2018; however, only nine per cent of the job was completed by March 2018. Subsequently, the completion date of the project costing Rs. (Pakistani) 14,061.79 million including a foreign exchange component of Rs. 13,542 million was shifted to October 2020. An interest-free loan is being provided by the Government of China for this project, but progress has been rather slow due to the prevailing security situation coupled with the remoteness of the site.[55] According to Lt-Gen Asim Bajwa, the then Chairman of the CPEC Authority, the Expressway was to be completed by October 2021.[56] However, it was finally inaugurated by Prime Minister Shehbaz Sharif on 3 June 2022.[57]

Similarly, Phase II of the Eastbay Expressway of Gwadar port, which had been approved by the fifth joint coordination committee as an 'early harvest project' of the China-Pakistan Economic Corridor (CPEC) at an approximate cost of PKR 6 billion, has simply failed to take off. The feasibility report for this phase was submitted to the Planning Commission in Islamabad on 7 November 2017, with a request for interest free funding from China. However, the Chinese have not yet agreed to provide the funding. Phase-II of the proposed Expressway will connect the new international airport being built at Gwadar with Phase I of the Eastbay Expressway.[58]

On 4 November 2019, a 300-megawatt coal-fired power plant was inaugurated at Gwadar as part of the CPEC by Ning Jizhe, deputy head of the National Development and Reform Commission of China. He also inaugurated the Gwadar Port Authority commercial complex project and the Faqeer Colony middle school expansion project, being funded by the China Foundation for Peace and Development (CFPD). The China-Pakistan Government primary school in Faqeer, which was built by donations from the CFPD, has been operating since 2016 and has around 600 students. The expansion of the school with new facilities is expected to be completed by 2020. The Chinese have been trying to showcase these CPEC projects as symbols of long-standing friendship between China and Pakistan. They have claimed that these will improve access to electricity, education, and commerce for local residents of Gwadar.[59]

The Gwadar Deep Sea Port project is being projected as a gateway to prosperity for not only Gwadar, but the entire region. To meet the power supply requirements of the project, a coal-fired plant is being developed by two Chinese companies jointly. The plant is expected to alleviate the severe electricity shortage at Gwadar. The projected investment of approximately $ 430 million is being met by the two companies.[60] Chinese Ambassador to

Pakistan Yao Jing has also said that the Chinese government is going to establish 19 factories in Gwadar, so as to provide jobs to the local youth. He also affirmed China's commitment to invest in the expansion of the Zhob - Dera Ismail Khan highway, which is considered a crucial link for the CPEC.[61]

The China Ocean Shipping Company (COSCO), launched a container liner service from Port Qasim - Karachi to Gwadar and then on to Jebel Ali - Sharjah - Abu Dhabi - Jebel Ali - Port Qasim. The first container vessel of the service *MS Tiger* arrived at Gwadar port on 7 March 2018. The vessel was welcomed in an elaborate ceremony and was escorted to the port by two warships. After unloading a cargo of frozen sea food, the vessel left for the port of Jebel Ali in the United Arab Emirates. The start of the first container cargo shipping service between Gwadar and several ports in West Asia, known as the Karachi Gwadar Gulf Express, marked a significant milestone for Gwadar. The service started by using Karachi, Jebel Ali and other Emirati ports as transit ports to integrate the new liner service into its 16 established international routes to provide services for its global clients. The COPHC, accordingly, issued a statement stating that "This is also the only shipping line in and out of Gwadar in the global shipping market. It means Gwadar will be connected to almost all major ports in the world and represents a big leap forward in the development of Gwadar".[62]

On 14 December 2019, the port was officially operationalised for exports, when a vessel carrying three fish containers with an average estimated value of $ 50,000 each for a Far-Eastern country, started seafood exports through Gwadar port. Authorities in Islamabad believe that this would relieve congestion at the Karachi port and also reduce time for overseas trade. They are hoping that the port gets a sizeable chunk of the trade to Afghanistan and Central Asia. The port has already been included in the rules framed for transit under the Afghanistan-Pakistan Transit Trade Agreement 2010. In order to facilitate the development of the port, the government has set up a committee to draft transit and transhipment rules.[63]

Gwadar offers enormous possibilities as far as business is concerned; a number of economic activities are possible including fisheries and tourism. The Pakistani elite believe that the Gwadar port project holds immense promise for progress and prosperity and will generate huge economic activity paving the way for the progress and development of Balochistan. It is widely believed that this mega project will boost trade with Central Asian states, help attract foreign investment and create new job opportunities. The project is considered of vital importance for Pakistan's economy. This project could also open up opportunities to export the natural resources and minerals of Balochistan.[64]

Limitations

Although, the project aims to kick start economic activities in a hitherto neglected region and create jobs, the Baloch are not happy with the Gwadar Deep Sea project. Although the Pakistani government has ambitious plans for developing Gwadar, and it could be the harbinger of prosperity in the region, the Baloch insurgents have been regularly targeting the work and the personnel associated with the project. As early as in 2004, three Chinese engineers working for a Chinese construction company in Gwadar were killed and nine others were injured when their vehicle was targeted by the insurgents. During the attack, rockets were fired on Gwadar airport.[65]

Baloch nationalists feel that the fruits of Gwadar will not reach the Baloch people; on the contrary, they feel it will lead to a large-scale influx of outsiders in Balochistan,[66] which would make them a minority in their own province. The channelling of funds has mainly been in the hands of the non-Baloch and the Baloch plea for control over decisions pertaining to development activities has been ignored by the Punjabi bureaucracy. More significantly, Gwadar is being connected to Karachi, but has not been connected to Quetta, the provincial capital, through Turbat, Panjgur, and Khuzdar. As a result, the rest of the province will not derive any benefit from these projects. This is leading to unrest within the Baloch community as they perceive that Balochistan is being turned into a landlocked province, in spite of possessing the longest coastline in Pakistan.[67]

The fact that cargo being offloaded at Gwadar has to travel almost all the way up to Karachi by the Makran Coastal Highway makes the port extremely unattractive to traders, as the transportation costs by road are much higher and it makes more sense to use Karachi or Port Qasim instead. Baloch resistance and Pakistan's acute financial crisis has already slowed down the progress of Phase II. This has resulted in a dip in Chinese investment as well. The COSCO Shipping Lines of China, which had started a weekly container liner service between Karachi and Gwadar in March 2018, terminated it on account of the slow progress of the Gwadar Free Trade Zone, which has resulted in inadequate volume of exports and imports from there.[68]

Gwadar's inability to tap the markets of Afghanistan and Central Asia, coupled with the inefficiency of Gwadar Customs, high cost of inland shipping and rejection of transit items by the Karachi port have led to this decision by COSCO. The company has alleged that the Pakistan government's inadequate policies and measures have adversely impacted market development and consequently, the yield of COSCO's liner service to Gwadar. Even the port operator, the Gwadar International Terminal Limited, a subsidy of the COPHC, is believed to be unhappy with the recent developments and have conveyed their discontentment to the federal authorities in Pakistan.[69]

The port also suffers from critical water and power shortages. There has been no rain in the Gwadar region for the last five-six years and most of the dams have apparently dried up. At present, the water crisis for the local inhabitants is so acute that each household is given 30-40 gallons each week. Water is therefore being brought from Mirani Dam in Turbat, 142 km away, by tankers, which costs Rs. (Pakistani) 15,000-18,000. Subsequently, the water is stored in three large underground tanks, which are inter-connected. The three tanks can store 500,000 gallons, 300,000 gallons, and 200,000 gallons of water which is distributed from there by tankers. The water is then provided by the officials of the Union Councils (UCs), who allot water to their respective UCs. There is enormous discontentment and apprehension amongst the locals about the foul play in distribution of water. Consequently, a police constable and a clerk from the Public Health Engineering (PHE) Department guard the entrance of the water works and record the number of tankers supplying water to various UCs. Like any other part of Pakistan, an army official also stays with them for supervision, to ensure transparency.[70]

Gwadar presently needs around 6.3 million gallons per day (MGD) of fresh water, whereas the total supply is only 2.9 MGD, of which 2.7 MGD comes from the Ankara Kaur Dam, while 0.2 MGD is being supplied by the COPHC from its desalination plant. It is intended to augment it to 12 MGD by 2020, which entails building a 67-km long pipe line from Swad Dam to Gwadar. Further augmentation of water supply is intended by a 4-MGD desalination plant being built by the Frontier Works Organisation (FWO) and a 5-MGD reverse osmosis sea water Plant for Gwadar city, which has been included in the public sector development programme (PSDP) 2017.[71]

For its power needs, Gwadar relies on the 132-kV high-voltage power distribution network from Iran, which supplies 100 MW for the coastal belt; of this, the current demand of Gwadar city is about 45 MW, which will increase exponentially as the city and the port infrastructure grows. As mentioned earlier work on a 300-MW coal-fired power plant is in progress by two Chinese companies and once commissioned, it should theoretically meet the demand till 2030.[72] However, coal-based plants are going out of vogue the world over and environmental concerns may force its closure much before 2030. Similarly, pipelines and transmission lines have been the favourite targets of Baloch nationalist groups, many of whom are vehemently opposed to the Gwadar port project.

Conclusion

Situated at the cusp of the Strait of Hormuz through which most of the world's oil flows, the Gwadar Deep Sea project being constructed with financial assistance from China is the largest developmental project being undertaken in Pakistan and has enormous economic potential. At a time when the energy demand in both South Asia and China are experiencing a sharp spike and is expected to double in the coming decade; the port along with the Trans-Karakoram pipeline creates huge potential for business and opens up new opportunities for tapping the energy resources of the landlocked Caspian region.[73] The port has the potential to become another business hub like Dubai and change the landscape of Balochistan. The port and other associated economic activities have the potential to take the Pakistani economy to great heights.

Despite Gwadar's enormous potential, there is no dearth of sceptics doubting its ability to deliver. The underlying reason is that despite its huge potential Gwadar cannot attain economic viability till it is connected to Quetta by road or rail for it to emerge as a bridgehead to Central Asia. Similarly as far as China or even access to Central Asia through China is concerned, its viability depends on timely completion of the Gwadar-Ratodero motorway. The use of the Makran coastal highway to transport goods does not make commercial sense because it almost amounts to taking goods to Karachi by road which could be done much more economically by sea.

Gwadar's prospects of emerging as the future hub of trade and energy transportation for the vibrant economies of East, South and West Asia as well as landlocked Central Asia, therefore depends totally on cutting down transportation costs and time taken to reach the port. However, this cannot be achieved as long as the restive population of Balochistan does not feel enthusiastic about its potential. As long as violence continues, Pakistan cannot emerge as an energy corridor to China nor can a direct road link to Central Asia be established. Not only does violence affect investor confidence, it also affects the implementation of infrastructural projects, especially the pipelines, roads and rail links, which cannot be perpetually defended in their entirety.[74]

The success of the project at the moment is an uncertainty but if successful it will result in the emergence of an ideal gateway for the landlocked states of Afghanistan and Central Asia. It could yield enormous benefits to Pakistan; however, its viability will depend upon Pakistan's ability to handle discontentment in Balochistan and to some extent in Gilgit-Baltistan through which the Karakoram Highway traverses and provides access to Xinjiang and the Central Asian Republics. This will eventually decide the viability of the Gwadar Port Project because as far as access to Central Asia is concerned, it has to get off the block fast because Chabahar is already operational and can give Gwadar a run for its money.

NOTES

1. Robert D. Kaplan. "Pakistan's Fatal Shore," *The Atlantic*, May 2009.
2. Ibid.
3. Mir Sherbaz Khetran. "The Potential and Prospects of Gwadar Port", *Strategic Studies*, Islamabad: Institute of Strategic Studies, 34(4)/35(1), Winter 2014 and Spring 2015, p. 71.
4. "Gawadar" from Govt of Pakistan Board of Investment website http://www.pakboi.gov.pk/News_Event/Gawadar.html (Accessed 22 June 2005).
5. Khetran, op. cit.
6. Azhar Ahmad., "Gwadar: Potential and Prospects", Research Paper presented on 29 January 2015 at one-day seminar on Gwadar by PICSS and FPCCI at Serena Hotel Islamabad.
7. "First phase of Gwadar port completed", *Dawn*, Karachi, 4 December 2004.
8. President of Pakistan General Pervez Musharraf's Address at the Ground-Breaking Ceremony of Gwadar Deep Sea Port on 22 March 2002.

9. "China-Pakistan Economic Corridor: Opportunities and Risks", International Crisis Group Asia Report No. 297, 29 June 2018, p. 17.
10. Ayesha Siddiqa on 13 September 2020 by personal email, in reply to a questionnaire sent by the author.
11. Azhar Ahmad, op. cit.
12. Ibid.
13. Ibid.
14. Noor ul Haq. "Balochistan: its past and present", *The Kashmir Times,* 8 February 2005.
15. Tarique Niazi, "Gwadar: China's Naval Outpost on the Indian Ocean", Association for Asian Research website http://www.asianresearch.org/articles/2528.html (Accessed on 22 June 2005).
16. Ibid.
17. Noor ul Haq, op. cit.
18. "Gwadar to be linked with Quetta through railway: minister" *Dawn*, 23 October 2018.
19. Amin Yusufzai, "Rail Connectivity of Gwadar with other Parts of Pakistan Not a Priority: Officials", from https://propakistani.pk/2019/04/06/rail-connectivity-of-gwadar-with-other-parts-of-pakistan-not-a-priority-officials/ (accessed on 10 December 2019).
20. Note 4. ibid.
21. Note 7. ibid.
22. "Pakistan to decide operator for Gwadar Port next Week", from *Khaleej Times* website http://www.khaleejtimes.com/DisplayArticleNew.asp?xfile=data/business/2006/August/business_August318.xml§ion=business (Accessed on 14 August 2006).
23. Ihtashamul Haque, "Tax-free zones in Gwadar planned: Wooing foreign investment", *Dawn*, Karachi, 17 June 2005.
24. Alok Bansal. "Gwadar: A Chinese Gibraltar", *India Strategic*, vol. 1, February 2006, p. 53.
25. Ministry of Ports & Shipping, Gwadar Port Authority presentation to Parliamentary Committee on CPEC on "Gwadar Port & CPEC" at Gwadar on 28 November 2015.
26. TEU (twenty foot equivalent unit) is an approximate unit of cargo capacity, which is usually applied to state the carrying/handling capacity of container ships and terminals handling them. It is based on the volume of a 20-foot-long (6.1 m) container, which is a standard-sized metal box easily transferrable between various modes of transportation, like ships, trucks, trains and other vehicles.
27. Ammad Hassan. "Pakistan's Gwadar Port – Prospects of Economic Revival" Naval Postgraduate School Monterey Thesis submitted in June 2005, p. 14.
28. Note 22, ibid.
29. Syed Fazl-e-Haider. "Gwadar Project in second phase" *Dawn*, 27 June 2005.
30. Behram Baloch. "Senate panel resents slow pace of work on Gwadar port", *Dawn*, 17 January 2019.
31. B. Raman. "The Baloch Cause", Opinion, Outlook.com (accessed on 19 April 2005).
32. Tahir Rathore. "Pak, Chinese presidents to open Gwadar Port", *The International News*, Internet Edition, 27 November 27, 2004.
33. "President for completing Gwadar port by June 2006", *The International News*, Internet Edition, 11 June 2005.
34. Zaheer Abbasi. "Gwadar Port Terminal Expansion Plan", *Business Recorder*, 19 March 2018, from https://epaper.brecorder.com/2018/03/19/20-page/705796-news.html

(accessed on 19 February 2020).

35. Ibid.
36. From Gwadar Port Authority website http://www.gwadarport.gov.pk/portprofile.aspx (accessed on 31 December 2019). The information has since been removed from the website. There has been substantive change to the details.
37. Ibid.
38. Ibid.
39. Rathore, op. cit.
40. "Gwadar's rich potential", Editorial, *Dawn*, Karachi, 13 June 2006.
41. Ibid.
42. Ibid.
43. Malik Siraj Akbar. "Who leads the Baloch", *The Nation*, Lahore, 29 December 2004.
44. "Gwadar rail track would be completed soon", *The Frontier Post,* Peshawar, 19 November 2004.
45. "Aziz directs acceleration of Gwadar work", *Daily Times* website http://www.dailytimes.com.pk/default.asp?page=story_5-6-2005_pg7_28 (Accessed on 8 June 2005).
46. "New Gwadar International Airport' from official website of China Pakistan Economic Corridor http://cpec.gov.pk/project-details/33 (accessed on 27 December 2019).
47. Adnan Aamir, "Is it wise for China to build Pakistan's largest airport at Gwadar?" from *Asia Dialogue*, the online magazine of the University of Nottingham, Asia Research Institute at https://theasiadialogue.com/2019/05/21/is-it-wise-for-china-to-build-pakistans-largest-airport-at-gwadar/ (Accessed on 28 December 2019).
48. Ibid.
49. Ashfaq Ahmed. "Pakistan's Gwadar International Airport will be the largest in the country" from *Gulf News* website https://gulfnews.com/world/asia/pakistan/pakistans-gwadar-international-airport-will-be-the-largest-in-the-country-1.63033953 (Accessed on 28 December 2019).
50. Ibid.
51 "Gwadar Port City Projects", from CPEC website https://obortunity.org/cpec-news/gwadar-port-city/ (Accessed on 28 December 2019).
52. Summer Zhen. "Chinese firm takes control of Gwadar Port free-trade zone in Pakistan", *South China Morning Post,* from https://www.scmp.com/business/companies/article/1877882/chinese-firm-takes-control-gwadar-port-free-trade-zone-pakistan (Accessed on 28 December 2019).
53. "Development of Gwadar Free Zone" Special Report on CPEC Projects (Transportation Infrastructure: Part 4), 1 October 2018 from Embassy of the People's Republic of China in the Islamic Republic of Pakistan website http://pk.chineseembassy.org/eng/zbgx/t1627112.htm (Accessed on 29 December 2019).
54. Zhen, op. cit.
55. Abbasi, op. cit.
56. "Eastbay Expressway Gwadar expected to complete in October, says Asim Bajwa", *The Nation*, Lahore, 3 May 2021.
57. "Shehbaz Sharif inaugurates road, development projects in Gwadar", *The News*, 4 June 2022, p. 1.
58. Abbasi, op. cit.

59. "Projects inaugurated in Gwadar to help implement China-Pakistan Economic Corridor" from http://www.xinhuanet.com/english/2019-11/05/c_138530508.htm (Accessed on 29 December 2019).
60. Ibid.
61. Dipanjan Roy Chaudhury, "PoK projects suffer as China focuses on Gwadar' *The Economic Times*, 12 November 2019.
62. "Under CPEC: First container vessel anchors at Gwadar", *The Express Tribune*, 8 March 2018.
63. Haseeb Hanif. "Gwadar port operationalised for exports", *The Express Tribune*, 15 December 2019.
64. "Expectations from Gwadar", Editorial, *The News,* Internet Edition, 7 October 2004.
65. Shahzada Zulfiqar. "Port of Terror", *Newsline*, June 2004, p. 56.
66. "Terrorism in Balochistan", Editorial, *Dawn,* Karachi, 18 December 2004.
67. Abdul Hakim Baluch. "Bringing development to Balochistan', *Dawn*, Karachi, 13 December 2004.
68. Dipanjan Roy Chaudhury, "China-Pakistan Gwadar Port runs into rough weather" *The Economic Times*, 10 September 2019.
69. Ibid.
70. Syed Muhammad Abubakar. "Welcome to thirsty Gwadar", *The News on Sunday*, 1 July 2018, Political Economy supplement, p. III.
71. Hassan Daud, "Gwadar: the economic gateway", *The News,* 21 November 2018, p. 6.
72. Ibid.
73. M. Ismail Khan, "The Trans-Karakoram Oil Pipeline", *The News*, Internet Edition, 31 October 2006.
74. Alok Bansal, "Gwadar Port: A South Asian Gateway for Central Asia" in K. Warikoo (ed.), *Central Asia and South Asia: Energy Cooperation and Transport Linkages*. New Delhi: Pentagon Press, 2011, p. 265.

3

Security Implications for Pakistan

This chapter delves into the various security implications, external as well as internal, of the Gwadar Deep Sea Port project in Pakistan. It also looks into the maritime security challenges Pakistan faces as well as the internal security problems that have a bearing on Gwadar or those that are impacted by this port. However, before analysing security implications, it would be prudent to define the term 'security' as a state of being free from threat or danger. Accordingly, maritime security could be defined rather simplistically as a state when the seas and the waters connected to the seas around a territory remain free from activities that could threaten their use for military, economic or scientific purposes. Some of these could be 'activities' like terrorism, piracy, armed robbery, human smuggling, drug trafficking, gun running, poaching, acts causing marine pollution, etc., which are often termed as 'non-traditional' threats along with traditional threats from hostile militaries requiring a response by naval forces to maintain maritime security. Ninety per cent of the global trade measured by volume and 80 per cent by value is carried by seaborne commerce and this dependence on the sea of the human race is growing and necessitates measures to safeguard it from both traditional and non-traditional threats.[1]

Unlike on land, the strategic, economic and even political interests of different countries intersect and even overlap at sea. Consequently, maritime security is often a 'shared concern' and, to that extent, non-traditional threats are seen as a 'common adversary'. In this pursuit of 'shared concern and common adversary', the Pakistan Navy also strives to be at the forefront to create a secure maritime environment in and around its waters, where economic, scientific and commercial activities may be pursued unhindered and without any interruption.[2] Ports are one of the most significant components of maritime security and consequently, the establishment of any new port changes the security dynamics around it.

Accordingly, the Gwadar port has huge security implications for Pakistan. According to Hussain Haqqani, former Pakistani Ambassador to the USA, right from the 1970s, Gwadar has always been conceived by Pakistan as a strategic military base.[3] On the one hand, it has removed a critical vulnerability for Pakistan as the port has provided it with another option to unload vital supplies as Pakistan's two domestic ports of Karachi and Port Bin Qasim are extremely susceptible to a naval blockade. Pakistan realised this in 1971 and has been looking for an alternative port to handle its cargo in case of any accident, blockade or any other emergency. Gwadar has fulfilled that critical void.[4] According to Shuja Nawaz, Distinguished Fellow, South Asia Centre, Atlantic Council, Washington DC and author of *The Battle for Pakistan: The Bitter US Friendship and a Tough Neighbourhood*, the port could potentially establish a lifeline for movement of goods and services away from the Indian border. India had the potential to effectively split Pakistan into two, by snapping its main upcountry link from Karachi by a military penetration from Eastern Pakistan during a conflict.[5]

On the other hand the local residents, the Baloch, who inhabit the region around the port, are not happy with the Gwadar project for various reasons. Baloch nationalism has been rearing its head right from colonial times and has manifested in violent insurrections many times since Pakistan's emergence on the global map. Although the Pakistani government has ambitious plans for developing Gwadar, which could change the landscape of the region and usher in prosperity, the Baloch have serious apprehensions about the project and perceive it as a conspiracy against their long-term interests. Accordingly, they have been opposing the project, which has fuelled a fairly widespread insurgency in Balochistan. The Baloch insurgents have been targeting the work, assets and various personnel associated with the Gwadar project regularly. The Pakistani government has failed to assuage their anger and has often used state machinery to rein them in. Consequently their alienation and their apprehensions about this project have only grown with the passage of time.

The various security implications of this port project have been further analysed in subsequent paragraphs.

EXTERNAL DIMENSION

For a state like Pakistan, maritime security is paramount as 95 per cent of its trade is dependent on the sea and the country can be delivered a debilitating blow if this medium is denied to it. The non-availability of this medium would result in its industries, exports and imports coming to a grinding halt. Transporting goods and raw material to and from other countries via land or air routes is not only expensive, but also highly inconvenient. Pakistan has a sea frontage of around 11,000 km and over 36,000 ships pass through Pakistan's waters.[6]

It is estimated that over 15 million barrels of crude oil moves from the Persian Gulf through Pakistan's waters daily to various destinations. Over half of China's crude oil imports, around 60 per cent of India's crude oil, 90 per cent of Japanese and almost the entire crude oil import of Pakistan comes from the Middle East. In the foreseeable future, the Indian Ocean and the Arabian Sea, in particular, would remain extremely significant on account of overwhelming dependence of the world on oil from the Middle East. Apart from various non-traditional threats, Pakistan always faces a traditional threat from India. This threat was clearly manifest in 1971 during the liberation war of Bangladesh as well as during the 1999 Kargil conflict. It is also perceived that India could use hybrid warfare, which combines conventional, irregular and cyber warfare; to aid, abet or sustain various non-traditional elements of instability and chaos, including terrorism, to harm Pakistan's critical security interests.[7]

Maritime Security

After the liberation of Bangladesh, despite having a long sea coast, Pakistan was primarily reduced to being a one-port country, which depended on Karachi for practically all its entire trade. During the 1971 war, the port of Karachi was targeted by the Indian Navy, thereby exhibiting its extreme vulnerability.

The port is just 200 nautical miles from the Indian port of Okha and is therefore extremely susceptible to a naval blockade. It was also clearly evident that shipping bound for Karachi could easily be interdicted by either the Indian Navy or Indian Air Force, as ships heading for Karachi needed to pass close to Indian waters or had to come close to India before entering the port.

In order to reduce its dependence on Karachi, Pakistan commissioned Port Muhammad Bin Qasim with one iron and coal berth in September 1980. It was initially constructed to meet the various requirements of bringing in heavy equipment for the Pakistan Steel Mills, which was being set up there. Subsequently, it was used for handling the massive imports of raw materials for steel production by Pakistan Steel Mills. From a captive port for Pakistan Steel Mills, it was developed into a full-fledged port. Currently 68 per cent of Pakistan's trade is via the Karachi port while the remaining 32 per cent is dealt with by Port Qasim.[8]

The emergence of Port Muhammad Bin Qasim as Pakistan's second commercial port, however, did not reduce its security vulnerabilities; as Port Qasim was even closer to India than Karachi. More significantly, the proximity of Karachi and Port Qasim to each other makes it easier to blockade both of them together.[9] More significantly, it could also enable any powerful navy to keep Pakistan's naval assets bottled up within these two ports. As a result, Pakistan's strategic and naval thinkers have always been looking at ports on the Makran coast away from Indian waters to reduce this critical vulnerability of Pakistan and its navy.

The first step towards eliminating this critical vulnerability was achieved when a naval base with basing facilities for warships was planned at Ormara on the Makran coast at a distance of about 130 nautical miles from Karachi. Pakistan's Ministry of Defence approved this proposal to construct a naval base at Ormara away from India's maritime boundaries and consequently, a contract was awarded to Sezai Turkes Ferzi Akkaya (STFA) Group and STM Savunma Teknolojileri Mühendislik ve Ticaret A.S. from Turkey and Jan De Nul from Belgium to start the work. The project estimated to cost approximately $ 500 million also involved the Frontier Works Organisation and Military Engineering Service. The ground-breaking ceremony was accordingly performed by Pakistan's prime minister on 17 March 1994.[10]

Ormara naval base was initially planned to be commissioned by March

1997, but the project was delayed and eventually commissioned by General Pervez Musharraf, the then Chief Executive on 22 June 2000. Ormara located at a road distance of 350 kilometres from Karachi and 285 kilometres from Gwadar, to a great extent, eliminated the Pakistani Navy's mortal fear of being bottled up inside the Karachi-Bin Qasim complex during a war like 1971. Ormara has since been connected with the China-Pakistan Economic Corridor (CPEC). According to the Pakistan Navy, the development of Jinnah Naval Base at Ormara has given it the capacity to secure its trade in the waters off the Makran coast. It has also enabled it to expand its reach towards its western coast and towards the Strait of Hormuz, through which a significant part of global oil flows.[11]

The base at Ormara, which has facilities to berth warships of different sizes, submarines as well as naval aircraft, has reduced the Pakistan Navy's reaction time to deal with eventualities in the Makran coast by six to eight hours. The base will cater for the security of Gwadar and surrounding waters and monitor the entire coast from Ormara to the Persian Gulf. Apart from Ormara, the Pakistan Navy has also built bases at Pasni, Jiwani, and Gwadar. These bases have helped the navy to expand its strategic 'outreach' towards the West Coast. The construction of these new naval bases provided the Pakistan Navy with considerable flexibility, as it could disperse its warships and base them at any of these locations. It also provided its ships at sea with alternative venues for shelter and logistics facilities, in case the Karachi-Bin Qasim Port was blockaded by a hostile power.[12]

Although projected as an exclusively commercial port, a huge tract of land in the vicinity of the Gwadar deep sea port has also been allocated for the Pakistan Navy, where various naval facilities are coming up. According to author Ayesha Siddiqa, who has worked with the Pakistan Navy, "Gwadar is considered critical for Pakstan's security." It intends to use it as an alternative port in case of war between India and Pakistan.[13] The naval assets based in the port could also enable Pakistan to monitor and prevent any ship entering or leaving the Persian Gulf, thereby giving it valuable strategic leverage. The disruption of oil and gas supplies from the Gulf could pose a major strategic threat for any of Pakistan's potential adversaries.

For India, it poses a major security challenge as the bulk of Indian refining facilities are located in the Gulf of Kutch and the Sea Line of Communication

(SLOC) from the Persian Gulf to the Gulf of Kutch passes just 40 nautical miles from Gwadar. Consequently, even a rudimentary gun boat or a missile boat based at Gwadar can easily interdict a ship moving along this SLOC. It has also succeeded in selling China the idea that the Gwadar port could be an alternative port for disembarkation of China's energy imports in case of any blockage of the Malacca Strait or other straits in South-East Asia, by powers that are inimical to China.

Gwadar, along with other naval bases, has transformed the security dynamics of the Makran coast. According to Rear Admiral Pervez Asghar, a retired admiral of the Pakistan Navy, in the past Pakistan's military installations were extremely vulnerable to Indian attacks, as had been demonstrated by the attack on the naval base at Karachi in 1971. However, after the establishment of new naval bases on the Makran coast, the situation has changed, as these bases provide the Pakistan Navy with not only alternative ports to operate from and defend its assets, but the presence of naval assets there had also increased the reaction time available to it in times of an attack. He added that with Ormara, Pakistan had a new submarine base and the navy had also developed a marine corps to thwart any hostile amphibious operations on the Makran coast. He also claimed that with the new bases, the Pakistan Navy was comfortably placed to secure all SLOCs between the Persian Gulf and Pakistan. The coverage of various radars and communication networks now overlap each other, thereby providing complete coastal coverage, a capability, which Pakistan had lacked earlier.[14]

The new bases on the Makran coast are also intended to provide both onshore and offshore security to the Gwadar port. The presence of special forces at Ormara and other bases on the Makran coast help the Pakistan Navy to secure Gwadar and nearby sea routes. The Pakistan Navy has already constructed an airstrip at Jiwani, 90 km west of Gwadar, which can be used as a staging post for maritime aircraft. This naval base at Jiwani, just 60 km from Iran, permits Pakistan to extend its reach well into the waters of the Persian Gulf. It also serves as a major point to keep track of all seaborne traffic in the Arabian Sea. Another naval air base named PNS Siddiq has been commissioned at Turbat for P3C Orion aircraft, which is a versatile aircraft for maritime reconnaissance and has an endurance of 14 hours.[15] All these naval facilities are centred around Gwadar, which is the 'centre of gravity' for all developments on the Makran coast.

Elimination of Economic Vulnerability

The new naval bases at Ormara, Jiwani, Pasni or for that matter even the naval base at Gwadar, did not provide Pakistan with any alternative avenue for trade or economic sustenance as Ormara was purely a naval base and had no facilities for trade or handling of bulk cargo and the other bases were meant to house naval personnel, air strips, radar stations or other maritime surveillance equipment. As a result, a blockade of Karachi and Bin Qasim ports could still land a debilitating blow on the country and its economy. The Gwadar project was envisaged to remove this critical vulnerability. This being the first major commercial port outside the Karachi-Bin Qasim complex, it has eliminated to a great extent the total dependence of Pakistan on the other ports for its economic survival. It is approximately 460 kilometres from Indian waters and that, according to many Pakistani strategists, reduces Pakistan's vulnerability and increases its strategic depth. It allows Pakistan more warning time against any air or naval threat emanating from India. With the development of the Gwadar port, Pakistan aims to prevent any 'bottling up' of its navy as was witnessed during the Indo–Pakistan conflict in 1971 and also during the Kargil crisis. The port will afford strategic depth to Pakistan's marine assets, both commercial and military.[16]

The port is connected to the rest of Pakistan by the newly constructed Makran coastal highway (653 km long) from Sheikh Raj, approximately 105 km north of Karachi to Gabd near the Pak-Iran border. This highway links the ports at Ormara, Pasni, Gwadar, and Jiwani with Karachi and has the potential to boost trade between Pakistan and Iran. Another road link in the pipeline is the Gwadar-Ratto Dero motorway which would join the Indus highway through Turbat, Awaran and Khuzdar. A rail link is also being planned to connect Gwadar to Quetta and Zahidan.[17] The port along with the communication links is expected to kick up economic development in a region that has remained Pakistan's most backward region.

The Gwadar deep sea port is perceived as the second greatest monument to the Pakistan-China friendship after the Karakoram Highway. Chinese involvement in the construction and operation of the port binds the interests of the two countries together. As highlighted earlier, China was involved in the construction of the project right from the beginning and even provided funding for it. However, the operations of the port were initially entrusted to the Port of Singapore Authority, which operated the port from 2007 to 2012. There were differences between the operator and the government, with each accusing the other of not fulfilling contractual obligations. Consequently, Pakistan unilaterally handed over the port operations to the China Overseas Port Holding Company (COPHC) in 2013.[18] Since then, the port project has become the pivot of the entire CPEC project, which is an important component of the Belt and Road Initiative (BRI) of China. There has been consequent enhancement of the infrastructural project at Gwadar and its completion has become essential for the success of the CPEC.

The location of the Gwadar deep sea port at the cross-junction of important and busy international sea shipping and oil trade routes and the Chinese presence there has created its own security implications. Chinese presence, coupled with the development of advanced infrastructure and surveillance facilities, implies that Gwadar would be in a position to help both Pakistan and China to monitor the SLOCs emanating from the Strait of Hormuz.[19]

The port and its monitoring facilities will enable Pakistan to track its energy imports and escort tankers bringing in these vital supplies. It also makes it easier for Pakistan to keep an eye on oil supplies to other countries from the Persian Gulf. The port gives its maritime forces greater reach inside the economically significant but volatile Persian Gulf. This could foreseeably lead to an enhancement of Pakistan's influence on the countries of the Persian Gulf, where its influence has been waning for some time. The region is extremely significant for Pakistan, because it not only supplies most of its energy needs, but also a major chunk of remittances received by Pakistan come from this region. For a country like Pakistan not only are remittances a major source of foreign exchange, but also contribute a lot to its economy. The ratio of remittances to GDP is 6.78 per cent, making it one of the first 40 countries in the world that are extremely dependent on remittances for their economic sustenance.[20]

The advent of the Gwadar port as a vibrant regional economic hub in the Arabian Sea has the potential to make it the preferred gateway for Afghanistan and the Central Asian Republics (CARs). This could give Pakistan enormous leverage over the resource-rich countries of Central Asia and enhance Islamabad's influence on these countries. Numerous regional and extra-regional powers may like to advance their strategic interests by infrastructural development at Gwadar Port, so as to access the enormous resources and vast markets of the energy-rich Central Asian Republics (CARs).

Entwining China in Pakistan's Security

Pakistan lacks strategic depth in the maritime domain of the Arabian Sea along the east-west axis. This vulnerability in the overall security calculus of the Pakistan Navy will be eliminated considerably by Gwadar, which, being a strategic port, is significantly distant from India. Pakistan's strategic thinkers perceive that the naval bases at Gwadar and Ormara and the Chinese naval presence there, could check Indian naval aspirations to emerge as a blue water navy as well as prevent the domination of the Arabian Sea by the US Fifth Fleet. They perceive that this will strengthen Sino-Pak naval cooperation in the Indian Ocean and thereby deny the Indian Navy manoeuvring space and also make China dependent on this port and thereby on Pakistan. This would strengthen the Sino-Pak strategic alliance.[21]

Pakistan's policy makers keep proclaiming to the world that Gwadar is purely a commercial port; however, it has enormous security implications. It was clearly evident when *MS Tiger*, the first ever container ship belonging to a Chinese company, which started a container service to Gwadar connecting it to Karachi and other ports in the Persian Gulf; arrived at the Gwadar port. The ship was escorted by two warships of the Pakistan Navy. Rear Admiral Moazzam Ilyas, the Commander West Coast of Pakistan Navy welcomed the container ship and said "The CPEC is a game changer for Pakistan and its success is just a prelude to the economic prosperity of the country and hence has taken central stage in the economic, political and security calculus of not only Pakistan but the entire region".[22] He stressed on the security dimension and stated that the Gwadar Deep Sea Port is the focal point of the CPEC, and consequently, its security was paramount. He stated that to meet this requirement, the Pakistan Navy had established Task Force 88, a new task force to provide maximum possible security to Gwadar port and its surrounding areas.[23]

Growing worldwide religious radicalization and the emergence of West Asia and contiguous parts of South Asia, as the hub of international jihadi terrorism have impacted the security dynamics. The emergence of this region as the citadel of transnational terrorist outfits like the al-Qaeda and the Islamic

State, have created global concerns and impacted Pakistan's maritime security in two ways. Firstly, there is an external threat that could manifest in the form of various terrorist organisations or their factions attacking a sea port or vessels therein, which could lead to floating bombs in the port, and bring port operations to a grinding halt. Gwadar is being projected as a hub port, which will have a large volume of trade from different ports across the globe. Its proximity to the main breeding grounds of global terror outfits makes it extremely vulnerable to such an attack, which could bring the entire trade from the port to a standstill.[24]

Secondly, being a hub of container traffic, Gwadar is also vulnerable to smuggling of weapons, drugs and even human trafficking by non-state actors through containers. Terrorist outfits or even insurgents can smuggle weapons, drugs and conduct human trafficking operations to finance their activities or get new recruits. This could seriously threaten Pakistan's core interests as well as endanger its national security.[25] There is a fear in Pakistan that India could take measures to destroy Sino-Pak joint strategic interests by resorting to hybrid warfare in the maritime domain and to that extent could provide covert support to maritime terrorism. Changing geopolitical milieu also complicates the security environment for Pakistan.[26] Islamabad and, more significantly, Rawalpindi want Beijing to perceive a threat to its assets in Gwadar from forces inimical to Pakistan, thereby forcing China to involve itself in the security dynamics of the port and in Pakistan's security.

Finally, like any other country, Pakistan also uses maritime security as an essential component of its foreign policy and intends to utilise it to enhance its diplomatic relations as well as its influence. The strategic location of Gwadar deep sea port allows Pakistan to emerge as a 'net security provider'[27] in this volatile region to countries with limited maritime capabilities. Its growing collaboration with China has helped it in undertaking various quasi-diplomatic projects regarding promotion of maritime trade through the Gwadar port. It has been extremely supportive of the Chinese 21st-century maritime silk road concept, which aims to expand regional economic cooperation and global interdependence "where a win-win situation is achieved by the notion of one belt/one road".[28]

Since 2018, the availability of Gwadar and other naval facilities on the Makran coast has allowed Pakistan Navy to undertake regional maritime security patrols (RMSP) aimed at ensuring the safety and security of its main sea lanes, through which a majority of the regional as well as Pakistan's commerce passes.[29] Despite riding piggyback on Chinese economic and military might to spread its influence in the region, Pakistan has continued to be a part of the US-led combined task force 150 (CTF-150), a multi-national naval task force, which is part of the 33-nation coalition of Combined Maritime Forces based in Bahrain. It patrols the northern Indian Ocean from the Red Sea to the Strait of Hormuz including the waters off the Horn of Africa, with the avowed objective of monitoring, boarding, inspecting, and stopping suspicious shipping in pursuance of the 'Global War on Terror'. The task force functions in support of operations in the Indian Ocean. Gwadar has considerably eased the Pakistan Navy's ability to participate in CTF-150. Consequently, on 20 January 2022, when Commodore Waqar Muhammad of the Pakistan Navy (PN) assumed command of CTF 150, the responsibility was being shared by the PN for the 12th time, a unique distinction, which no other country in the task force has achieved.[30]

On the whole, Pakistan perceives that its external security environment has improved considerably with the operationalisation of the Gwadar port project. It has reduced its critical vulnerability and given it a greater reach as well as flexibility to deploy its naval assets. It has given Pakistan a plausible role in the affairs of the Persian Gulf. It has also tied up China's interests with the port, thus ensuring some sort of security insurance for itself, even though it has antagonised the USA and other Western powers by this step. According to Hussain Haqqani, Pakistan's former ambassador to the USA, the Gwadar port allows China and Pakistan to exercise influence all over the Middle East and the Indian Ocean region from this strategic location.[31]

According to him, the significance of the port lies in the belief that a foreign power (China) can be induced to support Islamabad to project power and develop economically, while setting up naval facilities for its (Chinese) own use. "The CPEC and Gwadar are seen by Pakistanis not purely in economic terms but as a security guarantee of China's commitment to their country. This reflects the historic pattern of Pakistan's insecurity and presumption of Pakistan's global strategic centrality".[32]

INTERNAL DIMENSIONS

Apart from external diplomatic and security considerations, the Gwadar port project has enormous internal implications. Pakistan wishes to use Gwadar to kick-start economic development in an area, which has hitherto been out of the economic mainstream. The deep sea port and associated infrastructure are located at Gwadar, which is a part of Balochistan, the most under-developed province in Pakistan. The port and associated infrastructure has failed to meet local aspirations and has led to a low level insurgency in the region since 2004. The insurgency in Balochistan gives the project a different dynamics. The implications of the Gwadar port project for the internal affairs of Pakistan have been analysed and elaborated in subsequent paragraphs.

Gwadar's Role in the Development of Balochistan

Ports have traditionally been the nucleus of socioeconomic activities and consequently human settlements have often evolved around them. Consequently, most major cities and commercial hubs are located near ports, which are seen as engines of growth and development for the region. Like all other sea ports, Gwadar has the potential to contribute significantly in transforming the entire region around it through development and prosperity. The economic activities that Gwadar could initiate would include firstly the activities that are directly related to any commercial port, namely, handling of cargo/passengers, storage and distribution of cargo, ship repairs, bunkering, etc. Secondly, a set of processing industries are visualised that add to the value of imported goods before domestic consumption or re-export. Thirdly, a set of economic activities, which include those that depend on import of bulk commodities like oil refineries, steel mills, etc. Fourthly, activity that could provide employment encompasses tourism and recreational facilities. All these could generate employment and usher in prosperity. Policy makers in Pakistan visualise that these activities at Gwadar could create around two million jobs by 2025. As per the estimates of the Gwadar Development Authority, over 1.7 million people are expected to move to Gwadar by 2045.[33]

Balochistan being a vast province has abundant resources, which include huge hydrocarbon reserves and precious minerals, most of which have yet to be exploited optimally. This has naturally drawn a lot of international interest in this vast untapped region. Consequently, a large number of both investors and developers are keen to participate in the development process and reap a rich harvest. Balochistan possesses a large portion of Pakistan's energy and mineral resources and accounts for 36 per cent of Pakistan's total gas production. It also has huge deposits of gold, copper, silver, platinum, aluminium, and above all, uranium.[34]

The Saindak copper mines being operated by the Metallurgical Corporation of China (MCC) are estimated to contain over 400 million tons of gold and copper. In 2015, 13,056 tons of copper was produced. The total mineral content at the largest copper mine in the world, the Reko Dik mines, which is also in Balochistan was estimated to be 1.27 billion metric tons according to a feasibility study carried out in August 2010. Another copper and gold mine is being developed in the Chagai hills of Balochistan by an Australian firm.[35] There are iron ore deposits of almost 200 million tons in the province.[36] It also has coal deposits of around 217 million tons,[37] which can be used to generate power through small power plants of up to 25 MW capacity.[38] Despite such vast resources, Balochistan has always lacked proper infrastructure to extract and transport them. The Gwadar port project and the infrastructure associated with it will enable these resources to be harnessed and exported, thereby creating potential for both generating employment and development.[39]

In addition, the Makran coast also provides Pakistan with a huge exclusive economic zone (EEZ) of around 180,000 square kilometres, which is extremely rich in marine resources. Although most of the population that lives along the Makran coast has been traditionally involved in fishing, these resources could never be harnessed optimally for want of a port and supporting infrastructure for processing and packaging. Of the 50,000 active fishermen in Balochistan, around 9,000 each are concentrated in Gwadar and Pasni itself. At present, the catch brought in by these fishermen needs to be taken to Karachi for processing, packaging and further marketing. This results in a lot of wastage, and consequently, lesser profits for the fishermen. As the Gwadar port project moves forward, a large number of fish processing and packaging plants are expected to come up in the area. In addition, with a thriving port and a good network of roads, the produce can easily be marketed in the hinterland directly or exported abroad, thereby fetching for the fishermen a much better price for their catch. This in turn could usher in a huge transformation in the lives of these people, who reside in the region and live off fishing. This could bring all-round prosperity to Balochistan.[40]

With the passage of time, the Gwadar port could earn enormous revenues for Balochistan by providing transit and transhipment facilities to China, Afghanistan, the Central Asian Republics and even parts of Russia (especially in winter when most of the ports in the North Sea are closed). Continuing turmoil in Afghanistan is unlikely to subside in the near future and this will prevent worthwhile transit trade from Gwadar to and from Central Asia and Afghanistan. However, with China's growing economic power and the Gwadar port being part of the CPEC, even if a portion of China's transit trade passes through the Gwadar-Kashgar corridor, it would generate a lot of economic activities in the region through which the trade passes. If and when the roads to Gwadar through the Baloch hinterland materialise and the trucks and trade convoys start moving on them, numerous economic activities will be triggered, thereby, generating huge employment opportunities for the locals and others.[41]

Policy makers in Islamabad expect that as Gwadar thrives, it should be able to see a huge rise in the trade from the port, which in turn should attract large-scale foreign direct investment (FDI). They expect that it could eventually result in the emergence of Gwadar as a business centre and a hub of all economic activities, thereby drawing both capital and human resources from other parts of Pakistan and the world. This would lead to huge investments coming in for both infrastructural development and social development in the areas around Gwadar port.[42]

Local Unrest

A mega developmental project that triggers huge economic activity and generates employment should normally be welcomed by the local residents as it should usher in prosperity by generating economic activities and creating jobs. Both Islamabad and Beijing have ambitious plans for infrastructural development at Gwadar, and logically there is no reason why any rational individual should not be enthusiastic about the construction of a deep sea port there. However, the local residents, especially almost all Baloch nationalists, have been opposing the project tooth and nail. Consequently, armed members of various Baloch insurgent outfits have been regularly targeting the developmental work associated with the project and the personnel working on it ever since work began on the Gwadar deep sea port in 2002. The first major attacks on the Gwadar project and the personnel associated with it started in 2004.

On 4 May 2004, a team of 12 Chinese workers along with their Pakistani driver and a police guard were proceeding to the project site in a Mercedes van from the camp, where they had been residing. However, a powerful blast hit the van as soon as it slowed down to negotiate a speed-breaker on the fish harbour road. The blast was triggered by remotely detonating explosives planted in a small car. Three Chinese engineers were killed instantly, nine others were injured and four of those injured, including the police guard, were serious enough to be shifted to Karachi for better medical aid. Though the provincial administration subsequently beefed up security, yet the insurgents attacked again within three weeks when they fired rockets at Gwadar airport around midnight on 21 May 2004. Although all the rockets missed the intended target, which was the airport building, the security forces panicked and opened indiscriminate fire in all directions, thereby injuring a driver of an oil tanker at the airport.[43] Since then, attacks on various projects associated with the port, the companies involved in implementing them and their personnel have become a regular feature.

The port rightly or wrongly has exacerbated a sense of deprivation amongst the Baloch and has provided a fillip to Baloch nationalism, which has been rising from the colonial period. The rising nationalism ever since Baloch territories were incorporated in Pakistan has manifested itself in at least four violent insurrections before the current one which arguably was triggered because of Gwadar in May 2004. Before delving on the ongoing insurgency, it would be appropriate to track the trajectory of Baloch nationalism right from post-colonial times. The incorporation of Baloch territories in Pakistan and its subsequent treatment of Baloch is a saga of deceit and betrayal. These details have been covered in subsequent paragraphs to understand the Baloch response to this mega-developmental project at Gwadar and other such projects.

Balochistan and its Status in the Post-Colonial Era

Balochistan is a province that is flush with guns and is ruled by them. The insurgency has erupted in the province in virtually every decade of Pakistan's existence.[44] Most Baloch never wanted to join Pakistan in the first place. Way back in the 1930s, some Baloch leaders, foreseeing the eventual departure of the British from the subcontinent, had staked their claim for independence.[45] Balochistan under the British had been fragmented into British Balochistan, which included Quetta and other areas under direct British control, the Baloch states of Kalat, Kharan, Lasbela and Makran[46] and the tribal areas which were only notionally under the British but ruled by their *Sardars* autocratically.[47] Though sporadic resistance to the British rule continued throughout the colonial period, yet the fact that Baloch society was highly fragmented did not allow the emergence of a nationalist movement.

The first successful Baloch nationalist campaign was launched against state recruitment in 1929 and soon turned into an armed mutiny. The next year, several underground organisations emerged and an anti-colonial 'Quit Balochistan' movement was launched.[48] The demand for independence was the strongest in the State of Kalat, which was the strongest and most powerful of all Baloch princely states. The other three states, namely Kharan, Makran, and Lasbela, historically had been a part of Kalat state and had accepted its suzerainty in the past. Much before the advent of colonial rule, Naseer Khan, the Khan[49] of Kalat had managed to unite most of the Baloch under his rule.[50]

During the British rule, in 1920, a movement, *Anjuman-e-Ittehad-e-Balochistan,* was started to reunite the fragmented Baloch polity. The movement strongly propounded the cause of 'Greater Balochistan' and declared that the establishment of an independent and united Balochistan with a democratic government structure was its objective.[51] To propagate its objectives, the organisation came out with the weekly '*Al-Baluch*', which was published from Karachi. In a significant move to reiterate its objective, it printed in its issue dated 25 December 1932, a map of Greater Balochistan, which included the entire area of the Kalat confederacy, the Baloch territories of Iran, the Baloch areas leased to the British Indian government as well as the traditional Baloch lands in Sindh and Punjab.[52]

Anjuman-e-Ittehad-e-Balochistan was subsequently transformed into the Kalat State National Party and was allied to the All India States Peoples' Conference, which was a subsidiary organisation of the Indian National Congress (Amin, 1988:71).[53] After declaration of independence by the Khan of Kalat in 1947, when elections were held for the *Darul - Awam* (the House of Commons or the lower house of parliament), the members of the Kalat

State National Party won 39 out of 52 seats (including five nominated members) in *Darul - Awam* (Bresseg, 2004: 234).[54]

The British had a paramount relationship with all the princely states. It entailed the rulers of princely states to maintain their loyalty towards the British authorities and, in return, they were allowed substantive autonomy in managing the internal affairs of their states. Mir Ahmad Yar Khan Baloch, the Khan (ruler) of Kalat, who was undoubtedly the most powerful ruler of Balochistan and widely acknowledged liege lord of all Baloch tribes,[55] wanted to unite all the Baloch areas under his rule.[56] He was looking for independent status and claimed that his status was similar to that of the king of Nepal,[57] as both maintained their treaty relations with Whitehall rather than the British Indian government. In 1946, he submitted a memorandum to the Cabinet Mission, wherein he brought out that the governments succeeding the British authorities could only incorporate those states that had treaty relations with the British Indian government based in New Delhi and not those who had treaty relations with London. The Cabinet Mission did not question the legality of the argument, but it left this crucial issue unresolved.[58]

However, by the time the British started packing their bags to leave Indian shores, the once powerful state of Kalat had lost much of its former glory. Even then, it had a fully functioning administrative-set up and all the vestiges of an independent state. It had a government responsible to the parliament and which like the British parliament comprised of two houses, an upper house and an elected lower house. It had a council of ministers, which even included a Britisher, Douglas Fell, who was carrying out the duties of Foreign Minister of the State of Kalat.[59]

On top of it, the state had Mr. Mohammad Ali Jinnah as its legal adviser, who, according to Baloch historians, had agreed with the premise that the status of Kalat was quite distinct from other princely states of India. On 4 August 1947, a round table conference was held in Delhi, which was attended by the Viceroy, Lord Mountbatten; Mir Ahmad Yar Khan, the Khan of Kalat; his chief minister and Mohammad Ali Jinnah, as the legal advisor of Kalat. It was decided that Kalat would be independent from 15 August 1947 and would enjoy the status it had before entering into treaty relations with the British. This was followed by the Britishers returning the tribal regions inhabited by the Marri and Bugti tribes to Kalat and informing the rulers of Kharan and

Lasbela that their control had been transferred to the Khan of Kalat. These actions virtually unified the entire Balochistan under the suzerainty of Kalat's ruler, Khan Mir Ahmad Yar Khan Baloch (Rahman, 2005).[60]

Annexation of Kalat

As the British paramountcy ended over India, the Khan of Kalat declared independence on 15 August 1947 and offered a special relationship to Pakistan in the field of defence, foreign affairs and communications.[61] Much before declaring its independence, it had signed a 'Standstill Agreement' with Jinnah and Liaqat Ali Khan, on behalf of the 'yet to emerge' government of Pakistan on 4 August 1947. By signing the agreement, both Jinnah and Liaqat accepted Kalat as an independent state with bilateral relations with the British Government, quite distinct from the other princely states of India.[62]

Immediately after independence, both the houses of parliament in the state of Kalat unanimously rejected the proposal to accede to Pakistan. The leader of the Kalat State National Party, Mir Ghous Bakhsh Bizenjo, made a speech in the parliament, questioning the very rationale of the 'two-nation theory'. He stated, "We have a distinct culture like Afghanistan and Iran, and if the mere fact that we are Muslims requires us to amalgamate with Pakistan, then Afghanistan and Iran should also be amalgamated with Pakistan. They say we Baloch cannot defend ourselves in the atomic age. Well, are Afghanistan, Iran and even Pakistan capable of defending themselves against the superpowers? If we cannot defend ourselves, a lot of others cannot do so either. They say we must join Pakistan for economic reasons. Yet we have minerals, we have petroleum and we have ports. The question is what would Pakistan be without us?" Bizenjo's speech was the highpoint of Baloch national consciousness.[63]

Bizenjo, while rejecting the proposal to merge with Pakistan, had declared, "This means signing the death warrant for 15 million Baloch in Asia. We cannot be guilty of this major crime to humiliate the Baloch nation with a merger with a non-Baloch nation".[64] The State of Kalat in 1947, may not be representing all the people in Balochistan but there is no doubt that at that point of time most Baloch supported Khan's bid for independence.[65]

However, with the passage of time, the position of Kalat weakened considerably as the Muslim League managed to win over the other states under his suzerainty. Lasbela and Kharan were two vassals under Kalat State, whereas Makran was just a district with half its revenue permanently assigned to the State of Kalat. However, the newly-established Government of Pakistan raised their status to the level of separate sovereign states and thus divided the State of Kalat's historical territory into four pieces.[66]

Subsequently, these states as well as British Balochistan were covertly amalgamated into the newly-formed state of Pakistan. Although, the future of British Balochistan was to be decided in a 'referendum', it was limited to the members of Quetta municipality, a body that was overwhelmingly dominated by outsiders[67] and the *Shahi Jirga*, a council of elders from various tribes. The meeting was scheduled for 30 June 1947; however, it was advanced and surreptitiously held a day earlier without even informing the members. Consequently, only eight of the 55 representatives (43 of the *Shahi Jirga* and 12 of Quetta municipality) attended and voted. Baloch believe that no one from the *Shahi Jirga* actually voted.[68]

Despite these measures, it was not easy for the Pakistani Government to incorporate Kalat into Pakistan and it could only be achieved by the use of force. Pakistan mobilised its troops on 27 March 1948, for operations against Kalat, which had been converted into a landlocked area after Makran and Lasbela were merged. The mobilisation and the threat of war forced the Khan of Kalat to sign the instrument of accession. On 28 March 1948, after 225 days of independence, the State of Kalat became a part of Pakistan and a political agent was positioned to administer the state and guide the prime minister of Kalat in all its internal matters. Consequent to the military operation, the legal entity of the Khan of Kalat was eliminated and most of the ministers were incarcerated or deported from Balochistan.[69]

The forcible occupation of Balochistan by Pakistan resulted in a short-lived revolt by Prince Agha Abdul Karim, the brother of the Khan of Kalat. On 16 May 1948, after some clashes with better armed and better trained troops of the Pakistan Army, he crossed over to Afghanistan along with 1,000 of his followers. He organised a guerrilla campaign and managed to harass the Pakistani forces for some time. However, in the absence of any material support from Afghanistan and the Union of the Soviet Socialist Republic (USSR),[70] the movement withered away. By June 1948, the Pakistani Army had managed to secure Kalat as well as the rest of Balochistan, although the sporadic incidents of violence continued till 1950.[71]

Although the fighting in 1948 cannot be characterised as a Baloch-wide rebellion, it was extremely significant as the armed conflict took place at a time when the rest of Pakistan was celebrating the emergence of a new state.[72] The revolt did not last long, but it did give an enormous boost to the Baloch national movement, which kept resurfacing from time to time later.[73] This first encounter between the Baloch and Pakistani forces played a crucial role in shaping the Baloch nationalist discourse. It created a sense of national insecurity and fear of repression by the foreigners. The Baloch had managed their internal affairs even during the colonial period, but the post-colonial powers wanted to establish order and centralised rule, which the Baloch tribes were unwilling to accept.[74]

Early Rebellions

After the annexation of the State of Kalat, the government of Pakistan assumed power in the whole of Balochistan and officials administered the province from Karachi. In the late 1950s, the government broached the idea of forming the 'Balochistan States' Union' by merging the states of Las Bela, Makran and Kharan into Kalat. The Kalat State National Party was banned by the Pakistan Government in 1948. Consequently, in 1950, the Baloch nationalists formed the 'Balochistan Peace Committee' with the aim of struggling for the self-determination of the Baloch people. This was in due course replaced by another party, *Ustaman Gall* (Peoples' Party),[75] with Prince Karim, the brother of the Khan of Kalat,[76] as the president and Ghous Bakhsh Bizenjo of the Kalat State National Party as the secretary. The party had a red flag with three stars on it, representing the Baloch in Pakistan, Iran and Afghanistan. The aim of the party was described as the formation of 'Greater Balochistan'.[77]

A Balochistan States Union with the Khan of Kalat as its president and a Pakistani civil servant as its prime minister was established in 1951. However, within two years, serious differences erupted between the Khan and the Punjabi-Mohajir dominated Central government. Many Pakistani leaders believed that the Khan was working towards creating an independent Balochistan and this led to the dissolution of the Balochistan States Union's assembly in 1954 and almost a year later the Union itself was dissolved to form a single unit of West Pakistan[78]

The formation of one unit in 1955 sounded the death knell for the political aspirations and ethnic identity of the Baloch people. After the formation of one unit,[79] the tribal chiefs in Balochistan, who had historically enjoyed considerable autonomy, fearing an intrusion over their inherited powers by an overbearing and strong centre, came together to initially form *Ustaman Gall.* However, in due course, *Ustaman Gall* merged with six other nationalist parties from all over Pakistan to form the National Awami Party (NAP), which was working towards the dissolution of one unit and provision of greater provincial autonomy. At the political level, it performed an important role as the carrier of Baloch nationalism.[80]

On the other hand, the successive Pakistani ruling elite perceived Baloch nationalism as a threat to the state's suzerainty over the province. The incident that strengthened the centre's threat perception was an attempt in 1958, by the Khan of Kalat to convene a Jirga of the Baloch sardars for consolidation of a Baloch state on a linguistic basis.[81] In a panic reaction by the state, the Khan of Kalat was re-arrested. Consequently, in retaliation, several hundred Baloch men led by 80-year-old Nauroz Khan, the chief of the Zehri tribe, took to the arid hills and fought back. Nauroz Khan led a guerrilla force of around 1,000 men against the Pakistan Army to reinstate the Khan to power and withdrawal of One Unit.[82]

Nauroz Khan had participated in a number of armed revolts against the British in the 1920s and 1930s and was soon joined by a number of Baloch guerrilla warriors cutting across the tribal divide. The revolt spread across the entire Jhalawan sub-division and the army was actively involved in the counter-insurgency operations. As part of the operations, Baloch villages were bombed and a reign of terror was unleashed in the region. However, when even that failed to break the will of the Baloch rebels, the establishment resorted to deceit. It promised to meet the Baloch demands and persuaded Nauroz Khan to surrender but as soon as the rebels came down from their sanctuaries in the hills, they were taken into custody.[83] Nauroz Khan was imprisoned and seven others including his son were hanged for treason. This treacherous act of the state further strengthened the Baloch national movement. The nationalist feeling grew deeper and Nauroz Khan emerged as the archetypical hero and the Baloch were depicted as being exploited by the anti-Baloch federal forces.[84]

Despite severe repression by the state, the Baloch did not give up and by the early 1960s, Pakistani troops in Balochistan were subjected to a series of attacks, which included ambushes, raids and attacks by snipers.[85] As the centre resorted to indiscriminate use of force against the tribes, the latter developed a guerrilla organisation, *Parari* (non-believers in negotiations), and structured the organisation based on the experiences of Cuba, Vietnam, China and other socialist countries. Sher Muhammad Marri led the *Pararis* who, by July 1963, had set up 22 base camps across 45,000 square miles of Baloch territory. Although the camps varied in size, each of them could mobilise hundreds of local part-time reserves. The *Pararis* were organised into two commands, with the northern command being responsible for the Marri-Bugti area and the southern command for areas dominated by the Mengal tribes in Jhalawan district.[86]

In 1967, the Baloch Students Organisation (BSO) came into existence; though primarily confined to schools and colleges it played an important role in familiarising the younger generation with the Baloch ethno-national symbols. The NAP, the *Pararis* and the BSO along with a number of cultural organisations produced literature that identified common heroes from Baloch history with the purpose of reinforcing the common historical origin and identity. It also identified common villains and was a curious mix of Baloch history and Marxist literature. The aim was to re-emphasise the fact that the Baloch are a distinct nation and have a right to self-determination. The literature led to the growing radicalisation of the Baloch youth along Marxist-Leninist lines, who believed in an all-out military struggle for independence.[87]

The centre responded with oppressive measures to weaken the group's political and economic position. It started discriminating against Baloch youth in providing government jobs and reduced Balochistan's allocation of funds for development. More significantly, the state tried to settle Punjabis in traditional Baloch areas, with the intention of gradually changing the demographic profile. All these actions coupled with the exploitative attitude of the federal government in harnessing the natural resources of the province, led to an acute feeling of deprivation and powerlessness amongst the Baloch population.[88] This resulted in sporadic violence all over the tribal areas (inhabited by Mengal, Marri and Bugti tribes) of Balochistan. The resistance movement from 1963 to 1969 led by Mir Sher Muhammad Marri was not very intense but exhibited the continuing expression of Baloch resentment against the central rule.

Balochistan as a Province

The situation in Balochistan improved considerably as the one unit was dissolved and elections were ordered by Yahya Khan. During the 1970-71 elections, the Baloch leadership attempted to mobilise public support by stressing the underdevelopment of the province at the hands of a Punjabi-dominated centre. In the ensuing elections, the NAP won three out of four National Assembly seats from Balochistan. It also won the largest single block of seats in the provincial assembly and managed to form a provincial government led by Ataullah Mengal in coalition with the Jamiat Ulema-e-Islam (JUI).

After Ayub Khan's downfall, his successor General Yahya Khan dissolved One Unit of West Pakistan and granted Balochistan the status of a full-fledged province in 1970, almost 23 years after its creation. However, while demarcating the new province, Baloch majority districts in Sindh and Punjab like Jacobabad and Dera Ghazi Khan were excluded, despite severe opposition from the local population.[89] The situation in Balochistan improved considerably as the one unit was dissolved and elections were ordered by Yahya Khan. During the 1970-71 elections, the Baloch leadership attempted to mobilise public support by stressing the underdevelopment of the province at the hands of a Punjabi dominated centre.[90] In the ensuing elections, the NAP won three out of four National Assembly seats from Balochistan. It also won the largest single block of seats in the provincial assembly and managed to form a provincial government led by Ataullah Mengal in coalition with Jamiat Ulema-e-Islam (JUI).[91]

With the formation of the NAP-JUI coalition government in Balochistan in 1972, socio-economic cleavages amongst the Baloch were subdued and the contradictions between the central and regional elites assumed pre-eminence. The NAP had come to power after projecting the underdevelopment of the province and a glaring lack of Baloch representation in the higher echelons of the government, both in the central as well as the state administration. The provincial government headed by Sardar Ataullah Mengal tried to redress Baloch grievances by giving them preferential treatment in the provincial services. It also made arrangements for the return of Punjabi bureaucrats to Punjab as had been agreed upon by the previous central government in the aftermath of the break-up of one unit. At the same time, some militant Baloch tribes also attacked Punjabi settlers in the Pat Feeder area to evict them,[92] where they had been settled by the previous administrations of West Pakistan, when one unit was in place. The provincial government also raised a new provincial security force, *Balochistan Dehi Muhafiz* (BDM), consisting mostly of loyal tribesmen, and strengthened its tribal militia.[93]

At that time, Zulfiqar Ali Bhutto's Pakistan People's Party was in power at the centre and had a clear majority in both Punjab and Sindh but it had only three seats in the North West Frontier Province (NWFP)[94] provincial assembly and none in Balochistan. Bhutto was as authoritarian as his predecessors and wanted power to be concentrated in his hands. The fact that the administration of two strategically important provinces was not in his control was not an acceptable situation for him. Bhutto's authoritarian tendencies and his support base in Punjab made it imperative that the Baloch nationalists could not be permitted to continue with their administrative reforms.[95]

In 1973, despite some compromises made by the NAP government, Balochistan's first representative provincial government was brought to an early end, ironically, by the first popularly elected federal government of Zulfiqar Ali Bhutto. Incidentally, Baloch nationalists had supported Bhutto and his 1973 constitution, which promised substantial provincial autonomy. The dismissal of the Mengal government and the resignation of Mufti Mahmud's government in the NWFP in protest precipitated a serious political crisis which, among other things, brought influential sections of Baloch society to the conclusion that it was futile to seek redress within the framework of Pakistan.[96] This also added to the restlessness of the Baloch youth, making them lose faith in moderate leadership and the constitutional process. They took it upon themselves to arrest the decline of their community. An armed insurrection took place in Balochistan from 1973 to 1977, and the military was used to brutally suppress it. Bhutto had no hesitation to call on the troops to fire against their own countrymen just two years after the creation of Bangladesh.[97]

The insurgency was a reasonably well-organised military operation that was led by an organisation called the Popular Front for Armed Resistance (PFAR). The insurgent numbers increased rapidly from about 400 Mengal and 500 Marri tribesmen to an estimated 55,000 men at the height of the war in 1974. Of these 55,000, nearly 11,500 cadres were organised into hard-core units, which operated in small bands of 30 to 50 men equipped with light weapons (rifles, machine guns, etc.) and were based in hideouts in the mountains. They were well-trained and did not face shortage of arms and ammunition.[98] In order to crush the rebellion, the Pakistan Army deployed about 80,000 troops armed with modern sophisticated weapons, which were procured from Iran under an emergency military and financial aid worth $ 200 million.[99]

The military operations led to a brutal confrontation between 55,000 Baloch insurgents and almost 80,000 Pakistani troops. The fighting became intense when the security forces resorted to the liberal use of heavy artillery and air power in its combat operations in the mountainous region against the insurgents who had laid road blockades to de-link Balochistan from other provinces. The insurgents also attacked some oil exploration centres and conducted raids on military encampment, besides ambushing army convoys.[100]

Apart from hitting hard at the militants, the army's operational task was to either flush them out or force them to surrender by denying avenues of sustenance and blocking their escape routes. French Mirage and F-86 Sabre jet fighters and Huey Cobra helicopters undertook indiscriminate aerial bombings of Baloch villages. Iran deputed a 13-member team of the Iranian Army Aviation along with US-supplied Huey Cobra combat helicopters to support the Pakistan Army in crushing the Baloch rebellion. The team actively participated in ruthlessly suppressing the Baloch nationalists. The intense conflict resulted in heavy loss of life and enormous destruction of property. It was estimated that at least 5,000 militants and over 3,300 soldiers were killed in hundreds of armed encounters that continued till 1977. The Pakistan government spent about one million Pakistani rupees on military operations per day.[101]

Contrary to the expectations of the Baloch leadership, the Soviet Union did not intervene in support of the Balochistan separatist movement. This crisis in Balochistan was quite similar to that in erstwhile Bangladesh, to the extent that over-reaction by the centre transformed a movement for autonomy into a separatist movement.[102] The results however were quite different as the Baloch, unlike the Bengalis, failed to elicit any external armed intervention in their support.

The Pakistan government's policy of using brute force had failed in East Pakistan; yet, it did not feel deterred from pursuing the same strategy against Baloch militants from 1973 to 1977. The fact that the government did not hesitate to use troops to fire on its own citizens, just two years after the civil war in East Pakistan; shocked the nation.[103] Yet, it persisted with the policy and its renewed confidence in bringing them into abject submission stemmed from the army's superior firepower supported by Iran vis-à-vis the ill-prepared Baloch People's Liberation Front (BPLF) and the BSO. The outcome of the Bangladesh war itself set tremendous pressure on the ruling elite for an outright victory: having presided over the country's disintegration two years earlier, they did not want to tolerate any further challenges from any quarter to the territorial integrity of Pakistan.[104]

The Baloch nationalists had planned prolonged guerrilla warfare with the active military support of Afghanistan. As the insurgency progressed and the military apparatus of the insurgents crumbled, their strategy of wearing out the army through sustained harassment did not work. Consequently, a major part of the insurgency was over in 1974 itself and only sporadic incidents of violence continued till 1977. This clearly showed that the insurgents had overestimated their strength against a highly determined and powerful adversary. The economic hardship that the people of Marri and Mengal areas faced due to the total economic blockade imposed by the government also worked against the war strategy of the insurgents. After facing severe hardships in the mountains, the people grew disenchanted with their military mission and many reportedly gave up arms or preferred to cross over to the relative safety of Afghanistan. Most of the insurgents returned to the plains after availing general amnesty and rehabilitation assistance offered by the government of Gen. Zia-ul-Haq. Finally, a significant military event in the annals of Baloch history ended disastrously.[105]

Zia, opting to end an un-winnable war, withdrew the army, but resorted to divide-and-rule policies. The military then opted to empower Pakhtoon Islamist parties in Balochistan with the aim of countering the Baloch nationalists and to provide recruits for Pakistan's jihad in Afghanistan. Since then, the Baloch nationalist leaders, as well as the moderate Pakhtoon political parties have had to face two adversaries—an overbearing central government, directly or indirectly dominated by the Army and, closer to home, Islamic political parties backed by the military (International Crisis Group, 2006:7).[106]

It is thus evident that right from the time Pakistan came into being, the Baloch did not perceive themselves as part of the new state. Their alienation with the state has found expression in their frequent violent outbursts. With the passage of time their alienation has increased as the attempts by the Pakistani leadership to integrate them into the mainstream have failed miserably.

Gwadar and Baloch Insurgency

Gwadar has been the trigger for the ongoing insurgency in Balochistan, which started in 2004. Although, there have been many other reasons why the insurgency has sustained itself, the Gwadar deep sea port project, the CPEC and associated development continue to be most relevant. The Baloch, in general, view all developmental projects being under taken in Balochistan with suspicion. They believe that Islamabad is undertaking these projects at the behest of security agencies to draw people from different parts of Pakistan to the project sites in Balochistan. They perceive that all 'the mega projects' are primarily aimed at changing the demography of Balochistan.

Of all the mega projects, nothing agitates the Baloch mind as much as the Gwadar project, which is the largest infrastructural one being undertaken in Pakistan. Unfortunately, the state government has no say in the development of the project and Islamabad has been unilaterally taking all decisions regarding the Port and large tracts of land have been seized by State agencies like the navy, the coast guard and the paramilitary forces.[107]

The large-scale presence of security forces and building of security infrastructure in the region creates suspicion in the minds of the Baloch regarding the primary objective of Gwadar and associated developmental projects. They strongly believe that economic development is not the primary consideration of the government while undertaking the work and the government is more interested in gaining strategic superiority over the insurgents. In the past, the location of many of the new roads was not determined in accordance with economic priorities or local requirements, but in accordance with the government's overall military calculations. Since its undeclared objective was to subdue the insurgents at any cost, the army built roads where they were badly needed to penetrate inaccessible guerrilla strongholds.[108]

The fact that a proposal has been put up by the military to acquire more than 11,000 acres of land around the Gwadar port to build a 'Combined Defence Complex' (CDC), has again raised apprehensions of the local residents. The proposal moved by the General Headquarters (GHQ) in Rawalpindi aims at providing foolproof security for the entire deep sea port project by ensuring adequate presence of defence forces at this strategically located port. The GHQ note even talks of 'foreign interference' in Balochistan and the need for extraordinary measures to ensure that the authority of the state is not challenged by anti-Pakistan elements. It projects that the presence of defence forces would give a clear and loud message to the forces involved in the nefarious design of destabilising Pakistan by acting in Balochistan. The establishment of the 'Combined Defence Complex' at Gwadar would mark a significant move towards making the Gwadar Deep Sea project safe and secure for global trade.[109]

The Pakistani government has tried to impress upon the locals that Gwadar will provide a lot of opportunities of not only employment but also business, trade and investment for everyone, but according to Abdul Hakim Baloch, a former chief secretary of Balochistan, the primary issue is ownership and not the construction or operation of the Gwadar port project. The government land around Gwadar and along the coastal highway has been grabbed by the land mafia in association with the members of the underworld from the Makran region, including those who had infiltrated the government and the legislative bodies. This huge corruption has resulted in the provincial government of Balochistan losing trillions of Pakistani rupees, which could have legitimately brought in the much-needed finance for the impoverished province.[110]

More significantly, Gwadar is being connected to Karachi through the coastal highway, but has not been connected through Turbat, Panjgur and Khuzdar to Quetta, the provincial capital or other parts of the Baloch hinterland. As a result the rest of the province will not derive any benefit from these projects coming up at Gwadar. This is agitating the local residents as they feel that their homeland is being converted into a landlocked province even though it possesses the longest stretch of the coastline in Pakistan. On the other hand non-Baloch people from outside the province due to better connectivity on account of the coastal highway would derive economic benefits and eventually settle down, thereby colonising the coastal regions.[111]

The authorities claim that local people are being given employment in this project on a preferential basis and have been trained to operate the machinery and equipment installed at the port. Many of them have been sent to Karachi and Islamabad for training but Baloch leaders complain that the manpower for the project, which is being run by the federal government, is drawn predominantly from outside the province.[112]

The channelling of funds has mainly been in the hands of the non-Baloch, as the provincial government has been completely dissociated from the project. It has been alleged that the Baloch plea for control over decisions pertaining to development activities have been ignored by the Punjabi bureaucracy in Islamabad. Besides this, a perception has been created in the Baloch minds that their land is being colonised by the Punjabi real estate cartel. The Baloch have been complaining that Punjabi settlers have been grabbing prime land and property in and around Gwadar.[113] The targeting of the project often baffles Western analysts as well as other Pakistanis who feel that the rebels do not have the wellbeing of Balochistan at heart.

Baloch nationalists feel that the benefits of Gwadar will not reach the local residents; on the contrary; they feel it will lead to a large-scale influx of outsiders in Balochistan,[114] thereby reducing them to a minority in their own province."There are also fears that unbridled foreign investment and development projects will bring too much foreign influence, threatening the indigenous social and cultural patterns".[115]

According to Sardar Ataullah Mengal, former chief minister of Balochistan, "If there are jobs in Gwadar, people would flock there, Pakistanis and foreigners alike. With time, they would get the right to vote. The problem is that one Karachi in Gwadar is sufficient to turn the whole population of Balochistan into a minority. Gwadar will end up sending more members to the Parliament than the rest of Balochistan, we would lose our identity, our language, everything.[116] That's why we are not willing to accept these mega projects".[117]

Consequently, this is one of the issues that have agitated the Baloch mind the most, although Gwadar and other mega developmental projects being undertaken in Balochistan are purportedly for the economic development of the province. However, the primary concerns about underdevelopment with respect to the Baloch and Balochistan have lost their relevance in the flux of politics, which include certain deep-rooted biases. Various political forces are attempting to derive mileage out of this discontentment and are trying to malign one another in their efforts to gain power and pelf. These machinations have worked to the detriment of the poor masses of the province and have led to repeated bouts of violence in Balochistan and severe opposition to all the developmental projects in the province.[118]

Apart from Gwadar Deep Sea Port project, the other 'mega' developmental projects include the Makran coastal highway, which connects Gwadar with Karachi through Pasni and Ormara, Mirani Dam on the Dasht river and the Saindak copper-gold mines. All these projects have suffered delays in Pakistan's most under-developed province. These projects could have contributed enormously towards the socio-economic upliftment of the province, but have completely failed to do so. To give an example, the Mirani dam, was meant to irrigate 33,000 acres of barren land in Balochistan and provide water to Gwadar port, but the irrigation targets have never been met.[119] In 2007, Cyclone Yemyin caused a reverse flow in upstream rives which resulted in huge loss of life and property with over 6,000 houses demolished.[120] The project has appropriately been termed as a 'mega disaster'. Similarly, the coastal highway could have given a boost to much-needed tourism in this isolated region, but has totally failed. Similarly, the Gwadar Deep Sea Port has failed to evolve as a major port and has thus failed to emerge as a gateway for the Central Asian Republics or Xinjiang,[121] or even as a regional hub of economic activities.

The port unfortunately will not be able to attain commercial viability till the local aspirations are met. Regrettably, the Pakistan government has not taken adequate measures to assuage the apprehensions of the local population and consequently, Baloch nationalism has only grown with time. Baloch nationalist outfits continue to target the port project and the people associated with it. On 19 April 2019, a bus travelling from Gwadar to Karachi was stopped near Ormara and 14 non-Baloch travellers were segregated and shot dead. The Baloch Raaji Aajoi Sangar (BRAS), an alliance of three armed ethnic Baloch separatist groups. Balochistan Liberation Front (BLF), Baloch Liberation Army (BLA) and Baloch Republican Guard—claimed responsibility for the attack and declared that all those killed were personnel of the Pakistan Navy and Coast Guard.[122]

It would be prudent to sum up that while the influence of the Gwadar port project on Pakistan's external security has been quite good, as it has given its navy greater flexibility and eliminated its economic vulnerability; its impact on internal security has been, at best, mixed. Ideally, a port which brings about so much economic development should have been welcomed by the locals, but to the contrary, it has raised their apprehensions about being marginalised.

NOTES

1. Sohail Azmie. "Maritime security: Pakistan's perspective', *Pakistan Today*, 24 September 2017 from website https://www.pakistantoday.com.pk/2017/09/24/maritime-security-pakistans-perspective/ (Accessed on 28 December 2019).
2. Ibid.
3. In a personal interaction with the author by e-mail on 4 September 2020.
4. Ammad Hassan. "Pakistan's Gwadar Port – Prospects of Economic Revival" Naval Postgraduate School Monterey Thesis submitted in June 2005, p. 3.
5. In reply to a questionnaire sent by the author by e-mail on 15 July 2020.
6. Hasan Yaser Malik. "Strategic Importance of Gwadar Port", *Journal of Political Studies*, vol. 19, issue 2, 2012, p. 57.
7. Sohail Azmie. "Maritime security: Pakistan's perspective", *Pakistan Today*, Lahore, 24 September 2017.
8. Hasan Yaser Malik. op. cit., p. 58.
9. Port Muhammad Bin Qasim also known as Port Qasim is just 35 kilometres from Karachi city centre and the approach channels of the two ports are quite close to each other.
10. Muhammad Anwar, *Role of smaller navies: a focus on Pakistan's maritime interests*, Islamabad: Directorate of Naval Educational Services, Naval Headquarters, 1999, p. 133.
11. Mian Abrar, "Jinnah Naval Base – Navy expands strategic outreach to West Coast, Persian Gulf", from https://www.pakistantoday.com.pk/2016/01/13/jinnah-naval-base-navy-expands-strategic-outreach-to-west-coast-persian-gulf/ (Accessed on 28 December 2019).
12. Ibid.
13. Reply to author's questionnaire from Dr. Ayesha Siddiqa by e-mail dated 13 September 2020.
14. Abrar. op. cit.
15. Ibid.
16. Hasan Yaser Malik. op. cit., p. 58.
17. Noor ul Haq, "Balochistan: its past and present", *The Kashmir Times*, 8 February 2005.
18. "Pakistan hands over Gwadar port to Chinese company", *Deccan Herald*, 18 February 2013, from https://www.deccanherald.com/international/pakistan-hands-over-gwadar-port-to-chinese-company-304229.html (Accessed on 28 December 2019).

19. Hasan Yaser Malik. op. cit., p. 58.
20. Sabir Shah, "Pakistan among nations that depend substantially on foreign remittances", *The News*, 25 December 2019, pp. 2, 9.
21. Hasan Yaser Malik. op. cit., p. 58.
22. "Under CPEC: First container vessel anchors at Gwadar" *The Express Tribune*, 8 March 2018.
23. Ibid.
24. Mohid Iftikhar. "Challenges to Pakistan's maritime security", from Centre for Security Governance Website https://secgovcentre.org/2015/06/maritime-security-in-the-indian-ocean-challenges-for-pakistan/ (Accessed on 28 December 2019).
25. Ibid.
26. Sohail Azmie. op. cit.
27. The term Net Security provider was first used by Robert Gates, the US Defence Secretary in India's context during 2009 Shangri-la Dialogue in Singapore. Although there is no established definition of the term, it broadly implies a state capable of not only looking after its own security but also of providing security to others both directly or indirectly by building up their capacity.
28. Sohail Azmie. op. cit.
29. Sohail Azmie. "Pakistan Navy's evolving maritime security concept", *The Nation*, 28 June 2019.
30. "Pakistan Navy assumes command of multinational CTF-150", *The Express Tribune*, 21 January 2022.
31. Hussain Haqqani in a personal response to a question posed by the author in September 2020.
32. Ibid.
33. Azhar Ahmad, *Gwadar: Potential and Prospects*, Islamabad: Pak Institute for Conflict and Security Studies, 2015, pp. 13-14.
34. Ibid., p. 14.
35. Karnie M. Renaud. "The Mineral Industry of Pakistan" in *2015 Mineral Year Book*, US Department of the Interior, US Geological Survey, November 2018 (Advance Release), p. 22.2.
36. Azhar Ahmad. op. cit., p. 14.
37. Faisal Mushtaq et al. "Coal Fired Power Generation Potential of Balochistan", in *Petroleum and Coal 1337-7027*, volume 54, June 2012, p. 133.
38. Ibid., p. 141.
39. Azhar Ahmad. op. cit., p. 14.
40. Ibid., pp. 14-15.
41. Ibid., p. 15.
42. Ibid., pp. 15-16.
43. Shahzada Zulfiqar, "Port of Terror", *Newsline*, June 2004, p. 56.
44. "The tribes arise", *The Economist*, London, 7 May 7, 2005, p. 25.
45. Owen Bennett Jones, *Pakistan: Eye of the Storm*, New Delhi: Penguin Books India (P) Ltd., 2002, p. 132.
46. Lasbela, Kharan and Makran were vassals of Kalat but during the British rule they had more or less become independent and were dealing with the British directly though a modicum of suzerainty by Kalat was maintained.

47. Even though the region was under the British and the tribal sardars were administering their regions independently with minimal interference from the British, they still considered the Khan of Kalat as their notional overlord.
48. Adeel Khan. *Politics of Identity: Ethnic Nationalism and the State in Pakistan,* New Delhi: Sage Publications, 2005,114.
49. The ruler of Kalat was called the Khan of Kalat.
50. Jones, op. cit., p. 132.
51. Taj Mohammad Breseeg, *Baloch Nationalism: Its Origin and Development*, Karachi: Royal Book Company, 2004, p. 213.
52. Ibid., p. 215.
53. Tahir Amin, "Ethno National Movements of Pakistan", Islamabad: Institute of Policy Studies, 1988, p. 71.
54. Breseeg. op. cit., p. 234.
55. Sylvia Matheson. *The Tigers of Balochistan.* Oxford University Press, Karachi, 1998, p. 62.
56. Tahir Amin. op. cit., p. 71.
57. Veena Kukreja. *Contemporary Pakistan: Political Processes, Conflicts and Crises.* New Delhi, Sage Publications, 2003, p. 131.
58. Selig S. Harrison, *In Afghanistan's Shadow: Baloch Nationalism.* New York, Carnegie Endowment of International Peace, 1981, p. 23.
59. Owen Bennett Jones. op. cit., p. 132.
60. Asad Rahman. "Focus on Balochistan Part III – After Independence" at http://www.balochvoice.com/asad_rahman.html#Part%20III (Accessed on 19 May 2005).
61. Adeel Khan. op. cit., p. 115.
62. Breseeg. op. cit., pp. 232-233.
63. Tariq Ali, *Can Pakistan Survive? The Death of a State.* Suffolk, Penguin Books, 1983, pp. 115-116.
64. Breseeg. op. cit., p. 238.
65. Owen Bennett Jones. op. cit., p. 133.
66. Mir Ahmad Yar Khan Baluch. "Inside Balochistan – A political Autobiography of His Highness Baiglar Bagi : Khan-e-Azam XIII", Karachi, Royal Book Company, 1975, p. xvii.
67. Quetta was a military dominated town. It had many military establishments including the Staff College and a large percentage of its population depended directly or indirectly on the military.
68. Tilak Devasher, *Pakistan: The Balochistan Conundrum.* New Delhi: Harper Collins Publishers India, 2019, p. 83.
69. Breseeg. op. cit., pp. 238–239.
70. Afghan authorities refused to provide any help and the Soviet Embassy at Kabul, though sympathetic, did not offer any material assistance.
71. Adeel Khan. op. cit., p. 115.
72. Owen Bennett Jones. op. cit., p. 133.
73. Kukreja. op. cit., p. 131.
74. Ibid.
75. Breseeg. op. cit., p. 260.

76. Prince Karim led the first rebellion in Balochistan in 1948.
77. Breseeg. op. cit., pp. 260-261.
78. Ibid., p. 261.
79. One Unit was a scheme under which the Govt. of Pakistan merged all the provinces of West Pakistan under one province called West Pakistan. Similarly, East Bengal, Sylhet and the Hill Tracts were merged to form a province of East Pakistan. It came into being on 30 September 1955 and continued till 1970. It gave the two provinces parity in parliament, which was meant to balance the numerical majority of Bengalis.
80. Tahir Amin. op. cit., pp. 94-95.
81. P. Sahadevan, "Coping with Disorder – Strategies to End Internal Wars in South Asia ", *RCSS Policy Studies 17,* Colombo, Regional Centre for Strategic Studies, 2000, pp. 16-17.
82. Adeel Khan. op. cit., p. 116.
83. Breseeg. op. cit., pp. 288-289.
84. Ibid., pp. 290 - 291.
85. Owen Bennett Jones. op. cit., p. 133.
86. Breseeg. op. cit., pp. 291-292.
87. Tahir Amin. op. cit., p. 95.
88. Sahadevan. op. cit., p. 17.
89. "Pakistan: The Worsening Conflict in Balochistan", International Crisis Group, Asia Report No. 119, 14 September 2006, p. 6.
90. Kukreja, op. cit., p. 134.
91. Adeel Khan. op. cit., p. 116.
92. Tahir Amin, op. cit., p. 125.
93. Hasan-Askari Rizvi, *Military, State and Society in Pakistan.* London, Macmillan Press Limited, 2000, p. 155.
94. North West Frontier Province (NWFP) was a province of British India and later of Pakistan. It was established on 9 November 1901 and renamed as the province of Khyber Pakhtunkhwa on 19 April 2010.
95. Adeel Khan. op. cit., p. 117.
96. Mary Ann Weaver. *Pakistan in the Shadow of Jihad and Afghanistan.* New York: Farrar, Straus and Giroux, 2002, p. 127.
97. Lawrence Ziring. *Pakistan in the Twentieth Century: A Political History.* Karachi, Oxford University Press, 1999, p. 391.
98. White Paper on Balochistan published by the Pakistan Government, 1974..
99. Harrison. op. cit., p. 36.
100. Sahadevan. op. cit., p. 38.
101. Ibid.
102. Christophe Jaffrelot *Pakistan Nationalism without a Nation*?, Manohar Publishers & Distributors, New Delhi, 2002, p. 29.
103. Ziring. op. cit., p. 391.
104. Sahadevan. op. cit., pp. 66-68.
105. Ibid.
106. International Crisis Group, 2006, op. cit., p. 7.
107. Ibid., pp..14-15.

108. Harrison. op. cit., p. 166.
109. Arif Rana. "'Defence Complex' at Gwadar", from http://www.gwadarnews.com/newsdetail.asp?newsID=1052 (Accessed on 19 April 2008).
110. Abdul Hakim Baluch. "Bringing development to Balochistan', *Dawn*, Karachi, 13 December 2004.
111. Ibid.
112. "Balochistan's Grievances", Editorial, *Dawn,* Karachi, 9 November 2004.
113. Urmila Phadnis. "Ethnic Movements in Pakistan" in Pandav Nayak (ed.), *Pakistan: Society and Politics* – South Asian Studies Series, 6, New Delhi: South Asian Publishers Pvt. Ltd., 1984, p. 195.
114. "Terrorism in Balochistan". Editorial, *Dawn, Karachi,* 18 December 2004.
115. "Confrontation No Solution to Balochistan Imbroglio", Editorial, *The News,* Internet Edition, 16 January 2005.
116. According to the 2017 Census, the population of Karachi city is 14,916,456, whereas the population of the entire province of Balochistan is 12,344,408.
117. Idrees Bakhtia. "Mega-projects are a Conspiracy to turn the Balochis into a Minority in their Homeland", an interview with Sardar Ataullah Mengal, *The Herald*, August 2004, p. 51.
118. "Terrorism in Balochistan". Editorial, *Dawn,* Karachi, 18 December 2004.
119. Ibid.
120. Naseer Memon. "Disaster unleashed by Mirani Dam", *Dawn*, Karachi, 20 August 2007.
121. Editorial, *Dawn,* Karachi, 18 December 2004.
122. Nazir Mahmood. "As Balochistan bleeds", *The News*, Karachi, 20 April 2019. Also see Asad Hashim, "Gunmen kill 14 bus passengers in Pakistan's Balochistan", *Al Jazeera* websitehttps://www.aljazeera.com/news/2019/04/gunmen-kill-bus-passengers-pakistan-balochistan-official-190418045138814.html (Accessed on 20 April 2019) and "14 people, including nine navy men, shot dead in Balochistan", *Pakistan Today*, 18 April 2019.

4

Significance for China

China's active involvement in the construction of the port and subsequently, the manner in which the operations of the port were handed over to China, has led many strategic analysts to perceive Gwadar as a Chinese outpost in South Asia. It has also provided China with an outpost at the mouth of the Persian Gulf, which may disturb the geopolitical balance in this geo-strategically important region. In fact according to the well-known Pakistani political analyst and author, Ayesha Siddiqa, the whole purpose of the Pakistan government under Pervez Musharraf behind promoting Gwadar was to build China's interests in Pakistan's security through the port. It has integrated China and Pakistan's security interests in the geopolitical domain.[1] Gwadar also provides China and Pakistan access to the Persian Gulf and gives them a significant capability to monitor their oil shipments from the Gulf. On the other hand, Baloch nationalists perceive it as a Chinese-aided Pakistani project to colonise their land.

Connectivity, along with associated infrastructural projects, has always transformed global geopolitics. Sir Halford Mackinder, who propounded the heartland theory, had visualised the geopolitical transformation that railway tracks could bring about. China proposes to bring about that transformation by building up connectivity across the Eurasian landmass under its Silk Road Economic Belt (SREB) project. The SREB along with its maritime counterpart, the Maritime Silk Road Initiative (MSRI), which are both massive connectivity projects of China, have since been collectively termed as the 'Belt and Road' or 'One Belt, One Road' (OBOR) initiative.[2] This is China's ambitious project to revive the ancient Silk Route for trade connecting China, Central Asia and Europe by establishing three trade corridors via southern, northern, and central Xinjiang, linking China with Pakistan, Russia, India and Europe.[3]

China in trying to enhance its land-based influence in the Eurasian land mass through the CPEC and a revamped Silk Road could finally prove Mackinder's contention that "trans-continental railways are now transmuting the conditions of land-power, and nowhere can they have such effect as in the closed heartland of Euro-Asia". China realises the overwhelming superiority of the US Navy and its domination of the oceans. The USA has been focussing on projecting power through the oceans, since the end of the Cold War. Consequently, the US Navy has received the bulk of the funding for defence. Its capabilities place the US Navy in a position where the PLA Navy will find it extremely difficult to match in the foreseeable future. In order to facilitate its trade, without interference from the USA, whose powerful navy dominates the oceans. China is creating a web of continental connectivity across Eurasia.[4]

The initiative involves enormous infrastructural development associated with connectivity, and consequently, it has generated huge concerns about its long-term geopolitical impact. Although, MSRI and SREB were conceived as two-separate projects in 2013, but they have since been clubbed together. On account of their massive geographical expanse, financial outlay, and economic impact, they have generated enormous interest amongst researchers, strategic analysts, as well as businessmen in China and other participating countries like Pakistan. The projects have also attracted the attention of other regional and extra-regional powers like India, the USA, Russia, and Japan, whose interests they are likely to impact.[5]

Transnational economic and infrastructure initiatives are often linked with a country's foreign policy objectives and thus incorporate a significant geostrategic impact. The biggest infrastructure initiative in recent history, the Belt and Road Initiative (BRI)[6] has accordingly, generated widespread international attention due to its perceived impact upon global geopolitics and economy. The BRI aims to economically integrate a vast territory that is inhabited by 4.4 billion people and generates 29 per cent of global economic volume amounting to $ 21 trillion (Hussain and Hussain, 2017:80). Each individual component of the BRI has the capacity "to transform the global geopolitical landscape through the construction of interrelated infrastructure projects including ports, highways, railways, and pipelines".[7]

According to official sources of the Chinese government, the BRI includes 60 countries, with over 70 per cent of the global population and includes over half the Gross Domestic Product (GDP) of the world. It also includes many emerging economies as well as major energy-producing and consuming countries. Since 2013, China has extended $ 284 billion for infrastructural projects in different countries across the globe and has pledged an additional amount of $ 100 billion in May 2017. The huge investments clearly show that the project is extremely significant for China and its present leadership.[8]

The China Pakistan Economic Corridor (CPEC) is undoubtedly one of the most significant components of the BRI and the Gwadar port is the seaward terminal of this important component of the BRI. Gwadar port is also an ideal example of how China's strategic ambitions and objectives inherent in infrastructural projects being undertaken as part of BRI have often been masked under the charade of the economic aims of BRI in general and the CPEC in particular.

China Pakistan Economic Corridor (CPEC)

The CPEC constitutes one of the six corridors that form the landscape of the Belt and Road Initiative (BRI) and, geo-strategically, is considered one of the most important components of the BRI. It is broadly a combination of various projects in different sectors like roads, railways, ports and airports in the transport sector; oil and gas pipelines along with hydro and thermal power plants in the energy sector; fibre optics and telecommunications infrastructure in the communication sector and special economic zones. These projects are being established along a network of highways, railways, fibre optic cables, and pipelines that connect the trading town of Kashgar in the Xinjiang Uyghur Autonomous Region in western China to the Gwadar port on the Arabian Sea in the Balochistan province of Pakistan.[9]

This network will comprise three parallel routes from Xinjiang to the Arabian Sea along the eastern, central, and western alignments. The Chinese investments in the CPEC are huge and are equivalent to 20 per cent of Pakistan's annual GDP. The total amount slated for investment has since gone up and the bulk of the investment is for power plants being set up as part of the CPEC.[10]

Much before the idea of the BRI and CPEC took firm shape, China had started working on its first transportation corridor connecting Kashgar in Xinjiang to Abbottabad in Pakistan through the Khunjerab Pass in the Karakoram Mountain range. The corridor named Karakoram Highway was completed in 1979 and has been open to the public since 1986. Subsequently, General Musharraf, who was then Pakistan's President, proposed linking it to Gwadar, but the ongoing political instability in Pakistan in general and Balochistan in particular, prevented it from materialising.[11]

It was only in 2013 that the idea of a full-fledged economic corridor along this road evolved and the authorities in China agreed to finance the project, which would include a transportation corridor with many energy and infrastructure projects along it. The proposal eventually fructified in April 2015, when President Xi Jinping visited Pakistan and China and Pakistan signed an agreement to start working on the CPEC. The two countries agreed to work with a scheme for a projected outlay of $ 46 billion and it was anticipated that the 'early harvest' projects amounting to approximately half the total outlay would be completed by 2018.[12]

According to the official estimate of the total outlay, $ 10 billion were allocated for rail, road, and port infrastructure and included concessional financing by the Chinese government and associated banks. On the other hand, a sum of $ 18 billion was allocated for-energy related projects, which were to be funded by foreign direct investments (FDI) by various Chinese companies and banks. These power projects were assured of guaranteed tariffs by way of pre-negotiated power purchase agreements.[13]

Most significantly, as the corridor will pass through volatile regions, a special security division has been set up by the Pakistan Army,[14] to ensure the security of various projects and Chinese workers along the CPEC.[15] The 34th Light Infantry Division with more than 15,000 personnel has been established to provide security to CPEC and its workforce. The division commanded by a major-general comprises nine infantry battalions[16] and six paramilitary wings of the Frontier Corps and Pakistan Rangers.[17]

To provide maritime security, Special Task-Force 88 led by the Pakistan Navy has been created,[18] which has personnel from the Pakistan Marines and Maritime Security Agency. It has also set up a coastal security and harbour defence force to deal with coastal threats. In addition, to provide security to Chinese companies and workers, a force protection battalion of the Pakistan Marines has been established at Gwadar. Furthermore, Pakistan has enhanced its collaboration with the People's Liberation Army Navy (PLAN) and has established a 'Joint Maritime Information and Coordination Centre' (JMICC) and 'Coastal Watch Stations' (CWSs) to improve maritime domain awareness. Apart from these, the federal government has qualitatively and quantitatively enhanced the police force to maintain law and order along the CPEC.[19] It is expected that the cost of raising this division as well as its remunerations would further add to the overall cost of the project.[20]

The project also incorporates upgradation of the 1,300-km long Karakoram highway, which connects China to Pakistan. In addition, it includes laying a fibre optic cable from Rawalpindi to Khunjerab Pass, on China's border with Gilgit-Baltistan. The fibre optic link would expedite data transmission between the two countries. Rawalpindi is the actual power centre of Pakistan as it hosts the Pakistan Army's General Headquarters. China's Exim Bank is providing a concessional loan for the cross-border optic fibre project, which will be undertaken by Huawei, the Chinese telecom firm.[21]

The core idea of the CPEC is to link China's restive Xinjiang province with the Gwadar port through a network of infrastructural and energy projects, along with gas and oil pipelines. This overland route is being primarily envisaged to create an alternate supply channel for China's energy imports from the Middle East and Africa as against the existing maritime route that passes through the Indian Ocean and the South China Sea. The rationale for establishing this route emanates from China's much-debated 'Malacca Dilemma', wherein the Straits of Malacca is perceived as a potential chokepoint that can be used by China's adversaries to block its energy and trade supplies thereby paralysing its economy in times of hostilities. The CPEC also creates opportunities in remote, landlocked, and under-developed Xinjiang by opening up its access to sea thus encouraging both state and private enterprises to enlarge their economic activities in the region to create jobs.[22]

On account of such fears, China's investments in the CPEC and Gwadar present it with a much greater degree of energy security by allowing it to diversify or bypass the existing energy routes. Although, the 'Malacca Dilemma' has been used by China to justify its energy security concerns, there is a strong viewpoint that rejects this analysis by presenting alternative sea routes that can be used by China in case of a blockade. This viewpoint also contests the logic of a blockade of Chinese ships by the USA at Malacca, as America, with its military presence in the Gulf, could much more easily interdict the energy supplies bound for China from the Persian Gulf, at the Strait of Hormuz itself.

Another rationale for China's economic interest in the CPEC and Gwadar relates to the issue of correcting regional imbalances in the country's domestic development dynamics. Due to its landlocked nature, China's western provinces continue to remain much less developed than the eastern provinces. This development imbalance has not only compromised economic prosperity but has also posed a serious threat to the political stability of China's western regions. Under its 'Western Development Strategy', China now plans to connect its western region with a trade and energy route to the Middle East, Africa, and Central Asia through the CPEC. In addition, taking advantage of the Greek economic crisis, the China Ocean Shipping (Group) Company (COSCO) has taken over a majority stake in the strategically-located Greek port of Piraeus. Greece has one of the largest shipping tonnages in the world. China is planning to build a high-speed rail link from Piraeus to important destinations in Western Europe.[23] This could help China to start a regular liner service between Gwadar and Piraeus port thereby turning Gwadar into a gateway between Xinjiang and Europe later. Further, this trade channel is being envisaged by China to rein in the East Turkmenistan Islamic Movement (ETIM) in Xinjiang by bringing much-needed economic prosperity to this impoverished region. Moreover, by deepening economic cooperation with Pakistan and Central Asian states, China wants to increase its geopolitical clout in these countries and enlist their support in quelling any sympathy and institutional support for the Uighur separatist insurgency. As such, Gwadar becomes an important pivot of China's internal security strategy.

China has tried to project the CPEC and Gwadar as instruments of regional economic integration, growth, and prosperity. However, there have been questions about the economic rationale of the CPEC on account of geographic difficulties, cost calculations, and security issues. The transportation of oil and gas from Gwadar to China would entail crossing the entire length of Pakistan, including the treacherous Karakoram Mountains, before entering China through the Karakoram Highway. This route from the Pakistani side includes terrain with extremely difficult geomorphic features. Moreover, sections of the Karakoram Highway are subject to frequent landslides and rockslides since it crosses the geological fault line where the Eurasian and Indian plates collide. In addition, transporting oil and gas along this route through high-altitude pipelines becomes costlier as they require extra heating and insulating equipment, and high-power pumping stations to pump fuel uphill.[24] These doubts give rise to the suspicion that the CPEC is not purely an economic venture, but has a much deeper geo-political objective.

The CPEC for China could be an outlet for deploying excess capacity of its infrastructural firms and absorbing its huge surplus, but policy makers in Pakistan perceive it as Chinese insurance for Pakistan's security rather than a pure economic venture. Islamabad perceives it to be the centrepiece of China's strategic interests in their country and a panacea for all its ills. Consequently, even though China keeps reiterating that the aims and objectives of the CPEC are purely economic, almost everyone in Pakistan assumes it to be a strategic project that would strengthen their national security.[25]

The corridor technically became operational on 31 October 2016, when Chinese trucks carrying the first Chinese consignment of goods from Kashgar reached Sost[26] dry port in Gilgit-Baltistan, from where the shipping containers were taken to Gwadar port on Pakistani trucks. However, the fact that the consignment had to be received by the Pakistan army at Sost and then escorted in smaller convoys all the way to the Gwadar port by security personnel from the army, police and the special CPEC force, demonstrates the insecurities inherent in transporting cargo along this route. China, in order to augment security, had already donated 25 vehicles equipped with modern security gear to the local government in Gilgit-Baltistan (GB). This was done to ensure the safety of the convoys and their cargo from various armed groups operating in the region. In addition, the GB government also had to install 285 high-resolution close-circuit cameras with night vision capabilities to provide security.[27]

The extraordinary security arrangements made by both China and Pakistan for this inaugural movement of cargo along CPEC clearly show that it will be many years before transportation of goods along this route becomes secure and commercially viable. It has also been reported in the media,[28] that the Chinese authorities have also tried contacting various Baloch nationalist groups to buy security for the movement of their cargo along the CPEC in areas that are dominated by them.[29]

China plans to set up nine special economic zones (SEZ), as part of the CPEC in Pakistan and Pakistan-occupied Jammu and Kashmir (POJK).[30] In May 2017, a special incentive package was approved by the Pakistan government, for relocating industries from China to these SEZs. The package was aimed at incentivising Chinese investments and primarily dealt with those Chinese industries that were obsolescent and had been declared as sunset industries by Beijing, but were perceived to be still relevant and functional in Pakistan. It was projected domestically that it would create millions of new jobs. The Chinese authorities had demanded such a package at the sixth meeting of the CPEC Joint Cooperation Committee (JCC) held in Beijing in December 2016 and managed to get it from Islamabad.[31]

Chinese investments in the project have been revised upwards to $ 56 billion, which are almost equal to 20 per cent of Pakistan's GDP. The investment under CPEC is not only China's biggest overseas commitment, but also its most ambitious one. It aims to build a 3,218-kilometre route by 2030, which would include highways, railways, and pipelines to connect Gwadar deep sea port project to China's western province of Xinjiang. Most of the planned expenditure amounting to around $ 34 billion will be spent on numerous power generation facilities, which are anticipated to add 17,000 megawatts of electrical power to the Pakistani grid. Many of these are coal-fired plants being relocated from China. The remaining investment will be spent on transportation infrastructure, which includes upgradation of the railway line connecting Peshawar in the north-west to the port of Karachi. The corridor strives "to revive the earliest Silk Road with an emphasis on infrastructure, and establishes the strategic structure of bilateral cooperation" between China and Pakistan.[32]

The CPEC is perceived as a significant turning point for both Pakistan and the region, as it seeks to provide a strong stimulus to Pakistan's faltering economy, by promising rapid economic growth, development of infrastructure and creation of 700,000 new jobs by 2030-35. It is perceived that the CPEC is now ready to enter Phase II, where 27 projects are planned, which focuses on development of agriculture, industrial cooperation, and trade promotion. This phase also seeks to promote tourism. Consequently, it should lead to job opportunities for local residents. However, the way the CPEC is configured does not connect local towns, but bypasses them; consequently, there are serious questions about its capacity to create jobs.[33]

The Gwadar deep sea port project is the lynchpin of the CPEC and consequently, the success of the CPEC depends on Gwadar. As a result, the Chinese have identified a number of projects in and around Gwadar, which include the Gwadar international airport, the Gwadar east-bay expressway, development of the Gwadar free zone, construction of breakwaters, dredging of berthing areas and channels in the harbour, a freshwater treatment plant, water supply and distribution, a technical and vocational training institute, Bao steel park, Gwadar University, petrochemical and other industries, a friendship hospital and livelihood projects for the local population.[34]

Development of the port would provide China a secure and long-term foothold in the Arabian Sea. Besides development of the Gwadar port, the project also incorporates development of various infrastructure, which includes building roads and railway networks as well as industrial development in and around Gwadar as well as along the routes of the CPEC. The corridor aims to act as a conduit for the novel Maritime Silk Route that visualises connecting more than three billion people in Africa, Asia, and Europe.[35]

China's Interests in Gwadar

The Gwadar deep sea port is the flagship project of the CPEC. Almost all the economic activities associated with it converge at Gwadar port.[36] On account of its strategic location near the Persian Gulf, at the cross-section of South, West, and Central Asia, Gwadar holds immense strategic significance for both China's security as well as its economic interests. The political leadership at Islamabad has successfully used the strategic location of Gwadar to lure the Chinese leadership into the CPEC.[37] More significantly, as Gwadar connects the 21st-century maritime silk road with silk road economic belt, it can be regarded as the very fulcrum of the Belt and Road Initiative (BRI) in more ways than one.

Among the numerous ventures being undertaken under the CPEC, the projects at Gwadar have attracted the maximum international attention due to their obvious security and strategic implications. More significantly, out of the nine projects mentioned under the Gwadar subhead on the official CPEC website, the port facility has drawn the maximum attention from international analysts. Although, as mentioned earlier, the original idea of a port facility at Gwadar was based on recommendations by an American survey of the Balochistan coast way back in 1954, long before it became a key strategic component of the CPEC.[38]

China first evinced interest in developing a port at Gwadar in May 1999 by offering financial and technical support. However, the project did not take off. Eventually, Pakistan succeeded in drawing Chinese support in May 2001 when General Pervez Musharraf, during a visit to Beijing, elicited a commitment from Chinese Premier Zhu Rongji to help Islamabad in the construction of the port in exchange for setting up a Chinese radar station on the Pakistani coast.[39]

Although the Chinese master plan for Gwadar was ready by October 2001, the catastrophic events of 11 September 2001 and consequent US operations in Afghanistan delayed the project. It was only in March 2002 that an agreement could be signed by the two countries in Beijing. On 22 March 2002, the ground-breaking ceremony for the project was held, which was attended by the then President of Pakistan, General Pervez Musharraf, and the then Chinese Vice-Premier, Wu Bang Guo. The port was officially commissioned in 2005 and one of the largest port operators of the globe, PSA International Pte. Ltd.[40]of Singapore, was appointed as the operator. However, the first ship could enter the port only in March 2008 and that too after it had partially unloaded its cargo to another vessel at anchorage.[41]

The operator of the port was changed on 18 February 2013, when the China Overseas Port Holding Company (COPHC), a state-owned enterprise of China, was handed over the operations and development of the port for 43 years, although PSA International Pte. Ltd. had already been awarded the contract to operate the port for 40 years in February 2007. The official process of signing the documents to hand over Gwadar port to the Chinese was held in the official residence of the President of Pakistan in the presence of President Asif Ali Zardari and Liu Jian, the Chinese Ambassador to Pakistan.[42] This clearly indicated that the decision was not based on commercial considerations, but on political grounds and that too at the highest level of the government.

The Gwadar port received a significant impetus during Xi Jinping's maiden visit to Pakistan in 2015 when the CPEC project was beefed up with a corpus of USD 46 billion. Writing for a newspaper in Pakistan, President Xi identified the Gwadar port as one of the four pillars of the CPEC, "We need to form a '1+4' cooperation structure with the Economic Corridor at the centre and the Gwadar Port, energy, infrastructure and industrial cooperation being the four key areas to drive development across Pakistan and deliver tangible benefits to its people".[43]

In addition to security and economic dynamics, Gwadar allows China a strategic outpost in the Indian Ocean. In a significant move, the China Overseas Ports Holding Company (COPHC) officially took control of Gwadar Port's free-trade zone on 11 November 2015, further augmenting its presence in the Gwadar region. As per the agreement, the state-backed COPHC will manage the free-trade zone on a 43-year lease and the formal handing over indicates China's complete control over the business affairs of the port.[44] Pakistan's Prime Minister, Shahid Khaqan Abbasi, on 29 January 2018 inaugurated the first phase of the Gwadar Free Trade Zone (FTZ). He stated at the inauguration that "CPEC is turning into a reality today which will change the fate of the region". It was emphasised that the FTZ was a significant step to develop the coastal region around Gwadar, which would be a bridgehead on China's new Silk Road, through which Chinese goods destined for Europe and Africa would pass.[45]

The representatives from China and Pakistan also signed five agreements, which declared Gwadar and Piung in China as sister cities, at the same time declaring Gwadar Port and China's Tianjin as sister ports. A memorandum of understanding (MoU) for a poverty alleviation initiative was also signed between the COPHC and the Gwadar district government. COPHC chairman Zhang Baozhong, speaking on the occasion, stated that with the operationalisation of the FTZ, Gwadar would emerge as a big commercial hub for the entire region, and thereby improve Pakistan's economy and the lives of its citizens. He also claimed that some 30 companies in different fields like hotel, bank, logistics, and fish processing were already in the FTZ.[46]

In order to boost the growth of a business environment in and around Gwadar, China had sought and has succeeded in extracting huge tax concessions from Pakistan for the COPHC, as well as for other Chinese institutions and business ventures in Gwadar. On 23 May 2016, the day when a trilateral transit agreement was signed by Iran, India and Afghanistan to counter the China-Pakistan Economic Corridor (CPEC), Islamabad announced a complete income tax holiday for 23 years to all the businesses in the Gwadar Free Zone. In addition the COPHCL was exempted from paying a minimum of 1 per cent income tax and all the contractors and subcontractors of COPHCL were extended this concession for 20 years.[47]

In addition, the COPHCL and its operating companies, including the China Overseas Ports Holding Company Pakistan Private Limited, Gwadar Marines Services Limited, Gwadar International Terminals Limited, and Gwadar Free Zone Company Limited were given complete exemption from the 12.5 per cent tax on dividend income and withholding tax.[48] As if it was not enough, Islamabad also accorded tax exemption on profits on interest earned, for all Chinese financial institutions, which will be providing funds for the construction and development activities in Gwadar. The COPHCL, its operating companies and contractors were also exempted from sales tax and federal excise duty. Similarly, all the businesses set up within the Gwadar Free Zone were exempted from federal excise duty and sales tax for a period of 23 years. In the same way, all port-related businesses have also been granted this exemption.[49]

Besides, income tax, excise and sales tax exemptions, the COPHCL, its operating companies, contractors and subcontractors were accorded customs duty exemption for 40 years to import machinery, materials, plants, equipment, appliances and accessories required for the construction of the Gwadar port and the Gwadar free zone. In addition, customs duty exemption has also been granted to import bunker oils for supplying fuels and lubricants to ships, which visit the port and its terminals. The COPHCL was also accorded the liberty to import any vehicles from anywhere, without payment of any duty.[50] The massive tax exemptions are only indicative of China's complete control over Islamabad, as far as Gwadar and its development are concerned.

China's economic interests in Gwadar are threefold. Its first and foremost primary objective is to completely integrate Pakistan's economy into its own, by outsourcing low-end, labour-intensive, resource-absorbing and polluting industrial production to Islamabad. They hope to convert Gwadar and various other SEZs, being set up along the CPEC, into giant factory floors to produce goods for China and Chinese companies. Towards this end, many coal-fired power plants and other low end industrial hardware have already been transferred from China to Pakistan as part of the CPEC. The second objective is to obtain access to the vast markets of Central Asia for Chinese exports, as well as to tap their energy resources by developing transportation linkages from Gwadar through Pakistan and Afghanistan into Central Asia.[51]

Finally, China hopes to appease its restive Uyghur population in the Muslim-majority Xinjiang Uyghur Autonomous Region (XUAR). Uyghurs, who are Muslims, have often been protesting against Chinese occupation of their traditional lands and their cultural marginalisation. Beijing hopes that trade through Gwadar will lead to the development of this remote and isolated region, through massive infusion of development funds and enhanced economic linkages with predominantly Muslim Central Asian states as well as Pakistan and Afghanistan.[52]

Both China and Pakistan have long believed that the movement of trade and energy resources through the port will gain momentum when Gwadar is connected to the KKH through a direct route.[53] China aims to use Pakistan as an energy corridor between China and the Persian Gulf. It also aims to utilise this port to facilitate exports from Chinese factories located in the western part of China. It has accordingly constructed a dry port at Sost on the Karakoram highway in Gilgit-Baltistan,[54] 140 km north of Gilgit. The dry port was inaugurated by General Musharraf on 4 July 2006.[55]

At present, almost 80 per cent of energy imports of China transit through the narrow confines of the Malacca Strait, which has also been prone to maritime piracy in the past. A trans-Karakoram oil and gas pipeline as part of the CPEC provides China an opportunity to import its energy resources through Gwadar port in a much more secure and sustainable manner. As brought out earlier, it would also provide Beijing a safer alternative passage for its energy imports, in case of any hostile interruption to its shipments from the Gulf in times of war or conflict.[56]

The trans-Karakoram pipeline could also be used to connect landlocked Central Asia to the global markets, thereby opening up the vast hydrocarbon reserves of the region. It could set the stage for another new oil grid emanating from Turkmenistan or Kazakhstan and travelling to Xinjiang to connect with the pipelines of the CPEC for onward transportation to the Gwadar deep sea port.[57]

The pipelines being constructed as part of CPEC will enable oil from the Caspian Sea and its basin to reach the global markets, particularly the rapidly growing economies in Asia. In the process, the pipelines will circumvent the politically problematic or conflict-ridden countries like Afghanistan, Armenia, Chechnya, Iran, Russia, and even Georgia. The Caspian region has enormous reserves of oil and natural gas; "the proven natural gas reserves are estimated at over 236 trillion cubic feet, and estimated oil reserves range up to 243 billion barrels".[58]

In addition to the pipeline, plans are also afoot for a rail link between Pakistan and China by connecting Xinjiang's western city Kashgar to Gwadar deep sea port. According to Zhang Chunlin, Xinjiang's regional development and reform commissioner, the 1,800-km rail link to be funded mainly by China will pass through Islamabad and Karachi. He claimed that the cost of construction is likely to be high on account of hostile environment and difficult terrain, as the link would have to pass through the Pamir Plateau and Karakoram Mountains. However, once completed, it would be "one of the most strategically beneficial transportation infrastructures on the China-Pakistan economic corridor".[59] The rail line could facilitate a faster movement of cargo and personnel between the two countries. It also fits in with China's objective of gaining access to Central Asian markets for its exports, as well getting access to Central Asian energy reserves. As Afghanistan is likely to remain turbulent for at least some more years, this could also emerge as the trade route of choice for the countries of Central Asia. Pakistan is already considering the movement of goods to Central Asian States through the Chinese province of Xinjiang, thereby avoiding the need to transit through a hostile and unstable Afghanistan.

The trans-Karakoram pipeline predates the CPEC and is often glossed over that China and Pakistan had agreed to build the pipeline, much before the CPEC was even conceptualised. They had agreed to build the pipeline all along the Karakoram Highway to facilitate movement of hydrocarbons from West Asia to China's north-western provinces through Gwadar. In June 2006,

General Musharraf, while welcoming the Emir of Kuwait, had spoken about "Pakistan's plans to facilitate regional commerce through the Gwadar port which offers overland links with South Asia, Central Asia and the western parts of China with the Gulf region".[60] The statement clearly indicated that this was an integral part of Pakistan's long-term vision.

More significantly, Chinese President Hu Jintao, while welcoming General Musharraf during his visit to Beijing, stated that China would work "to develop Pakistan as an energy corridor through the Gwadar deep sea port".[61] Consequently, much before the BRI or CPEC was unveiled, China had evinced keen interest "in the construction of a pipeline from Gwadar to Xinjiang, a road linking Gwadar with the Karakoram Highway and a huge oil refinery complex at Gwadar, which would partly meet the requirements of Pakistan and Xinjiang".[62]

Chinese academics go out of their way to try and convince the global community that China's interests in the port are purely economic and are nothing but part of its strategy to boost domestic income and consumption by investing in various ports in Asia to access energy sources and to enhance its influence over maritime routes. The strategy according to them stems from the fact that the earlier Chinese policy of encouraging cheap exports is no longer feasible to sustain growth. However, apart from economics, Gwadar also has a huge security and geo-strategic significance for China. The Gwadar port gives China the shortest access to Africa and West Asia, where numerous Chinese companies are undertaking developmental projects and have employed tens of thousands of Chinese workers.[63]

The port, on account of its location, offers Beijing a strategically significant foothold in the Arabian Sea as well as the Indian Ocean. Coupled with China's first overseas naval base in Djibouti, it allows China a significant military presence in the Indian Ocean to monitor its cargo. The permanent presence of Chinese forces in the Indian Ocean will also enable it to further enhance its influence on most of the countries of South Asia, especially Bangladesh, Nepal, Pakistan, and Sri Lanka, to the detriment of India, which is the predominant regional power.

More significantly, the port, on account of its proximity to the Strait of Hormuz, gives Beijing the capability to monitor shipping passing through this geo-strategically significant choke point. Almost four-fifths of global energy exports flow though this narrow water way. The Chinese presence at Gwadar will enable it to track its energy imports from the Persian Gulf, and provide an alternative passage for them in case of any hostile interruption of its shipment from West Asia or Africa.[64]

Almost 60 per cent of China's energy imports originate from the Persian Gulf and a pipeline from Gwadar will reduce the transportation distance considerably and provide China with a land-based supply point, which is controlled by an ally, Pakistan.[65] The distance from the Strait of Hormuz via the Malacca Strait to Shanghai is around 10,000 km. On the other hand, Kashgar is only 2,800 km from the Gwadar deep sea port along the CPEC and just over 3,400 km from the Strait of Hormuz. More significantly, Kashgar is only 4,500 km from Shanghai.[66]

Another strategic use of the Gwadar port relates to its potential use as a naval base in case of a 'two-front' war scenario between India and the China-Pakistan alliance. Though there are no official documents in the public realm that presuppose a 'two-front' situation, it remains a key security concern for India. By posing a perennial security threat to India, Gwadar serves as a potential tool in China's classic geo-positional balancing against India. A Chinese naval presence at Gwadar can easily block energy supplies to India from the Persian Gulf. More significantly, Gwadar fulfils China's long-standing quest for a permanent presence in the Indian Ocean to safeguard its shipping and other interests.

China's Indian Ocean Strategy

The Indian Ocean, unlike the Atlantic and the Pacific, is primarily an enclosed ocean with a few widespread points of entry often called choke points. China's economic growth depends enormously on foreign trade, which in turn relies on trade via the Indian Ocean.[67] China faces significant strategic challenges in the Indian Ocean region as its sea lines of communication (SLOCs) across it, are critical for its economic well-being especially for the transportation of much-needed energy resources. As brought out earlier, the SLOC originating in the Persian Gulf, transiting through the Strait of Hormuz, and going round the Indian subcontinent to the Malacca Strait and the Pacific is the most important for China's energy security.[68]

Other important Chinese SLOCs in the Indian Ocean pass from the Suez to Malacca and from the Cape of Good Hope to Malacca. This makes China extremely vulnerable in the Malacca Strait, through which 82 per cent of its oil imports transit. This is China's Malacca Dilemma, which has been mentioned earlier in the chapter. The Chinese SLOCs however are vulnerable throughout the Indian Ocean from state as well as non-state actors. China's sense of vulnerability is further accentuated by the fact that it does not have a clear overland route between China and the Indian Ocean. Formidable geographical barriers block China's overland access to the Indian Ocean through which almost all of its trade with Europe, Africa, and West Asia passes.[69]

China's shipping and consequently its trade transiting through the Indian Ocean is extremely vulnerable to interference by local powers. This realisation has made China dependent on overseas bases and regional allies to support and sustain its naval presence in the region, which may be necessary to support its shipping in the region. Many analysts perceive that the Indian Ocean has emerged as a new arena of contestation for influence between various powers. Some analysts have even termed it as a new 'Great Game' between India and China, with India controlling access to the key choke points, ports and other maritime infrastructure.[70]

China's emergence as the second largest economy in the world with the largest foreign exchange reserves have contributed to its growing economic influence in the region. It not only has the largest bilateral trade with many states in the Indian Ocean Region, but is also among the biggest investors in the region. The dependence of many of these countries on this trade and investment, invariably enhances China's strategic influence, although in some cases it has led to local protests against China's overbearing influence. For example, in Sri Lanka, there were violent protests against growing Chinese influence and acquisition of land near Hambantota. Similarly, there have also been protests in Laos and Thailand against Chinese demands and debt.[71]

Similarly, China has emerged as one of the biggest arms suppliers to the region and supplies weapons to a large number of countries in the IOR. However, it hardly has any comprehensive security partnerships with any country, with the sole exception of Pakistan. Chinese armament and ammunition are a large component of defence procurement by countries like Pakistan, Myanmar, Bangladesh and Sri Lanka. This dependence on Chinese arms has increased as they are relatively cheap and often come without any linkages to a country's internal democracy or human rights record, as has been the case for Western arm supplies.[72]

Many island nations in the Indian Ocean Region use China to balance their relations with the USA and India or more significantly to garner aid from India. However, with the sole exception of Pakistan, no country in the region depends on China to provide or guarantee its security. In this aspect, the Indian Ocean Region has a similarity with East Asia, where many countries have tried to balance the growing Chinese influence by increasing their security cooperation with the USA and India. Consequently, it can be summed up that there is a huge divergence between China's growing economic influence and limited presence in the security architecture of the region. Therefore, in the near future, the USA would continue to be the single-most significant provider of security for most countries of the region.[73]

According to an assessment of the US Directorate of Net Assessment, China is pursuing a strategy of building relationships with countries along the sea lanes, all the way from the Middle East to the South China Sea, including Gwadar. They have termed the strategy as a 'string of pearls'.[74] It is not only confined to a purely defensive posture, but also incorporates an offensive positioning to defend China's energy interests, as well as serve its broad security objectives in the region. In their perception, China aims to achieve these objectives by building naval bases and strengthening its diplomatic relations with these countries. According to their communique, "Beijing has already set up electronic eavesdropping posts at Gwadar and is monitoring ship traffic through the Strait of Hormuz and the Arabian Sea".[75]

Gwadar is probably the most significant component of this 'String of Pearls' scheme, which, apart from meeting its economic interests, also provides China a significant strategic outpost in the Indian Ocean. It is important to note here that the COPHC, which not only controls and operates the Gwadar port, but virtually owns it, is also one of the largest state-owned enterprises (SOE) in China. In addition, Beijing also has a presence in Pakistan's Karachi-Bin Qasim port complex through another SOE, the China Harbour Engineering Company Limited (CHEC). The company already has a significant stake in the Karachi port and is currently undertaking many projects there, including a housing project and a container terminal yard. In addition, it also has a significant presence in Port Bin Qasim, where it is constructing the Qasim international container terminal (QICT) with an annual capacity of 1.17 million TEU.[76] Its presence at Karachi, Port Bin Qasim and Gwadar provides China a robust presence right at the mouth of the Arabian Sea.

More importantly, Chinese footprints in the IOR have increased with the establishment of a PLA base at Djibouti in 2017, ownership of Hambantota Port, development of Kyaukphyu Port and Special Economic Zone and acquisition of 50 per cent stake in UAE's Fujairah port. Gwadar along with these developments plays an extremely significant role in China's Indian Ocean strategy. While it has not been overtly acknowledged by China as a naval base, Pakistan's policy makers have often been suggesting that. In any case, all these commercial ports could easily allow the Chinese navy to use them as logistics bases. China is also aiming to bring small island nations of the Indian Ocean like the Maldives, Seychelles, and Comoros, under its influence by offering them loan and credit for various developmental projects.[77] There is no doubt about Gwadar's military significance and, at the very least, Gwadar, along with other ports where China has a stake, allows it to have a strong presence in the Indian Ocean Region (IOR). It therefore allows China to strengthen its position as a maritime power in the Indian Ocean.

Pakistan's relationship with China is premised on their common hostility towards India and makes it one of China's strongest long-term allies apart from North Korea. China has supplied arms to Pakistan since 1960s. The two countries have also collaborated in development and production of a number of military hardware, which include aircraft, ships, and tanks. It is widely believed that Pakistan's nuclear programme would not have fructified without support from China. Most significantly, Pakistan has clearly exhibited its willingness to host Chinese naval facilities at Gwadar. At this stage, China has reacted cautiously to this proposal, but it could eventually decide to position Chinese naval and air assets there.[78]

At one stage, Myanmar also appeared as a potential ally for China's access to the Indian Ocean. However, of late, Myanmar has tried to distance itself from China and has opened up to India, Japan and Western countries. This has further enhanced the significance of Gwadar for China. Of late, China has also been looking at Sri Lanka for a presence in the Indian Ocean, as well as for a security partnership. Hambantota port has already been leased to the

China Merchants Port Holding Company Ltd. (CM Port) on a 99-year lease. A maintenance facility to support Sri Lanka's Air Force is expected to come up near Hambantota and could eventually result in the presence of the PLA Air Force. However, unlike Gwadar, it could have only a marginal impact on reducing China's strategic vulnerability in the Indian Ocean.[79]

Persian Gulf and the Middle East

Chinese involvement in Gwadar has led to numerous speculations about the Chinese motives behind such a heavy investment in this greenfield project. As brought out earlier, some analysts believe that Chinese would like to use it to supply the economically underdeveloped regions of Western China while others feel it could be used to supply energy to the Chinese hinterland without any feasibility of supplies being choked in the narrow straits of South East Asia. However, arguably the most significant dimension of the port is its location, just 120 km from the Iranian border; it provides China an extremely significant toe-hold in the crucial Persian Gulf. The deep sea port is virtually next to the Strait of Hormuz, which provides access to the Persian Gulf and through which a significant part of the global oil and gas exports transit.[80]

The Strait of Hormuz also has enormous significance for China, as almost 80 per cent of China's oil imports originate in the Middle East.[81] Similar to its Malacca Dilemma, China also faces a 'Hormuz Dilemma' as most of its oil imports come from the Persian Gulf and pass through the narrow confines of the Strait of Hormuz.[82] China being the largest importer of energy resources in the world needs to ascertain that the routes through which its shipping passes are secure and are not liable to be choked.[83]

Gwadar, coupled with the CPEC, provides China with an entry point to the Persian Gulf, as well as a foothold for its military presence in this vital region,[84] thereby enhancing its geopolitical and geo-economic influence not only in the Persian Gulf region, but in the entire Middle East. China has been trying to enhance its influence in this strategically important region, which is clearly reflected in its recent bonhomie with regional powers like Egypt, Iran, Saudi Arabia, and UAE. President Xi visited Egypt, Iran and Saudi Arabia in January 2016 and the UAE in July 2018. Saudi Arabia is the biggest supplier of crude to China and its oil company, Aramco and China's Sinopec signed an agreement in January 2016 for cooperation.[85] The bilateral trade between the two countries crossed $ 74 billion in 2012. During King Salman's visit to China in 2017, the two countries signed deals worth $ 65 billion. Although China's trade with Egypt is miniscule, Beijing considers Egypt significant due to its strategic location and the Suez Canal, which is a significant link in the maritime component of the BRI.[86]

China, while maintaining good relations with Saudi Arabia, the UAE and Egypt, has successfully transcended both the intra-GCC as well as Saudi-Iran tensions. Iran by virtue of its geographical location has already been integrated in China's Eurasian plans, which has caused some concern in GCC countries. However, China has managed to successfully allay their apprehensions by maintaining a neutral stance while seeking economic partnership with all.[87] President Xi became the first world leader to visit Tehran after the Iran nuclear deal. This allowed China to derive full mileage for future economic engagements with the Islamic Republic.[88]

China and Iran signed an agreement in 2016 to bolster defence and military cooperation between the two countries and to cooperate in fighting terrorism. China is Iran's biggest trading partner and the total bilateral trade in 2018 was $ 35.13 billion, of which crude oil alone accounted for almost half – $ 15 billion.[89] Despite US sanctions on Iran, China has continued buying oil from Iran.[90]

China considers Iran a key component of the BRI. During President Xi Jinping's visit, the two countries agreed to expand bilateral trade to $ 600 billion over 10 years, as part of a 25-year plan to enhance cooperation. Almost 100 major Chinese companies have invested in Iran's key economic sectors, predominantly in energy and transportation. Even the redesigning of Iran's Arak IR-40 heavy water reactor to make it compliant with the 2015 nuclear deal, is being done by the China National Nuclear Corporation. Chinese companies involved in building dams, power plants and other infrastructure in Iran have been provided $ 10 billion as loan by Beijing. The infrastructure being built by Chinese companies includes major railway connectivity projects linking Tehran with Bayannur in the Inner Mongolia Autonomous Region of China and railway links to Bushehr on the Persian Gulf and Mashhad in the north-eastern part of Iran.[91]

Iran is an important link in the Silk Road Economic Belt (SREB), which visualises the movement of railway traffic, emanating in China, to Iran through

Central Asia and from Iran travelling to Turkey and then to Europe. Iran has already indicated its willingness to be part of the CPEC. In February 2016, the first train from China arrived in Tehran bringing goods from the Chinese trading hub of Yiwu in eastern China.[92] On 10 May 2018, China announced the launch of a new rail link between Bayannur in China's Inner Mongolia Autonomous Region and Tehran. It claimed that it would reduce travel time for goods by 20 days as compared to the sea route.[93]

On 27 March 2021, during Chinese Foreign Minister Wang Yi's visit to Iran, the two countries signed a deal, whereby China agreed to invest in Iran a sum of around $400 billion over the next 25 years in lieu of a constant supply of oil from Iran, which would keep fuelling its growing economy.[94] By importing Iranian oil, China will be defying the American sanctions. In return, Iran will become an integral part of BRI connectivity projects. The deal provides Iran with great leverage against the USA, which, under President Biden, is keen to rejoin the nuclear agreement with Iran.[95] According to reports, Chinese investments in Iran are likely to be in various fields that would include banking, health care, information technology, ports, railways and telecommunications. It is also believed that the deal also includes closer military cooperation that includes intelligence sharing as well as joint exercises and cooperation in the fields of training, research and development of armaments.[96]

There are also reports of possibilities of deployment of Chinese troops in Iran to protect Chinese investments. There have also been some reports about Iran agreeing to lease out the strategically situated Kish Island in the Persian Gulf to China.[97] China also has a presence at Chabahar Port now and sees it as an alternative for its energy supplies to Gwadar. As a result, now Gwadar and Chabahar have accorded each other the status of sister city and most Iranians now perceive Gwadar as an opportunity rather than a rivalry. There are reports of Chinese interest in developing Jask Port, which is west of Chabahar and just outside the Strait of Hormuz, which could allow Beijing to keep an eye on the Fifth Fleet of the US Navy, which is based in Bahrain.[98]

Wang's visit was a part of China's new quest for outreach in the Middle East, although Iran was probably its lynchpin. He had visited Saudi Arabia and Turkey, before arriving in Tehran and travelled to the United Arab Emirates, Bahrain and Oman after Iran.[99] China sees itself as the emerging global power and perceives that the US decline is irreversible. The USA has for some time been trying to pivot away from the Middle East and wants to reduce its commitments. China is trying to move in and fill the void. According to *China Daily*, a party organ, Wang presented a five-point formula "for achieving security and stability in the Middle East by offering a constructive boost to the Palestine-Israel dialogue, resuming the Iran nuclear deal and building a security framework in this region".[100] China has carefully avoided taking sides in the Middle East, as it has been trying to cultivate relations with not only Iran but also the Arab states and Israel.[101]

Apart from Saudi Arabia and Iran, China has huge stakes in the United Arab Emirates (UAE). China is currently Dubai's number one trading partner and the UAE's second largest. The Jebel Ali port in Dubai has been expanding its ties with China in order to be a fulcrum of the BRI. A dedicated container terminal is being set up by the Chinese company, COSCO, at Port Jebel Ali with a capacity of 5 million TEUs approximately. More than half of the China-UAE trade comprises goods that are re-exported to Europe or Africa.[102] Once Gwadar emerges as a thriving port, China would like to plug into this existing trade from Dubai to Africa and Europe, till Gwadar is in a position to emerge as a regional hub in its own right. The growing cooperation between the two countries has also manifested in the form of the UAE emerging as the regional manufacturing hub for China's Sinopharm COVID-19 vaccine, consequent to the Gulf Pharmaceutical Industries signing a contract to start manufacturing the vaccine from April 2021. The deal signifies the growing Chinese influence in a country, which has always been perceived as a close ally of the USA.[103]

However, if the Gwadar port emerges as a viable gateway to Afghanistan and Central Asia, it could also emerge as the main transhipment hub of the region. At present, Dubai, the most populous city of the United Arab Emirates, enjoys this distinction of being the regional transhipment hub. Despite having poor natural resources, Dubai has emerged as a multi-cultural city and the business, trade and tourism hub of the region, which is visited by millions of visitors from across the world for both leisure and business.[104] This eminence is enjoyed by Dubai on account of its two big commercial ports, Port Jebel Ali and Port Rashid, which have emerged as huge transhipment ports for almost all the littorals of the Arabian Sea. Port Jebel Ali is the biggest artificial man-made harbour in the world, as well as the largest port in the entire Middle East. These ports provide businesses located in Dubai with enormous locational advantages, leading to various commercial entities setting up their offices there. As a result, most of the global corporations have their regional offices located at Dubai and consequently, over 5,000 companies from across the globe, based in 120 countries of the world, have their presence there.[105]

The Emirate of Dubai, a part of the UAE, unlike most other emirates in the Persian Gulf, is devoid of major hydrocarbon resources. As a result, most of the revenue for the Emirate of Dubai comes from sectors like aviation, tourism, and financial services. Its emergence as the tourism hub of the region as well as its commercial centre has resulted in a boom in the construction and real estate sector, which has emerged as another major source of revenue for the Emirate. Tall skyscrapers and iconic hotels draw many high-end investors from across the globe to Dubai. The Emirate not only has the Burj Khalifa, the tallest building in the world, it also has iconic hotels in the sea. The kingdom also organises major sports and cultural events and going by the standards of other countries in the region, pursues a rather liberal policy to draw in more visitors.[106]

Consequently, Dubai draws the maximum number of international tourists in the entire Middle East. In 2014, Dubai was ranked the fifth-most popular global destination for international travellers by the Master Card Global Destination Cities Index and is expected to attract 20 million tourists by 2020.[107] However, its varied sources of income are premised on the single most significant factor that Dubai is the regional transhipment hub just inside the mouth of the energy-rich Persian Gulf.[108]

As and when the Gwadar port emerges as a thriving and vibrant port, it would give a tough competition for Dubai and could pose a serious existential threat to its status as the main transhipment port of the region. Gwadar has certain inherent geographical advantages over Dubai, as it is closer to the Eurasian heartland and could reduce transportation time for goods slated for Western China and Central Asia.[109] It could enhance trade between the Middle East and the Central Eurasian landmass, as connectivity between these two energy and resource-rich regions has been extremely tenuous and long. More significantly, ships coming to Gwadar do not have to enter the Persian Gulf through the narrow Strait of Hormuz, a process, which considerably slows them down as they have to follow a traffic separation scheme and reduce speed.[110] This enhances the financial burden for ships entering Dubai. A substantive portion of the transhipment cargo is bound for ports outside the Gulf, thereby; requiring it to cross the Strait of Hormuz twice and it raises the transportation cost and time. This would be completely eliminated in the case of Gwadar.

To compound matters, on-going tensions in the Persian Gulf also give Gwadar a huge advantage over Dubai. Continuing acrimony between the USA and Iran poses a serious threat to the freedom of navigation in the Gulf. As the tensions rise, Iran keeps reiterating its threat that in case of hostility, it will close down the Gulf. This may make Gwadar, a much safer option for ships to disembark their cargo. As the UAE, which includes Dubai, is considered a strong ally of the USA and the Western powers, some countries aligned with Iran may prefer using Gwadar over Dubai for purely political reasons. This could include countries like Syria, Iraq and, more significantly, Qatar, whose relations with the UAE have taken a sudden dip. Consequently, Qatar is investing a huge amount estimated to be around 15 per cent of the total cost of the CPEC, in various infrastructural projects associated with the CPEC, especially the facilities coming up at Gwadar. Besides financial returns, the aim could as well be to put pressure on UAE, which includes the Emirate of Dubai.[111]

Consequently, both geo-economics and geo-politics have brought China, Pakistan and Qatar together in promoting Gwadar and making it a success, as all these countries hope to derive immense economic as well as geo-political benefits from this port becoming a thriving economic transhipment hub. On the other hand, India and the UAE, as well as its allies in West Asia, do not want Gwadar to emerge as another Dubai. To this extent, they are promoting investments by the USA and other Western powers in Dubai. The UAE, especially Dubai, will be a big loser if Gwadar really takes off as its revenue from transportation and tourism could be curtailed drastically.[112]

Another country with historical linkages with Gwadar and of significance to China is Oman, which has managed a neutral stance in the divided polity of the Persian Gulf between Sunni Arab sheikhdoms and Shiite Iran. On account of its location, Oman is extremely significant for the BRI. It is not only a major oil and gas exporter to China, but is also considered to be a strategic ally. China imports more than 75 per cent of the crude produced by Oman, which also makes it China's fourth-largest source of oil. Chinese companies are building an industrial city in Oman at a huge investment of $ 10.7 billion. The city coming up at Duqm between the Gulf of Oman and Aden, will have facilities that will include a plant for assembling automobiles, solar energy plant, factories for oil and gas equipment and an oil refinery. In trying to maintain their neutrality, the Omanis have refrained from taking Saudi assistance and have instead sought a $ 3.6 billion loan from China to meet the budgetary shortfall due to low oil prices.[113]

Gwadar Port, which is being run and developed by China, allows it to further its geopolitical and geo-economic interests in the Persian Gulf region. As stated earlier, even though primarily built as a commercial port, Gwadar has a military dimension and can be used by the Pakistan Navy as well as the Chinese Navy. A presence at the port allows China to monitor shipping entering and leaving the Persian Gulf; more significantly, even a small naval detachment at the port can easily be used to interdict any ship passing through the Strait of Hormuz.

The port therefore gives significant maritime capabilities to any naval power using it. The development of the port marks China's firm advent into the Persian Gulf and through it into the entire Middle East—an area of huge geo-strategic and geo-economic significance. China achieved a huge success on 10 March 2023, when representatives of both Iran and Saudi Arabia called on Beijing to restore diplomatic relations. The speed and secrecy with which China managed to create the rapprochement to end the four-decade-old hostility, clearly signals its emergence as a significant power in the region, which has traditionally been dominated by the USA.[114]

The deal may still not bring the two foes together, but it has had a huge impact and has established Xi Jinping, the Chinese President, as a global leader, especially in the eyes of people in the Middle East. According to a recent survey, more Arab youth see China as an ally rather than the USA. With 80 per cent approval rating, China is second only to Turkey in the region, whereas the USA is a distant seventh. China is already the largest trading partner of most of the oil-exporting countries in the Gulf.[115] Most countries in the region use oil and gas revenues, which is a major component of government revenue, to fund the state machinery and dispense patronage. Consequently, China, as the largest oil importer of the world, has enormous leverage over the Gulf countries dependent on oil revenues.[116]

Although China has been engaging with the region for some time and had established the China-Arab States Cooperation Forum (CASCF) in 2004 and the China-Gulf Cooperation Council (GCC) Strategic Dialogue in 2010, its footprint in the Middle East has increased rapidly in the recent past. On 9 December 2022, it held its first China-Arab States Summit and the first China-GCC Summit in Riyadh. China surpassed the EU as the largest bilateral trading partner of GCC countries in 2020 and is actively pursuing a free trade agreement (FTA) with them.[117] Apart from trade, it has emerged as the largest source of foreign direct investment in the region and most of the Arab states have joined the BRI.[118] Its economic push has been supplemented by deft diplomacy. After the Iran-Saudi détente, China has volunteered to mediate between the Israelis and Palestinians as well. After an economic and diplomatic push, Gwadar may provide China with a launch pad for a military push.

Pakistan has repeatedly expressed its willingness to host Chinese naval facilities at the port. Although China has till now been extremely cautious in responding to Pakistan's suggestions, it may eventually decide to base PLA's naval and possibly air assets there. At the moment the USA dominates the Persian Gulf with its overwhelming military presence and is able to ensure freedom of navigation through the Hormuz.[119] However, Chinese presence in Gwadar and rising tensions between Iran and the USA could give China a major stake in the region.

Chinese Influence in East Africa

Africa has been a key focus area for China for some time. In the post 'cold war' era, the People's Republic of China has established itself as an influential player in the African continent, which had hitherto been dominated by the USA, France and the UK. The African nations have found Chinese aid attractive, as it comes without any preconditions unlike the Western aid.[120] Almost half of China's concessional aid is destined for Africa, of which over 60 per cent is used for building infrastructure.[121] Africa has not only emerged as a big market for Chinese goods, but its abundant natural resources also provide China with raw materials essential for its economic growth, especially energy resources. Over one third of China's oil supplies come from Africa as also one fifth of its cotton.[122]

China established 'The Forum on China Africa Cooperation' (FOCAC) in 2000 and Chinese trade with Africa, which was merely $ 2 billion then, has since risen to $ 170 billion in 2017, making China Africa's largest trading partner.[123] Over 10,000 Chinese companies are currently operating in the continent, where the Chinese business is already over $ 2 trillion, with investments of over $ 300 billion in the pipeline. Africa has already overtaken Asia as the largest destination of China's overseas construction contracts. China's expertise in infrastructure development has ensured that it now has over 40 per cent share of Africa's infrastructure boom.[124] Although China is the fourth-largest investor in Africa, after the USA, the UK and France, its investments are rising much faster than the others.[125] Almost all African countries have either signed an MoU under the BRI or have extended support.[126] Its primary investments in Africa have been in ports and areas around ports along the coast.[127] Although, both East and West Africa are part of the BRI, China's focus is more on East Africa for historical reasons. East Africa is also the fastest-growing region in Africa with growth rates of 5.9 per cent in 2019 and 6.1 per cent in 2020.[128] Chinese presence at Gwadar will make a far greater impact as far as the countries of East Africa are concerned, as compared to the countries on the West Coast.

China already has a significant presence in Djibouti including a naval base, which should be able to provide naval resources to Gwadar in the initial phase. The two bases can also provide mutual support to enhance China's influence all along the East Coast of Africa. It has linked the Ethiopian capital, Adis Ababa, with Djibouti through a rail link, which has been built and financed by China. This cross-border electrified railway, primarily to carry freight, is going to be operated by Chinese personnel for at least next five years.[129]

China has already built special economic zones in Ethiopia, Mauritius and Zambia. One of the earliest Chinese infrastructural projects in the African continent was the Tanzania-Zambia railway line, which was built in the 1970s. The Chinese are at present funding railway lines, which connect the Kenyan port of Mombasa to the Kenyan capital, Nairobi, as well as from the Tanzanian capital, Dar-es-Salam to Rwanda with branches to Burundi and Uganda.[130]

As brought out earlier, the primary Chinese focus is on ports, as they can be used by the PLA Navy and ships based at Djibouti or Gwadar can enter these ports in pursuance of Chinese interests. Two major ports in East Africa are Mombasa in Kenya and Dar-es-Salaam in Tanzania. Both of them traditionally contested for business, but today, both are cooperating with China to expand their business avenues. Kenya is setting up a new port at Lamu as a collaborative venture between the China Communications Construction Company and the Kenya Port authorities, which will also operate the port. Tanzania on the other hand is developing Bagamayo Port, which will be financed by the China Merchant Holding Ports Company in collaboration with an Omani firm. The Chinese firm will be operating the port. Another Chinese firm, the China National Offshore Oil Corporation (CNOOC) has got the production licence for the Kingfisher oilfield in neighbouring Uganda. It plans to export oil from Bogmayo through a new pipeline. In Mozambique, the China Harbour Engineering Company Ltd. (CHEC), is part of an international consortium, which is developing a new port at Maputo, which will provide port services to land-locked Botswana, Eswatini, and Zimbabwe. Since September 2015, the CHEC is also engaged in developing the Beira fishing harbour.[131]

China is also involved in other projects in Mozambique, which include new terminals at the international airport at Maputo, a circular road for the city, a stadium as well as a three-kilometre long bridge. Chinese companies have stakes in oil and gas blocks in Mozambique and are financing and building a 2,600-km long pipeline to carry gas from Mozambique to South Africa. South Africa is amongst the major destinations for Chinese investment in Africa. The economic ties between China and South Africa have been growing and in return South Africa has been supporting China's viewpoint on contentious issues like Tibet and the South China Sea.[132]

China is also using the BRI and the investments under its rubric to enhance people-to-people contact so as to educate them and then indoctrinate them to the Chinese viewpoint. In countries like Ethiopia and Sudan, top officials are being trained by the Communist Party of China (CPC) in their totalitarian model and are being advised on how to mould public opinion and manage the media. Not only that the Chinese are also telling them about the surveillance technologies to be used and the legislations that need to be passed. Its utmost priority is to harmonize the development priorities of countries participating in the BRI with those of China's, which incidentally also includes human rights.[133] Many of these countries are now under the Chinese debt trap and are constrained to follow China's policy directives. It is pertinent to note that China's BRI projects in Africa are usually funded by large loans to governments, with commitments from the borrowers not to completely disclose the financial terms.[134]

Gwadar Port not only allows China a suitable port in the Indian Ocean to provide offshore security to its investments in East Africa, but can also be used as a port for export/import of goods from Africa. Raw material and energy resources could be disembarked at Gwadar for onward transfer to China. Similarly, goods manufactured by various industries being set up as part of the CPEC can also be exported to East Africa from Gwadar. The SLOC from Gwadar to East Africa will pass clear of any area where hostile powers could interfere with Chinese shipping easily.

Challenging US Influence in the Region

For quite some time, the USA has considered the Persian Gulf, to be an area of vital strategic interest for its national security. During the Cold War, the US objective in the region, like in any other part of the world, initially, was to check Soviet expansion. However, it soon realised its huge potential on account of its enormous energy resources and changed its outlook towards the region and designated it as a region vital to its interests. However, from the Second World War till the first Gulf War, the USA maintained a remote presence, and predominantly relied on its allies to establish order in the region. However, this changed with Iraq's invasion of Kuwait, which made the USA realise the need for having its troops present in the region and since then it has started positioning its forces there in significant numbers. The end of the Cold War, immediately after the first Gulf War, led to circumstances that pushed the USA to assume a far more overt and significant security role in the Persian Gulf region.[135]

The region, for the last five decades or more, has fulfilled a critical role in ensuring that the future energy needs of the USA and its Western allies were met. This critical role stemmed from the fact that although, the Middle East's contribution to global oil production is only around 25 per cent, when it comes to proven oil reserves, the estimate of the reserves in the region vary from around two thirds to three quarters of global reserves. Consequently, the

USA and its Western allies have defined the region as vital to their strategic interests.[136]

The large military presence of the USA in the region was necessitated by this vital importance of the Persian Gulf and the need to ensure the free flow of trade, which requires that the traffic moves in and out of the Gulf through the Strait of Hormuz without any hindrance. The huge military build-up by the USA in the region after the first Gulf War, gave it a political leverage, which was effectively used to help American companies win contracts in the region. The traditional strategy of the USA in the region was premised on its strategic need to ensure a continuous flow of oil at reasonable prices. This entailed reliance on states with excess capacity like Saudi Arabia to counter any spurt in prices on account of short-term interruptions in either production or transportation. In the process of doing so, it has consistently tried to deny its enemies or potential enemies control over these vital resources that could make them more menacing.[137] This is probably the prime reason behind its hostility towards Iran and its unbridled support towards the Gulf Cooperation Council (GCC) countries.[138]

After the British withdrawal from the region, the USA has been the dominant power in the North Arabian Sea, especially in the region surrounding the Persian Gulf. Currently, Bahrain, Qatar, Kuwait, Saudi Arabia, Jordan, Oman and the United Arab Emirates host a number of US troops on their soil. The US Central Command naval forces, as well as the US Fifth Fleet are based at Bahrain and are responsible for around 2.5 million square miles of ocean territory, which include the Persian Gulf, the Gulf of Oman, the Arabian Sea, the Red Sea and significant parts of the Indian Ocean. This vast expanse includes territories and waters belonging to 20 different countries and has three critical choke points. These critical choke points are at the Suez Canal, which connects the Mediterranean to the Red Sea; Strait of Hormuz, between the Persian Gulf and the Gulf of Oman and the Bab-el-Mandeb Strait which connects the Red Sea to the Gulf of Aden, near the southern tip of Yemen.[139]

It is estimated that there are over 41,000 American security personnel deployed in the GCC countries. There are five naval bases and 11 air bases of the USA in the region, including the Al-Dhafra airbase in the UAE, which is the busiest American air base for surveillance flights in the world. Similarly, the port of Jabel-e-Ali is the busiest naval port of the USA in the entire Persian

Gulf region. Almost all the Arab countries in the region, with the possible exception of Iraq, consider the US military presence as a guarantee for the stability of their non-representative regimes. The US military is also perceived as a deterrence against any threat that could emanate from Iran or its allies against their fragile regimes. Consequently, numerous agreements have been signed by the Arab states of the GCC with the USA to ensure its continued presence in their countries. On the other hand, Iran, right from the time of its revolution, has tried to project the continuing US presence in the region as a destabilising factor. It has tried to whip up public emotions against the American presence in Arab lands and has succeeded to some extent in the Arab streets. However, it has never been able to create that sort of mass upsurge that is necessary to force the removal of US troops from the region. However, after Qassem Soleimani's assassination, Iran has succeeded in creating huge demonstrations against the US presence in Iraq and has even led to Iraq's parliament asking for the US troop withdrawal.[140]

Most of the US troops that were deployed in Syria to support its Kurdish allies have since moved to Iraq, after President Donald Trump decided to pull out his troops from Syria. The USA presently has eight military bases in Iraq, which officially house 5,200 troops, but after enhancement of recent tensions and calls for their withdrawal by Iraqi protestors, the USA has announced that it is closing down three military bases. This is a clear indication that it is planning to reduce its footprint in Iraq under sustained pressure, both from the Iraqi government and population at large. The resentment against the USA is evident from the fact that over 160 rockets have been fired at the US military bases and its assets in Iraq since October 2019.[141]

The USA has numerous core interests in the Persian Gulf region, namely, ensuring reliable supply of oil, eradication of jihadi terrorism, prevention of nuclear proliferation, and protection of key friends like Israel and Jordan. In order to achieve these objectives, without deputing a large number of troops, the USA needs strong partners like Iraq. The US withdrawal could lead to enhanced Iranian influence in the region, especially in Iraq.[142] Fissures between Iraq and the USA could lead to a greater Iranian influence in the region and would require the USA to relocate its troops to other countries in the Persian Gulf. It is perceived that there are still some US troops in Syria to support its allies. More significantly, the USA has many operational bases in Afghanistan and has a credible military presence to support the government in Kabul. All these troops and bases are mainly supported from bases in the Persian Gulf region or by forces operating in the North Arabian Sea and the Persian Gulf.

In December 2018, after 75 years, the USA became a net exporter of energy, courtesy commercial exploitation by Shale Gas.[143] Even more significantly, it is estimated that soon the USA would be exporting more oil and liquids than the Kingdom of Saudi Arabia.[144] Consequently, the USA is no longer dependent on energy supplies from the Persian Gulf; however, its allies in Europe and Japan are still overwhelmingly dependent on supplies from the Persian Gulf.

As a result, the Persian Gulf will continue to remain important for the USA and it will have a stake in the free movement of goods in and out of the Gulf. It would need bases in the region to keep existing autocratic regimes, allied with it in power as well as support its forces operating in Afghanistan. This requires the USA to have free, unbridled access to the Persian Gulf. However, the Chinese presence at Gwadar gives China a unique capacity to monitor every vessel leaving or entering the Persian Gulf. It also gives China an opportunity to support Iran and bolster its regime, which has been under US sanctions. More significantly, this gives China the ability to intercept any shipping coming out of the Gulf and it would be well within its capacity to block the Gulf should it so desire. Gwadar provides China a strategic outpost, which it can use against the USA and its allies if tensions between the two aggravate to the extent of naval blockades, as the USA and China confront each other at sea.[145]

This has the potential to exacerbate existing tensions in the Persian Gulf, which originate from Donald Trump's decision to renege from Iran's 2015 nuclear deal with the world powers including the USA and impose 'maximum' economic sanctions (*Arab News,* 14 January 2020).[146] These sanctions have had a devastating impact on Iran's economy. However, Tehran's recent deal with Beijing coupled with Chinese presence at Gwadar and its connections with Xinjiang could easily enable Iran to breach these sanctions. China has consistently been importing oil from Iran, despite the sanctions imposed by the USA. Iran is accordingly exhibiting keen interest in laying an LNG pipeline to China all along the CPEC.[147] This would easily enable it to breach the crippling sanctions imposed on it by the USA.

Chinese stakes in Gwadar and the possibility of its military base there just outside the Strait of Hormuz would provide it with huge strategic benefits apart from the apparent economic and commercial gains. This could enable China to emerge as a net security provider for the Persian Gulf and Arabian Sea region, which could pit it directly against US interests. A naval base at Gwadar gives China anti-access/area denial (A2/AD) capabilities in the strategic waters adjacent to the Strait of Hormuz, and would enormously enhance China's capability to project power and gather intelligence. In conjunction with the Chinese military base in Djibouti, it could transform the strategic balance of power in the entire North Arabian Sea and Persian Gulf.[148] Consequently, the USA is already moving ahead with steps to contain China's influence in the region.[149] Accordingly, the US-led International Maritime Security Construct (IMSC) was set up, which apart from the USA, comprises Australia, Albania, Bahrain, Saudi Arabia, the United Arab Emirates and the United Kingdom. On 7 November 2019, the IMSC formally launched its operations by escorting ships transiting in international shipping lanes through the Strait of Hormuz.[150]

It is therefore quite clear that the Gwadar deep sea port, which is built with Chinese assistance and is being operated by a Chinese firm, could have Chinese naval facilities in times to come, which have the potential to threaten America's vital interests in the region.

Conclusion

It can therefore be concluded that the Gwadar deep sea port, despite its avowed economic objectives, is a geopolitical constituency for China. Developing infrastructure and transport facilities in the region allows China to address its two core practical concerns, namely, achieving energy security and ensuring economic development of its western regions. At the strategic level, a port facility at Gwadar allows China a strategic foothold in the Indian Ocean Region, which allows it to conduct geo positional counter-balancing against India. In addition, Gwadar serves as the common link between China's two earlier connectivity projects, namely, the Silk Road Economic Belt initiative and the 21st century Maritime Silk Road. As such, it entails a symbolic significance for China's most ambitious foreign policy project, the Belt and Road Initiative, which is nothing but a combination of the 21st century Maritime Silk Road and the Silk Road Economic Belt.

NOTES.

1. Ayesha Siddiqa in response to a question by the author in September 2020.
2. Jean-Marc F. Blanchard and Colin Flint. "The Geopolitics of China's Maritime Silk Road Initiative", *Geopolitics*, 2017, vol. 22, no. 2, p. 223.
3. Ashfaq Ahmed. "Pakistan's Gwadar International Airport will be the largest in the country", *Gulf News*, 31 March 2019.
4. Omar Alam. "China-Pakistan Economic Corridor: Towards a New 'Heartland'?" from https://isnblog.ethz.ch/international-relations/china-pakistan-economic-corridor-towards-a-new-heartland (Accessed on 1 April 2020).
5. Jean-Marc F. Blanchard and Colin Flint. op. cit., pp. 223-224.
6. The Belt and Road Initiative (BRI) was initially called the One Belt One Road (OBOR) initiative, although the name has been changed in English to dilute China's salience in the project In Mandarin, the project is still called One Belt One Road.
7. Jean-Marc F. Blanchard and Colin Flint. op. cit., pp. 223-224.
8. Srikanth Kondapalli and Hu Xiaowen (eds.). *One Belt One Road: China's Global Outreach*. New Delhi: Pentagon Press, 2017, p. 1.
9. Sudha Ramachandran. "China-Pakistan Economic Corridor: Road to Riches?", Jamestown Foundation, *China Brief*, vol. 15, issue 15, 31 July 2015.
10. Ibid.
11. Manoj Joshi. *The Belt Road Initiative aka One Belt One Road scheme*. New Delhi: Federation of Indian Chambers of Commerce & Industry, 24 January 2018, p. 35.
12. Ibid.
13. Ibid.
14. Ibid.
15. Shabana Fayyaz and Salma Malik. "China-Pakistan Economic Corridor (CPEC): Security Concerns", *Global Regional Review* (GRR) 4 (4), Fall 2019, p. 436.
16. Zahid Gishkori. "Army assigned security of Chinese engineers", *The Express Tribune*, Karachi, 22 April 2015.
17. Muhammad Ibrar et al., "The China-Pakistan Economic Corridor: Security Challenges", paper presented at the 2016 2nd Asia-Pacific Management and Engineering Conference (APME 2016).
18. Yen-Chiang Chang and Mehran Idris Khan. "China–Pakistan economic corridor and maritime security collaboration: A growing bilateral interests", *Maritime Business Review*, 4(2), p. 218.
19. Siegfried O. Wolf. "The Growing Security Dimension of the China-Pakistan Economic Corridor", Italian Institute for International Political Studies, 10 March 2020.
20. Manoj Joshi. op. cit., p. 35.
21. Naveed Butt, "Economic corridor: China to extend assistance at 1.6 percent interest rate", *Business Recorder*, 3 September 2015.
22. M Ilyas Khan. "Is China-Pakistan 'silk road' a game-changer?", from https://www.bbc.com/news/world-asia-32400091 (Accessed on 9 July 2018).
23. Shyam Saran. "What China's One Belt and One Road Strategy Means for India, Asia and the World', *The Wire*, 9 October 2015.
24. Rahul Jaybhay. "China's pipeline dream in Pakistan", The Lowy Institute, 30 June 2020.

25. Husain Haqqani. *Reimagining Pakistan: Transforming a Dysfunctional Nuclear State*. Noida: Harper Collins Publishers, 2018, pp. 240-241.
26. Sost or Sust at 2,800 metress above sea level is the last town on the Karakoram Highway, before the Highway crosses into China. It is part of Gilgit-Baltistan, a territory under Pakistan's control, but considered a part of the Union Territory of Ladakh by India. Besides the dry port, Pakistani customs and immigration offices are also located in the town.
27. Shabbir Mir. "First Chinese shipment rolls into Sost dry port in Gilgit-Baltistan", *The Express Tribune*, 1 November 2016.
28. Farhan Bokhari and Kiran Stacey (2018). "China woos Pakistan militants to secure Belt and Road projects", *Financial Times*, London, 19 February 2018.
29. Malik Siraj Akbar. "Beijing to Balochistan", *The News on Sunday*, Karachi, 4 March 2018.
30. The territories of the former princely state of Jammu and Kashmir, which were occupied by Pakistan in 1947-48 and have remained under its illegal occupation, and which have been politically and administratively divided into two parts. One is called 'Azad' Jammu and Kashmir (Mirpur-Muzaffarabad) and the other Gilgit-Baltistan.
31. Shahbaz Rana, "Chinese vow to make Gwadar more valuable than Karachi", *The Express Tribune*, 9 October 2019.
32. Ashfaq Ahmed. op. cit.
33. Nasir Iqbal. "CPEC: phases and challenges', *The News*, 3 January 2019, p. 6.
34. M.S. Pratibha. "China-Pakistan Economic Corridor", in Srikanth Kondapalli and Hu Xiaowen (eds.). *One Belt One Road: China's Global Outreach*. New Delhi: Pentagon Press, 2017, p. 191.
35. Ashfaq Ahmed. op. cit.
36. "Gwadar, a challenge for stakeholders to develop as successful economic city" *Pakistan Today*, 16 August 2018.
37. MS Pratibha. op. cit., p. 191.
38. "Gwadar port: 'history-making milestones'," *Dawn*, 14 April 2008.
39. Frederic Grare. "Along the road: Gwadar and China's power projection", European Union Institute for Security Studies, Issue Brief 7/2018, July 2018, p. 2.
40. PSA International Pte Ltd is a Singapore-based port management group that was formerly known as the Port of Singapore Authority.
41. "Gwadar port: 'history-making milestones'," *Dawn*, 14 April 2008.
42. Syed Irfan Raza, "China given contract to operate Gwadar port", *Dawn*, 19 February 2013.
43. "Pak China Dosti Zindabad (Long live China-Pakistan friendship)", *Daily Times*, 19 April 2015.
44. Summer Zhen. "Chinese firm takes control of Gwadar Port free-trade zone in Pakistan", *South China Morning Post*, 11 November 2015.
45. "The opening of Gwadar Free Trade Zone on China's new Silk Road disappoints New Delhi", *Asia News*, 30 January 2018.
46. Ibid.
47. Shahbaz Rana. "Pakistan approves massive tax exemptions for Gwadar port operators", *The Express Tribune*, 24 May 2016.

48. Ibid.
49. Ibid.
50. Ibid.
51. Tarique Niazi. "Gwadar: China's Naval outpost on the Indian Ocean" The Jamestown Foundation, *China Brief*, vol. 5, issue 4, 15 February 15 2005.
52. Ibid.
53. "Gwadar-KKH link", Editorial, *Dawn*, 6 July 2006.
54. Gilgit-Baltistan (GB) has been a part of Jammu and Kashmir. After 30 October, India considers it as part of the newly-constituted Union Territory of Ladakh. Its inclusion in Ladakh is based on its historical links as well as its status under the Maharaja's rule. It is presently under the occupation of Pakistan. Pakistan's constitution does not recognize GB as a part of its territory.
55. Safdar Khan. "Karakoram Highway's Gwadar link likely", *Dawn*, Karachi, 5 July 2006.
56. M Ismail Khan. "The Trans-Karakoram Oil Pipeline", *The International News*, Internet Edition, 31 October 2006.
57. Ibid.
58. The US Department of Energy estimates the oil reserves of Azerbaijan and Kazakhstan to be thrice that of the USA at around 130 billion barrels of oil.
59. "China tables railway project linking to Pakistan" *Dawn*, Karachi, 30 June 2014.
60. "Gwadar port as trade, energy corridor", *The International News*, Internet Edition, 20 June 2006.
61. "China sees Pakistan as energy corridor", *The International News*, Internet Edition, 17 June 2006.
62. B. Raman. "Let Down by India", from Outlook website http://www.outlookindia.com/full.asp?fodname=20060616&fname=raman1&sid=1&pn=2 (Accessed on 20 June 2006).
63. M Ilyas Khan. "Is China-Pakistan 'silk road' a game-changer?", from https://www.bbc.com/news/world-asia-32400091 (Accessed on 9 July 2018).
64. Tarique Niazi. op.cit.
65. Shabir Ahmad Khan. op. cit., pp. 94-95.
66. Azhar Ahmad. "Gwadar: Potential and Prospects" Research Paper presented at one-day seminar on Gwadar by PICSS and FPCCI on 29 January 2015 at Serena Hotel Islamabad, p. 5.
67. Sudha Ramachandran, op. cit.
68. David Brewster. "The Changing Balance of Power in the Indian Ocean: Prospects for a Significant Chinese Naval Presence" in David Michel and Ricky Passarelli (eds.). *Sea Change: Evolving Maritime Geopolitics in the Indo-Pacific Region*, Stimson Centre, 2014, pp. 71-72.
69. Ibid., pp. 71-72.
70. Ibid., p. 76.
71. Shihar Aneez. "China's 'Silk Road' push stirs resentment and protest in Sri Lanka", *Reuters*, 2 February 2017, from https://www.reuters.com/article/us-sri-lanka-china-insight-idUSKBN15G5UT (Accessed on 18 February 2021).
72. Brewster. op. cit., p. 76.
73. Ibid.
74. The term 'String of Pearls' was first used to describe Chinese naval bases in the Indian

Ocean in a report prepared by the Booz Hamilton consulting firm for the US Defence Department titled 'Energy Futures in Asia'.

75. Ronald Rourke, "China Naval Modernization: Implications for U.S. Navy Capabilities—Background and Issues for Congress" in Jerald D. Finn (ed.). *China-US Economic and Geopolitical Relations*. New York: Nova Science Publishers Inc, p. 146.
76. Andrew Erickson and Kevin Bond. "Essay: China's Island Building Campaign Could Hint Toward Further Expansions in Indian Ocean", *USNI News*, 17 September 2015, from https://news.usni.org/2015/09/17/essay-chinas-island-building-campaign-could-hint-toward-further-expansions-in-indian-ocean (Accessed 10 July 2020).
77. Bertil Lintner. "China eyes a Covid-19 edge in the Indian Ocean", *Asia Times*, Hong Kong, 23 April 2020.
78. Brewster. op. cit., p. 77.
79. Ibid.
80. Sudha Ramachandran. op. cit.
81. Summer Zhen. "Chinese firm takes control of Gwadar Port free-trade zone in Pakistan", *South China Morning Post*, from https://www.scmp.com/business/companies/article/1877882/chinese-firm-takes-control-gwadar-port-free-trade-zone-pakistan (accessed on 28 December 2019).
82. David Brewster. op. cit., p. 71.
83. Mushtaq Khan and Danish Hyder. "CPEC: The devil is not in the details", from https://herald.dawn.com/news/1153597 (accessed on 1 March 2020).
84. Mahwish Chowdhary. "China's Billion-Dollar Gateway To The Subcontinent: Pakistan May Be Opening A Door It Cannot Close" from https://www.forbes.com/sites/realspin/2015/08/25/china-looks-to-pakistan-to-expand-its-influence-in-asia/#3eeda9093de9 (Accessed on 1 April 2020).
85. Summer Said and Ahmed Al Omran, "Saudi Aramco Set for Chinese Energy Deals", *Wall Street Journal*, New York, 20 January 2016.
86. Manoj Joshi. op. cit., p. 37.
87. Ibid.
88. Jane Perlez. "Chinese Leader Is All Business in Middle East ", *The New York Times*, New York edition, 31 January 2016, Section A, p. 8.
89. Kristin Huang, "Iranian relations built on trade, energy and arms', *South China Morning Post*, 9 January 2020.
90. Alex Vatanka. "China's Great Game in Iran" *Foreign Policy*, 5 September 2019 from https://foreignpolicy.com/2019/09/05/chinas-great-game-in-iran/ (Accessed on 1 March 2020).
91. Ibid.
92. Manoj Joshi. op. cit., pp. 37-38.
93. Rick Noack. "China's new train line to Iran sends message to Trump: We'll keep trading anyway', *The Washington Post*, 12 May 2018.
94. Farnaz Fassihi and Steven Lee Myers. "Big Iran Deal Gives Beijing an Oil Supply and Influence", *The New York Times*, New York edition, 28 March 2021.
95. Jeremy Bowen, "China sets sights on Middle East with Iran co-operation deal", *BBC News*, 31 March 2021, from https://www.bbc.com/news/world-middle-east-56574336 (Accessed on 14 May 2021).

96. Fassihi and Myres. op. cit.
97. Dina Esfandiary, "Iran's 'New' Partnership with China is just Business as Usual", *World Politics Review*, 22 April 2021.
98. Kabir Taneja and Kalpit Mankikar "$400 bn deal an eye-catcher. But Iran is just a square in China's geopolitical chessboard', *The Print*, 2 April 2021.
99. Fassihi and Myres. op. cit.
100. Bowen, op. cit.
101. Taneja and Mankikar. op. cit.
102. Manoj Joshi, op. cit., p. 38.
103. "China picks UAE as regional production hub for Sinopharm Covid-19 vaccine", *The Strait Times*, Singapore, 28 March 2021.
104. Tariq Al-Shammari, "Dubai and Gwadar: the silent economic war in the Gulf of Oman', *Open Democracy*, 14 August 2017 from https://www.opendemocracy.net/en/north-africa-west-asia/dubai-and-gwadar-silent-economic-war-in-gulf-of-oman/ (Accessed 12 December 2019).
105. Ibid.
106. Ibid.
107. Mary Sophia. "Dubai Ranks Fifth Among Top Global Destinations for Travellers", *Gulf Business*, Dubai, 10 July 2014.
108. Al-Shammari. op. cit.
109. Ibid.
110. Chawla, Muhammad Iqbal (2018). "Belt and Road Initiative: Regional and Global Dimensions", *Journal of Political Studies*, 25 (1), pp. 83-85.
111. Al-Shammari. op. cit.
112. Ibid.
113. Manoj Joshi. op. cit., p. 38.
114. "The Impact of the Saudi-Iranian Rapprochement on Middle East Conflicts", International Crisis Group, 19 April 2023, https://www.crisisgroup.org/middle-east-north-africa/gulf-and-arabian-peninsula/iran-saudi-arabia/impact-saudi-iranian (Accessed on 4 July 2023).
115. Mohammed Abdelbary and Abbas Al Lawati. "China surpasses US in popularity among Arab youth as Beijing expands Middle East footprint", CNN website https://edition.cnn.com/2023/06/21/middleeast/china-surpasses-us-mideast-survey-mime-intl/index.html (Accessed on 4 July 2023).
116. Joseph Webster and Joze Pelayo. "China is getting comfortable with the Gulf Cooperation Council. The West must pragmatically adapt to its growing regional influence.", 5 April 2023, Atlantic Council website https://www.atlanticcouncil.org/blogs/menasource/china-is-getting-comfortable-with-the-gulf-cooperation-council-the-west-must-pragmatically-adapt-to-its-growing-regional-influence/ (Accessed on 5 July 2023).
117. Mohammad Eslami and Maria Papageorgiou. "China's Increasing Role in the Middle East: Implications for Regional and International Dynamics", *Georgetown Journal of International Affairs*, 2 June 2023.
118. Ishtiaq Ahmad. "China's growing footprint bodes well for the Middle East", *Arab News*, 18 May 18, 2022.
119. Brewster. op. cit., p. 77.

120. Denis M. Tull. "China's engagement in Africa: scope, significance and consequences', *The Journal of Modern African Studies*, 44 (30), September 2006, p. 459.
121. Manoj Joshi. op. cit., p. 29.
122. Wade Shepard. "What China is Really up to in Africa", *Forbes*, 3 October 2019, from https://www.forbes.com/sites/wadeshepard/2019/10/03/what-china-is-really-up-to-in-africa/?sh=6fc9362a5930 (Accessed 15 May 2021).
123. Although, the EU's trade with Africa is larger, none of its individual members have trade with Africa that can match China's trade with Africa.
124. Shepard. op. cit.
125. Joseph Ingram. "China's Presence in Africa: A Boon or a Bust?', African Development Bank Group, Africa Economic Brief, 10 (1), p. 3.
126. As of August 2020, only five countries, namely, Benin, Eritrea, Sao Tome and Principe, Eswatini (Swaziland) and Mali had neither signed an MoU nor expressed support for the BRI, but of these all except Eswatini, which recognises the Republic of China (Taiwan); have allowed Chinese projects within their countries.
127. Venkateswaran Lokanathan. "China's Belt and Road Initiative: Implications in Africa", Observer Research Foundation, Issue Brief 395, August 2020, pp. 2-3.
128. Ingram. op. cit., p. 2.
129. Manoj Joshi. op. cit., p. 29.
130. Ibid.
131. Ibid., pp. 29-30.
132. Ibid., pp. 30-31.
133. Ingram. op. cit., p. 5.
134. Harry G. Broadman, "Africa's debt dance with China in creating the Belt Road Initiative", *The Africa Report*, 21 April 2021.
135. Alex Edwards. *"Dual Containment" Policy in the Persian Gulf: The USA, Iran, and Iraq, 1991–2000*. New York: Palgrave Macmillan, 2014, pp.17-18.
136. Shibley Telhami, "The Persian Gulf: Understanding the American Oil Strategy", 1 March 2002 from Brookings website https://www.brookings.edu/articles/the-persian-gulf-understanding-the-american-oil-strategy/ (Accessed on 21 March 2020).
137. Ibid.
138. GCC countries include Bahrain, Kuwait, Oman, Qatar, Saudi Arabia, and the United Arab Emirates. The access to most of them is through the ports in the Persian Gulf.
139. "Crown Prince of Bahrain Visits NAVCENT', 4 March 2020, from US Naval Forces Central Command website https://www.cusnc.navy.mil/Media/News/Display/Article/2101160/crown-prince-of-bahrain-visits-navcent/ (Accessed on 19 March 2020).
140. Khurram Minhas. "Expulsion of US from the Persian Gulf?", *The Nation*, Lahore, 17 January 2020.
141. Nafiseh Kohnavard. "Iraq military bases: US pulling out of three key sites", 16 March 2020, *BBC* website https://www.bbc.com/news/world-middle-east-51914600 (Accessed 21 March 2020).
142. Michael E. O'Hanlon and Sara Allawi. "The relationship between Iraq and the US is in danger of collapse. That can't happen." 20 March 2020, Brookings website, https://www.brookings.edu/blog/order-from-chaos/2020/03/20/the-relationship-between-iraq-and-the-us-is-in-danger-of-collapse-that-cant-happen/ (Accessed on 21 March 2020).

143. Benjamin Roussey, "Is America Energy Self-Sufficient Yet?", 11 March 2019, Energy Central website, https://energycentral.com/c/gn/america-energy-self-sufficient-yet (Accessed on 1 March 2020).
144. "North America becomes Self-Sufficient in Oil", Rystad Energy website, 7 March 2019, from https://www.rystadenergy.com/newsevents/news/press-releases/North-America-becomes-self-sufficient-in-oil/ (Accessed 1 March 2020).
145. Maria Abi-Habib. "What China Gets for Building up Pakistan: A Military Toehold", *The New York Times*, New York edition, 20 December 2018.
146. "US warns vessels transiting Gulf amid tensions with Iran", *Arab News*, Riyadh, 14 January 2020.
147. Syed Fazl-e-Haider, "Shifting alliances in the Gulf a boon to China", *The Interpreter*, 18 November 2019 from https://www.lowyinstitute.org/the-interpreter/shifting-alliances-gulf-boon-china (Accessed on 12 December 2019).
148. Frederic Grare, "Along the road: Gwadar and China's power projection", European Union Institute for Security Studies, Issue Brief 7/2018, p. 3.
149. Fazl-e-Haider. op. cit.
150. "Maritime coalition launched to protect Gulf shipping after Iran attacks", *Arab News*, Riyadh, 8 November 2019.

5

Impact on Regional Security

The Gwadar Deep Sea Port project aims to become another Dubai, at the mouth of the Persian Gulf. If the project fructifies and attains its true potential, it will transform the regional dynamics. It has the potential to not only emerge as the ideal gateway for Afghanistan and Central Asia, but also as a major transhipment port for the region. It could be used to supply goods to the Persian Gulf, Central Asia, the Trans-Caucasus region, and South Asia. More significantly, the sovereign guarantees given by Pakistan to China and the fact that the port is being operated by a Chinese firm and the likelihood of Chinese naval facilities at the port have huge strategic and security ramifications. This chapter will deal with the impact of the Gwadar port project on the littorals and extra regional powers in Central Asia, the Persian Gulf, and the northern Indian Ocean, besides South Asia, which will be covered with India separately.

Afghanistan and Central Asia

After the disintegration of the Union of Soviet Socialist Republics (USSR) in 1991, there was a sudden rush to capture the enormous natural resources of land-locked Central Asian states, especially its energy resources.[1] Even after the collapse of the Soviet Union, these states have traditionally depended on Russian ports for their trade with other countries, as the Soviet era infrastructure, which included pipelines, railways and road networks, was so configured. After the disintegration, their linkages with China increased and many Central Asian countries have started banking on China for a substantive part of their trade. Similarly, pipelines and trade through the Caspian Sea have ensured that many states of the region trade with Europe and the West through Turkey and Caucasus. However, the shortest possible exit to the open oceans for the countries of the Central Asian Republics continues to be the warm water ports in Iran or Pakistan in the North Arabian Sea.[2] Unfortunately, despite geographical proximity, almost negligible trade to and from the Central Asian States transits through the ports in the North Arabian Sea.

In the case of land-locked Afghanistan, most of its overseas trade transits through Karachi and then winds its way up through Pakistan's territory to Torkham near Jalalabad. However its relations with Pakistan have always remained tense and, consequently, it has been in the forefront to seek free access to sea. On the other hand, Pakistan has always been strongly opposed to any free access to Afghanistan and has asked for it to be governed by bilateral or multilateral treaties. It has asserted that "the sanctity of a contract voluntarily arrived at was infinitely better than a contentious, nebulous right". In 1955, after the transit treaty signed between the UK and Afghanistan during the colonial times had lapsed, Pakistan subjected Afghanistan to a blockade that caused it immense economic hardships. Consequently, Afghanistan was in the forefront of seeking rights for the landlocked states at the United Nations.[3]

Afghanistan's relentless efforts eventually materialised in the form of the Convention on Transit Trade of land-locked States. The United Nations Conference on Transit Trade of Land-locked Countries, which was held at the United Nations Headquarters in New York, adopted the Convention. The conference had been convened in pursuance of the decision of the United Nations General Assembly (UNGA), which in its 1328th plenary meeting held on 10 February 1965 had recommended it. The convention was eventually signed in New York on 8 July 1965 and came into force on 9 June 1967.[4]

This was the first international agreement that dealt specifically with the unique problems of land-locked states and their transit trade. This agreement laid down the framework for a cooperative mechanism between the landlocked states and their neighbours through whose territory their trade transited. After this international agreement, Pakistan was legally bound to provide transit facilities to Afghanistan for its exports and imports. Consequently, the Afghanistan Transit Trade Agreement (ATTA) was signed in 1965, which was subsequently replaced by the Afghanistan Pakistan Transit Trade Agreement (APTTA) in 2010.[5]

Despite the agreements, Pakistan created numerous bottlenecks for trade to and from Afghanistan. In accordance with the ATTA, Afghanistan was permitted the use of two Pakistani ports, namely, Karachi, and Port Passim,[6] for its trade which needed to cross into Afghanistan at either Torkham or Chapman. It did not have any provision for Afghan trade with China through the Karakoram Highway, while conditions for trade with India through Wage could never be finalised. The agreement did not specify trade routes or crossing points and did not allow Afghan trucks to cross into Pakistan and the goods in Pakistan were initially carried by Pakistan Railway and subsequently by the National Logistics Cell (NLC), which is controlled by the Pakistan Army.[7]

However, there were significant changes in the world after 1965, both in the field of technology as well as geo-politics. On one hand, heavy-duty trucks, with advanced technology entered the market; on the other, the disintegration of the Soviet Union created new sovereign states in Central Asia, many of which were also land locked.[8] The CARs appeared as a significant source of hydrocarbons, as well as a lucrative market for manufacturers across the globe, but more specifically for those in South Asia. The energy-starved economies of South Asia optimistically looked at tapping the vast energy resources of this region, which was contiguous to South Asia. As a result, Pakistan started looking into tapping the Central Asian markets as well as accessing energy from the region. Consequently, the two countries initiated negotiations to revise ATTA. This resulted in APTTA being signed on 28 October 2010, which came into effect from 12 June 2011.[9]

The agreement gave Afghanistan access to a third port in Pakistan, the Gwadar Deep Sea Port, besides Karachi Port and Port Passim. It also provided Afghanistan with a third crossing point at Ghulam Khan in North Waziristan Agency, besides the existing border crossing points at Chaman and Torkham. More significantly, it also provided Afghanistan access to Sost in Gilgit-Baltistan,[10] on the Karakoram Highway for trading with China. The agreement, for the first time, allowed Afghan trucks to carry goods to Pakistan's sea ports as well as to its border with India at Wagah, but did not allow them to pick up Indian goods bound for Afghanistan. As a quid pro quo, the agreement allowed Pakistan to access Central Asia through specified trade routes in Afghanistan.[11]

Consequent to the signing of the APTTA, Pakistan has been eyeing trade with the Central Asian Republics and believes that if Gwadar emerges as the port of choice for these countries and a substantive part of their trade starts transiting through its territory, it might open vistas for Pakistan's own exports to these countries, as well as for importing hydrocarbons for its energy-starved economy. Islamabad has been aiming to widen the scope of its transit trade with Afghanistan to include transit trade to Tajikistan, Turkmenistan, and Uzbekistan from Torkham, Chaman, and Ghulam Khan through Afghan territory.[12]

Pakistan perceives that it is located at the crossroads of major trade corridors to tap Central Asian markets on account of its strategic location and three major ports. Consequently, it has proposed amendments to the existing framework, which aim to govern cargoes imported by Pakistan from Tajikistan, Turkmenistan, and Uzbekistan. This also plans to cover their imports from ports at Karachi, Gwadar, and Port Qasim, which would transit via Pakistan and Afghan territory. At the same time, it would also cover Tajikistan, Turkmenistan, and Uzbekistan's exports transiting through Afghanistan and Pakistan onwards to Karachi, Gwadar, and Port Qasim.[13]

Policy makers in Islamabad believe that as a significant logistics hub for transit trade, Pakistan would be able to usher in prosperity all along the trade routes, across the entire South Asia and even beyond. They believe that economic development in a region is invariably triggered by a good network of transportation and legal regimes that permit movement of goods and people along them. Pakistan's Federal Board of Revenue (FBR) has posted on its website that "By virtue of its geographical position, the importance of Pakistan cannot be undermined." It further adds that "Pakistan's geostrategic advantage lies in the fact that it shares borders with Iran, Afghanistan, China, and India while the Arabian Sea connects it with the rest of the world".[14]

Most of Afghanistan's imports originate from its immediate neighbours, whereas its primary exports of fresh and dry fruits, carpets, medical herbs, and animal skins are primarily destined for Pakistan, India, and Iran as its exports to other countries depends on the efficiency, reliability, and cost-effectiveness of transit facilities in Pakistan and its ports.[15] Unfortunately, transit through Pakistan is the most viable option for Afghanistan's trade with the rest of the world. As a result, its dependence on Pakistan, in absolute terms as far as the flow of cargo under Afghan transit trade is concerned, increased 44 per cent to 93,732 containers in 2018-19 as against 60,516 containers in the previous year. Similarly, the assessed import value of the transit goods also increased at a healthy rate of 55 per cent from $ 3.97 billion in 2017-18 to $ 5.715 billion in 2018-19.[16] However, the existing problems, which Afghan traders have been facing in Pakistan, have accentuated in recent years. This has resulted in attempts by Afghanistan to reduce its trade dependence on Pakistan.[17]

As a result of these efforts, Afghanistan's trade with Pakistan has been declining. This includes both Afghan exports to Pakistan as well as Afghan cross-border trade through Pakistan. The main reasons for the slowdown were the frequent interruptions and delay imposed by security agencies in Pakistan under the garb of monitoring the cargo,[18] which was also a result of adversarial bilateral relations between the two countries.

According to a report by the Trade Development Authority of Pakistan (TDAP), due to higher transit costs, Afghan trade is shifting to Iran and other neighbouring countries that provide better facilities for handling cargo at competitive rates, as well as cost-effective transportation. According to the report, "High cost of transportation and hefty deposits by shipping companies for transportation of containers are discouraging Afghan importers to deal with Pakistan".[19] To further aggravate matters, the Pakistani authorities tend to close border crossings between Afghanistan and Pakistan frequently under various pretexts. This results in thousands of containers being stranded at the check posts, which results in damage to perishable cargo. The customs authorities in Pakistan, earlier used to block carriers, which could not clear Pakistan's borders within 14 days, but of late they have been blocking virtually every carrier.[20] The situation has not really improved even after the return of the Taliban in Kabul, which was widely perceived to be Islamabad's proxies.

Gwadar was recognised as a port of entry for Afghan merchandise as part of the APTTA and even for Central Asia though Afghanistan. However, it has not really been able to emerge as a port of choice, primarily as the roads connecting Chaman and Torkham with Gwadar though the hinterland are non-existent. To further aggravate matters, continuing insurgency in Balochistan and the conflict in Afghanistan make transportation of goods from Gwadar to Afghanistan and Central Asia quite risky. Nevertheless, as and when the Gwadar port project fructifies and roads through the hinterland start functioning, it would lead to a greater dependence of Afghanistan on Pakistan. Not only that, even the dependence of Central Asian states on Pakistan will increase significantly. This could reduce their dependence on Russia and to some extent on China.[21]

Even within Afghanistan, the preferred border crossing would shift from Torkham to Chaman. This could result in most of the international trade of Afghanistan and Central Asia to transit through Chaman, because it avoids the perpetual turbulence that has prevailed in the erstwhile Federally Administered Areas (FATA) of Pakistan. Pakistan was hoping that the return of the Taliban would enable it to trade with Central Asia through Afghanistan. Unfortunately, Afghanistan has not been peaceful and economic activity has come to a standstill. With both Afghanistan and Pakistan facing severe financial crisis, bilateral trade has come to a grinding halt. The revival of the Tehrik-e-Taliban Pakistan (TTP) has resulted in increased tensions between the two neighbours and even firing between Afghan and Pakistani border guards. Consequently, Pakistan, to tide over its foreign exchange shortage, has now allowed barter trade with Afghanistan.[22] China has played a major role in resolving contentious issues between Afghanistan and Pakistan and on 7 May 2023, Chinese Foreign Minister Qin Gang held talks with both Bilawal Bhutto Zardari, Pakistan's foreign minister and the Taliban's foreign minister, Amir Khan Muttaqi. Subsequently, the two countries agreed to boost trade.[23]

Although Gwadar Port has been functioning for some time and has been included in the APTTA, there has been no trade to or from Central Asia through it. In the initial decades, the Central Asian infrastructure was linked to the Russian infrastructure, a legacy of Soviet days. Consequently, most of their trade moved west through it. Subsequently, connectivity with China and Turkey was established. However, trade through Afghanistan could not materialise due to conflict and tensions between Afghanistan and Pakistan. However, some day, when the situation improves, this could become a major transit route for goods to and from Central Asia. This could make the Central Asian Republics dependent on Pakistan and could enhance Islamabad's influence there. Traditionally, India has had a better influence in the region, but of late, increasing Turkish influence has been tilting some of it towards Pakistan. If Gwadar emerges as the gateway to this vast resource-rich region, the tilt would enhance significantly.

With the ascendance of the Taliban in Kabul, the possibility of Afghanistan emerging as an ideal transit for Central Asia for goods and personnel looks unlikely in the near future. Although, many Central Asian states have established reasonably good working relations with the Taliban, it is unlikely to result in significant trade with or through Afghanistan. Continuing turbulence and the Taliban's obscurantist ideology will remain a big deterrent for the free movement of goods and personnel through Afghanistan. However, if the CPEC becomes a major trade corridor, some of the Central Asian Republics, especially Kirghizstan, Tajikistan and may be, Kazakhstan could use the connectivity projects of the CPEC to trade through Karachi or Gwadar. This would further enhance China's influence in Central Asia, where it is already emerging as a major player after the weakening of Russian influence consequent to the Russia-Ukraine war.

Implications for Iran

As analysed in the previous section, before the Taliban's return to power, rising tensions between Afghanistan and Pakistan and increasing problems faced by Afghan transporters in Pakistan, had led to a significant chunk of Afghanistan's trade being routed through Iran. As a result, the transportation network within Iran, which connects Afghanistan's border towns with the main Iranian transportation grid and consequently to its ports, both in the Caspian Sea as well as the Arabian Sea, are being enhanced. More significantly, Iran is building a new port close to Gwadar at Chabahar in collaboration with India. The port is close to Iran's border with Pakistan and even more importantly is just outside the Persian Gulf, close to the main shipping routes to Asia and Europe.[24] One of the reasons for Iran to continue dealing with the Taliban, despite serious ideological differences and its treatment of Afghan Shias, is probably Tehran's desire that Afghan trade transits through Afghan territory. This is possibly an explanation for the change in Tehran's approach to Taliban 2.0, as compared to its previous version.

Railways are the preferred mode of communications in strife-torn countries and, consequently, attempts are being made to link Afghanistan with the Iranian railway network. A link connecting railway tracks in Iran with the western Afghan city of Herat is already under construction. The ongoing project includes a link from the main line from Mashhad to Bafgh in Iran, which was inaugurated in May 2005. The work on the project had already commenced on 29 July 2006 and has been grouped under four sections. Of these, two sections are in Iran and two in Afghanistan. The total length of the railway line is 191 km and stretches 77 km in Iran and 114 km in Afghanistan. There are 10 intermediate stations that have been planned and of these Ghurian will be the largest intermediate town served by the track on Afghan territory.[25]

There is also a proposal to extend this line within Afghan territory via Meymaneh and Sheberghan to Sher Khan Bandar, on its border with Tajikistan. This could help Iran to access Central Asia bypassing Turkmenistan. More significantly, it could boost Central Asia's trade with Iran and through it with the rest of Asia and Africa, as the line would pass though a relatively, more stable part of Afghanistan. This could also earn huge revenues for both Iran and Afghanistan by way of transit charges. The authorities expect traffic on this railway link to be 321,000 passengers and 6.8 million tons of cargo, annually.[26] According to sources in Afghanistan, the railway link to Herat from Mashhad is almost 90 per cent complete.[27]

Afghanistan is also in talks with India to extend this rail line further from Herat to Mazar Sharif, which is already linked with Uzbekistan and Tajikistan.[28] Herat is also linked with the railway corridors of Turkmenistan. India is also considering construction of a railway line from Chabahar to the Hajigak region of Afghanistan, which has huge deposits of iron ore. A consortium of seven Indian companies led by the Steel Authority of India Limited (SAIL), had acquired rights to Asia's largest iron ore mines in the Hajigak region of Central Afghanistan.[29] These rail links will help Uzbekistan and Tajikistan access Iran's rail network through Afghanistan and other Central Asian states to access Iran through them. A map showing various proposed and existing transportation links in Iran and Afghanistan along with their existing and proposed links with Central Asia is shown in Map 1.

All these investments by Iran and various other countries are aimed at making Iran as the preferred gateway for oceanic trade with Afghanistan and Central Asia. However, once Gwadar port becomes fully operational and emerges as a vibrant commercial hub, the huge locational advantage that it enjoys over any other port in the North Arabian Sea, with the possible exception of Chabahar, would make it the preferred oceanic gateway for Afghanistan and Central Asia. This could make huge infrastructural investments being made in Iran completely infructuous.

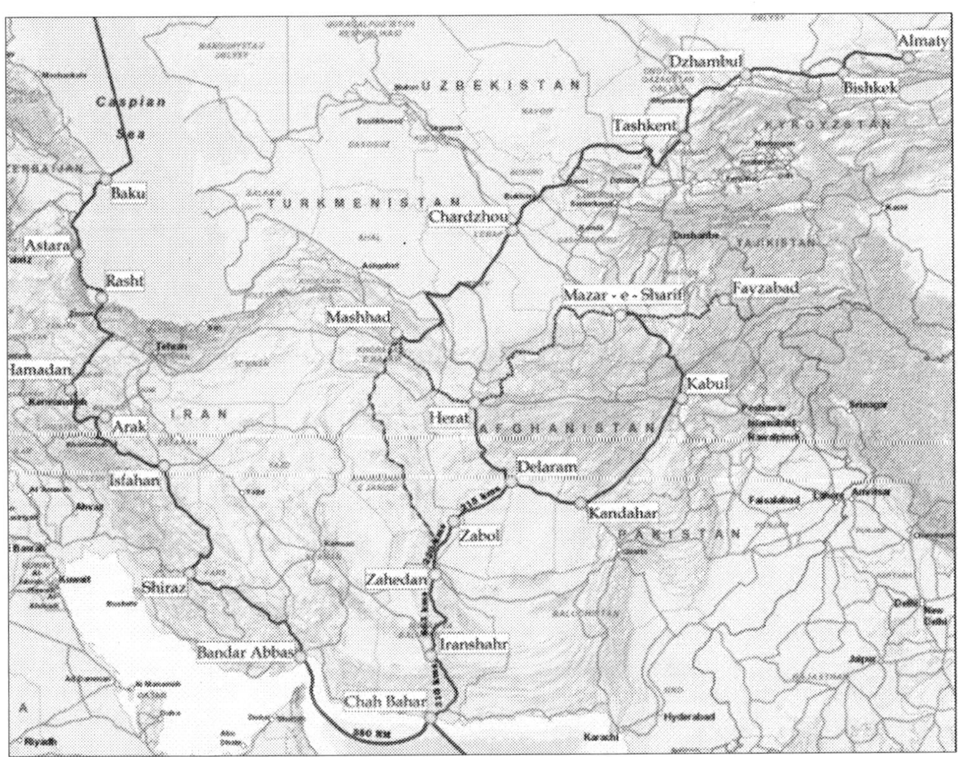

Map 1: Map showing existing and planned railway links through Iran and Afghanistan along with existing and proposed links with Central Asia

In order to counter this huge locational advantage which Gwadar, and to some extent, Karachi, enjoy over Bandar Abbas, the main Iranian port, for embarking and disembarking Afghan and Central Asian trade; Iran has collaborated with India to conceptualise the Chabahar port. The port, which is just outside the Strait of Hormuz, is almost as close to Afghanistan as the Gwadar port and has been projected as its rival.[30] Afghanistan and the Central Asian Republics are being linked to the Chabahar port through an intricate network of roads and railways.[31] A map showing the railway network in Iran is shown in Map 2.

Considering the huge investments in both Gwadar and Chabahar ports, Gwadar's emergence as the preferred gateway to Central Asia, could make the enormous investment in the Chabahar port and its associated infrastructure, a huge economic liability. It would also quash any hopes that Iran has about

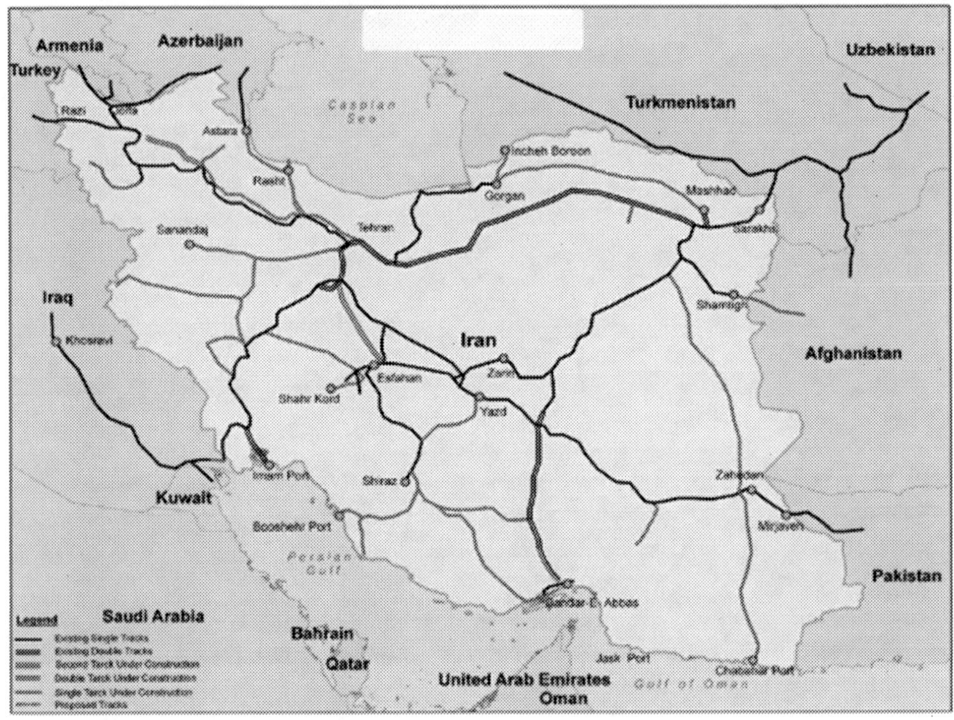

Map 2: Iranian Railway Network

Source: Roy, Meena Singh (2012), "Iran: India's Gateway to Central Asia', *Strategic Analysis,* 36(6), November–December 2012, p. 964.

emerging as the preferred gateway for Afghanistan and the Central Asian Republics and deriving huge economic benefits from this transit trade, which is expected to boom many fold, once peace returns to Afghanistan. Consequently Iran has vested interests in ensuring that the Gwadar port project does not emerge as the preferred oceanic gateway for resource-rich Afghanistan and Central Asian states.

Both Gwadar and Chabahar lie in territories dominated by the Baloch, who have been seeking autonomy and protesting against their respective governments. Consequently, the security situation in both Western Balochistan (in Iran) as well as Eastern Balochistan (under Pakistan) has been extremely tenuous. The Baloch will play a major role in determining which of these two ports emerges as the gateway to Afghanistan and Central Asia. The emergence of Gwadar or Chabahar as the preferred port for merchandise bound for Afghanistan and Central Asia may not be feasible, without co-opting the

Baloch. However, the operationalisation of these ports, with or without their support, will have a huge impact on the Baloch nationalist movement and the situation in Balochistan on both sides of Goldsmith Line.

The imposition of sanctions by the Trump Administration against Iran for perceived violations of the nuclear deal and the inability of the Biden Administration to withdraw them, despite professing to do so, has constrained India to reduce its trade with Iran and cut down its oil imports from there. Consequently, Iran has of late been gravitating towards China for some time, as China has managed to withstand the US sanctions against Iran. China continues to import oil from Iran, giving it a valuable source of revenue. Consequently, Iran has not only joined the BRI, but has also signed a memorandum of understanding (MoU) making Chabahar and Gwadar sister ports.[32] This action and the fact that traffic through Chabahar has not really picked up, could severely jeopardise India's position and strengthen Chinese influence in the region.

Implications for West Asia

The Gwadar Deep Sea port, if it emerges as a viable gateway to Afghanistan and Central Asia could also emerge as the main transhipment hub of the region. At present, Dubai, the most populous city of the United Arab Emirates (UAE), enjoys the distinction of being the regional transhipment hub. Despite having poor natural resources, Dubai has emerged as a multi-cultural city and the business, trade, and tourism hub of region, which is visited by millions of visitors from across the world for both leisure and business. This eminence is enjoyed by Dubai on account of its two major commercial ports, Port Rashid and Port Jebel Ali, which have emerged as huge transhipment ports for almost all the littorals of the Arabian Sea. Port Jebel Ali is the biggest artificial man-made harbour in the world, as well as the largest port in entire Middle East. These ports provided businesses enormous locational advantages leading to various commercial entities setting up their offices there. Most of the global corporations have their regional offices located at Dubai and consequently, over 5,000 companies from 120 countries have their presence there.[33]

Dubai, unlike other emirates in the Persian Gulf, is devoid of major hydrocarbon resources. Consequently, most of the revenue for the Emirate of Dubai comes from sectors like aviation, tourism, and financial services. Its emergence as the local tourism and commercial hub has led to a boom in construction and the real estate sector, which have emerged as another major source of revenue. Huge skyscrapers and iconic hotels draw many high-end investors from across the globe to Dubai. The Emirate not only has the Burj Khalifa, the tallest building in the world; it also has iconic hotels in the sea. The kingdom also organises major sports and cultural events and going by the standards of other countries in the region, pursues a rather liberal policy to draw in more visitors.[34] It draws the maximum number of international tourists in the entire Middle East. In 2014, Dubai was ranked the fifth most popular global destination for international travellers by the MasterCard Global Destination Cities Index and is expected to attract 20 million tourists annually.[35] However, its varied sources of income are premised on the single most significant factor that Dubai is the regional transhipment hub just inside the mouth of the energy-rich Persian Gulf.[36]

If the Gwadar port emerges as a thriving and vibrant port, it would be a major rival for Dubai and could pose a serious existential threat to its status as the main transhipment port of the region. Gwadar has certain inherent geographical advantages over Dubai, as it is closer to the Eurasian heartland and could reduce transportation time for goods slated for Western China and Central Asia.[37] It could enhance trade between the Middle East and the central Eurasian landmass, as connectivity between these two energy and resource rich regions has been extremely tenuous and long. More significantly, ships coming to Gwadar do not have to enter the Persian Gulf through the narrow Strait of Hormuz, a process that slows them considerably as they have to follow a traffic separation scheme and reduce speed. This enhances the financial burden for ships entering Dubai. A substantive portion of the transhipment cargo is bound for ports outside the Gulf, thereby; requiring it to cross Strait of Hormuz twice and it raises the transportation cost and time. This would be completely eliminated in the case of Gwadar.

To compound matters, on-going tensions in the Persian Gulf also give Gwadar a huge advantage over Dubai. Continuing acrimony between the USA and Iran poses a serious threat to the freedom of navigation in the Gulf. As the tensions rise, Iran keeps reiterating its threat that in case of hostility, it will close down the Gulf. This may make Gwadar, a much safer option for ships to disembark their cargo. As the UAE, which includes Dubai, is considered a strong ally of the USA and the Western powers, some countries aligned with Iran may prefer using Gwadar over Dubai for purely political reasons. This could include countries like Syria, Iraq and more significantly Qatar, whose relations with the Trump Administration in the UAE had taken a sudden dip. Consequently, Qatar is investing a huge amount estimated to be around 15 per cent of the total cost of the CPEC, in various infrastructural projects associated with the CPEC, especially the facilities coming up at Gwadar. Besides financial returns, the aim could as well be to put pressure on the UAE, which includes the Emirate of Dubai.[38]

Consequently, both geo-economics and geo-politics have brought China, Pakistan, and Qatar together in promoting Gwadar and making it a success, as these countries hope to derive immense economic as well as geo-political benefits from this port becoming a thriving economic transhipment hub. According to Hussain Haqqani, Gwadar positions China at the mouth of the Persian Gulf, which will impact its relations both with Iran as well as the Sunni sheikhdoms of the Persian Gulf. It could replace American influence in some of them. More significantly, it enables China to interrupt US oil imports as well as trade with these countries.[39] On the other hand, India and the UAE, as well as its allies in West Asia, do not want Gwadar to emerge as another Dubai. To this extent, they are promoting investments by the USA and other Western powers in Dubai. The UAE, especially Dubai will be a big loser if Gwadar really takes off, as its revenue from transportation and tourism could be curtailed drastically.[40]

Implications for the USA

Of various extra-regional powers, the USA is the pre-eminent power in the Indian Ocean. For long, it has considered the Persian Gulf to be an area of vital strategic interest for its national security. During the Cold War, the US objective in the region, like in any other part of the world, initially, was to check Soviet expansionism. However, it soon realised its huge potential on account of its enormous energy resources and changed its outlook towards the region. It designated it as a region vital to its interests, but from the Second World War till the first Gulf War, the USA maintained a remote presence, which predominantly relied on its allies to establish order in the region. However, this changed with Iraq's invasion of Kuwait, which made the USA realise the need of having its troops present in the region and since then it started positioning its forces there in significant numbers. The end of the Cold War, immediately after the first Gulf War, led to circumstances that led to the USA to assume a far more overt and significant security role in the Persian Gulf region.[41]

The region, for the last five decades, fulfilled a critical role in ensuring that the future energy needs of the USA and its allies were met. This critical role stemmed from the fact that although, the Middle East contributes to only around a quarter of the global oil production, when it comes to proven oil reserves, the estimate of regional reserves vary from two thirds to three quarters of global reserves. Consequently, the USA and its Western allies defined the region as vital to their strategic interests.[42]

The large military presence of the USA in the region was necessitated by this vital importance of Persian Gulf and the need to ensure that the traffic moved in and out of the Gulf through the Strait of Hormuz, without any hindrance. The huge military build-up by the USA in the region after the first Gulf War, gave it a political leverage, which was effectively used to help American companies win contracts in the region. The traditional strategy of the USA in the region was premised on its strategic need to ensure a continuous flow of oil at reasonable prices. This entailed reliance on states with excess capacity like Saudi Arabia to counter any spurt in prices on account of short-term interruptions in either the production or transportation. In the process of doing so, it has consistently tried to deny its enemies or potential enemies control over these vital resources that could make them more menacing.[43] This is probably the prime reason behind its hostility towards Iran and unbridled support towards the Gulf Cooperation Council (GCC) countries.[44]

After the British withdrawal from the region, the USA has been the dominant power in the North Arabian Sea, especially in the region surrounding the Persian Gulf. Currently, Bahrain, Qatar, Kuwait, Saudi Arabia, Jordan, Oman, and the United Arab Emirates host a number of US troops on their soil. The US Central Command naval forces, as well as the US Fifth Fleet is based at Bahrain and is responsible for 2.5 million square miles of ocean territory, which includes the Persian Gulf, Arabian Sea, Gulf of Oman, Red Sea and parts of the Indian Ocean. This vast expanse includes 20 countries and has three critical choke points at the Strait of Hormuz, the Suez Canal, and the Bab el-Mandeb Strait at the southern tip of Yemen.[45]

It is estimated that there are over 41,000 American security personnel in the GCC countries. According to US military websites, there are five naval bases and 11 air bases of the USA in the region, including the Al-Dhafra airbase in the UAE, which is the busiest American air base for surveillance flights in the world. Similarly, the port of Jabel-e-Ali is the busiest naval port of the USA in the entire Persian Gulf region. Almost all the Arab countries in the region with the possible exception of Iraq, consider the US military presence as a guarantee for the stability of their non-representative regimes. The US military is also perceived as a deterrent against any threat that could emanate from Iran or its allies against their fragile regimes. Consequently, numerous agreements have been signed with the USA to ensure its continued presence in their countries.

On the other hand, Iran right from its revolution, has tried to project the continuing US presence as a destabilising factor for the region. It has tried to whip up public emotions against the American presence in the Arab lands and succeeded to a great extent in the Arab streets. However, it has never been able to create that sort of mass upsurge that is necessary to force the removal of US troops from the region. After Qassem Soleimani's assassination, Iran has succeeded in creating huge demonstrations in Iraq against the US presence and it has even led to Iraq's parliament asking for withdrawal of the US troops.[46]

Most of the US troops deployed in Syria to support its allies had also moved to Iraq after President Trump decided to pull out its troops from there. The USA presently has eight bases in Iraq, which officially house 5,200 troops, but after the increasing tensions, the USA has announced closing down of three bases. This is a clear sign that the USA is reducing its presence in Iraq under sustained pressure from the Iraqi government. Since October 2019, there have been more than 160 rockets that have been fired at US military bases in Iraq.[47] The USA has numerous core interests in the region, namely, ensuring reliable supply of oil, eradication of jihadi terrorism, prevention of nuclear proliferation, and protection of key friends like Israel and Jordan. In order to accomplish these objectives, without deputing large troops, the USA needs strong partners like Iraq. The USA withdrawal could lead to enhanced Iranian influence in the region, especially in Iraq.[48] Fissures between Iraq and the USA could lead to greater influence of Iran in the region and would require the USA to relocate its troops to other countries in the Persian Gulf.

At present, around 2,500 US troops are present in Iraq and 900 others in Syria, primarily to assist local forces in combating the Islamic State (IS). Despite being vanquished, IS fighters frequently launch attacks in Iraq and Syria. US Secretary of Defence Lloyd Austin during his visit to Baghdad reiterated that the US troops were there at the invitation of the Iraqi Government to defeat the Daesh (IS).[49] The USA had many operational bases in Afghanistan till August 2021. All these troops and bases were mainly supported from the bases in the Persian Gulf region or by forces operating in the North Arabian Sea and Persian Gulf. In December 2018, after 75 years, the USA became the net exporter of energy, courtesy commercial exploration by Shale Gas.[50] Even more significantly, it is estimated that soon, the USA would be exporting more oil and liquids than the Kingdom of Saudi Arabia.[51] Consequently, the USA is no longer dependent on energy supplies from the Persian Gulf; however, its allies in Europe and Japan are still overwhelmingly dependent on supplies from the Persian Gulf. As a result, the Persian Gulf will continue to remain important for the USA and it will have a stake in the free movement of goods in and out of the Gulf. It would need bases in the region to keep existing autocratic regimes allied with it, in power, as well as to support its forces operating in Afghanistan. This requires the USA to have free, unbridled access to the Persian Gulf. However, growing Chinese influence coupled with Chinese presence at Gwadar gives China a unique capacity to monitor every vessel leaving or entering the Persian Gulf. It also gives China an opportunity to support Iran and bolster its regime, which has been under US sanctions. More significantly, this gives China the ability to intercept any shipping coming out of the Gulf and it would be well within its capacity to block the Gulf should it so desire. Gwadar provides China with a strategic outpost, which it can use against the USA and its allies if tensions between the two aggravate to the extent of naval blockades, as the USA and China confront each other at sea.[52] As brought out earlier, Chinese diplomatic and economic outreach has endeared it to the Arab masses in the region and the masses, unlike their regimes, clearly prefer China to the USA.

It could exacerbate existing tensions in the Gulf, which stem from Donald Trump's decision to withdraw the USA from Iran's 2015 nuclear deal with world powers and to impose 'maximum' economic sanctions. The sanctions have devastated Iran's economy. However, the Chinese presence at Gwadar and its connections with Xinjiang could easily enable Iran to breach these sanctions. China has consistently been importing oil from Iran, despite the sanctions imposed by the USA. Iran is accordingly exhibiting keen interest in laying an LNG pipeline to China all along the CPEC.[53] This would easily enable it to breach the crippling sanctions imposed on it by the USA or any such move in the future.

Chinese stakes in Gwadar and the possibility of its military base there just outside the Strait of Hormuz would provide it with huge strategic benefits apart from the apparent economic and commercial gains. This could enable China to emerge as a net security provider for the Persian Gulf and the Arabian Sea region, which could pit it directly against US interests. Gwadar Port provides China a listening post to monitor US naval activities in the Persian Gulf .[54] A naval base at Gwadar gives China anti access/area denial (A2/AD) capabilities in the strategic waters adjacent to the Strait of Hormuz, and would enormously enhance China's capability to project power and gather intelligence. In conjunction with the Chinese military base in Djibouti, it could transform the strategic balance of power in the entire North Arabian Sea and Persian Gulf.[55]According to a Pakistani defence analyst the presence of the PLA Navy, at this critical choke point not only prevents Indo-US domination of the Indian Ocean, but also makes China a credible naval power of the region.[56]

According to well-known Baloch journalist and former editor of *Baloch Haal*, Malik Siraj Akbar, China's growing presence in the region threatens American interests. However, the Americans and the Western countries have not offered much resistance to China as far the port project is concerned, possibly due to their lack of interest or as they have not yet understood the full impact of the project.[57] The USA is however, belatedly taking some steps to contain China's influence in the region.[58] Consequently, the US-led International Maritime Security Construct (IMSC) was set up which apart from the USA, comprises Australia, Albania, Bahrain, Saudi Arabia, the United Arab Emirates, and the United Kingdom. On 7 November 2019, the IMSC formally launched its operations by escorting ships transiting in international shipping lanes through the Strait of Hormuz.[59]

It is therefore quite clear that the Gwadar deep sea port, built with Chinese assistance, and operated by the Chinese could have its naval facilities that threaten America's vital interests in the region.

Implications for Other States

The countries and regions mentioned above are the primary actors who will be affected by the Gwadar port project. However, they are many other countries, which will be affected to varying degrees by this project. One of the other countries to be affected is going to be Russia. The radical Islamist ideology emanating from Afghanistan-Pakistan impacts Russia's soft underbelly. More significantly, at this moment, the countries of Central Asia and the trans-Caucasus region are overwhelmingly dependent on Russia for their economic sustenance as well as external trade. However, once Gwadar starts functioning as a major transhipment hub. These countries will find newer avenues of trading with Asia and Africa and this could reduce their dependence on Russia and reduce Russian influence on them. More significantly, the Russia-Ukraine war has led most countries in Central Asia and the Caucasus to be cautious of Russian unilateralism. Consequently, many traditional allies of Russia have maintained silence or have professed neutrality. They feel China could provide them some sort of security guarantee against any future Russian adventure.

More significantly, Russia, which has been promoting the International North-South Transport Corridor, in conjunction with India and Iran, to access the warm water ports on the Iranian coast for its trade with Asia and Africa, will also look at Gwadar to access these regions. It has already been reported that Russia has sought permission from Pakistan to use Gwadar port for its exports to the region. According to the Pakistani media, Islamabad has approved the usage of Gwadar port by Russia for trade to have round-the-year access to the warm waters of the Arabian Sea. More significantly, Russian has apparently shown a desire to join the CPEC "to reap the maximum dividends." This could lead to greater strategic ties between Russia and Pakistan.[60] Russia has already agreed to help Pakistan to construct a railway line from Quetta to Taftan on its border with Iran and is investing $ 14 billion in Pakistan's energy sector. It is also investing $ 2.5 billion in a north-south pipeline. The two countries have been coordinating their policies on Afghanistan and have started joint anti-terrorism drills.[61]

Russia and its predecessor, the USSR, have traditionally backed India in South Asia and it has been the largest supplier of defence hardware to India. Russia is generally perceived to be a time-tested ally in India, but all that seems to be changing and India could lose its long-term strategic partnership with Russia. A Russia-Pakistan Joint Military Consultative Committee (JMCC) was established in 2018 to boost defence ties and strengthen, expand and diversify mutual cooperation.[62] The Russian and Pakistani navies are already carrying out joint exercises called Arabian Monsoon, since 2014. The ships of the two navies have been visiting ports in each other's country.[63] Russia has already supplied Pakistan four Mi-35M combat helicopters and has agreed to train Pakistan's army officers.[64] According to the Russian authorities, Pakistan had also sought 50,000 AK 47 rifles from Russia, which apparently was rejected by Russia, due to Indian sensitivities. Pakistan has also shown interest in purchasing T90 tanks and new air defence systems from Russia.[65] Gwadar's emergence as the 'gateway to Central Asia' could bring the two countries closer at the cost of India.

More significantly, with Chinese presence at Gwadar, China will emerge as the principal challenger to the USA in the Middle East, a position that is presently enjoyed by Russia after its successful support to the regime of President Bashar-al-Assad in Russia. China's close relations with Iran and its growing military presence could see some of the countries in the region reaching out to China in order to counter the US influence. This could result in Russian influence in the region either getting replaced by the Chinese or remain as part of a collaboration between Russia and China.

Apart from Russia, the European powers have had a significant presence in Indian Ocean region, especially in the Persian Gulf. France still has a significant presence in the Indian Ocean both in terms of territory as well as forces. Similarly, the UK has territory in the Indian Ocean Region. Both these countries had a significant presence in West Asia. Many European countries import oil from the Persian Gulf and have huge commercial as well as strategic interests in this region. As colonial powers, many of them have historical linkages and strong people-to-people connect. Many citizens of these countries reside in the region and many European companies have their establishments here. Consequently, the security of the region is important for them and as a result many of them have sent their naval forces to patrol in the North Arabian

Sea and the Persian Gulf as part of Combined Task Force 150 and/or Combined Task Force 152.[66]

The presence of China in Gwadar presents the European nations with a new regional dynamic that will in all probability affect the power equation in the region. If Gwadar emerges as a fully developed vibrant port, with Chinese presence along with their anti-access and area denial capabilities, then it would definitely enhance China's leverage in the region, while reducing the influence of other traditional powers including the European countries. In case of any conflict with Iran, Gwadar could easily threaten the sea lanes passing through the Strait of Hormuz, thereby affecting vital European interests. Fully developed, the Gwadar port with Chinese presence, therefore, poses direct as well as indirect conventional and non-conventional threats to European interests.[67]

As brought out earlier, China has emerged as a big player in Africa. It is Africa's largest trading partner, bilateral creditor and an extremely significant investor in its infrastructure. Almost 15 per cent of Africa's industrial production is by Chinese companies and African communication links are based on Chinese-built digital infrastructure. China's defence, security and political bonds with the countries in the African continent are growing by the day.[68] Africa is the second largest source of China's energy imports after the Middle East. China is the source for 14 to 20 per cent of sub-Saharan Africa's imports and destination for 15 to 16 per cent of its exports.[69] China has already surpassed the USA as the largest economic player in the continent. China's first overseas naval base is in Djibouti in the Horn of Africa.[70] This, coupled with its presence in Gwadar, could easily provide military muscle to its diplomatic and economic push, especially in North and East Africa.

To sum up, the Gwadar deep sea port project will create a huge impact not only for China and Pakistan, but for all the countries of the region, as well as for extra regional powers like the USA and Russia.

NOTES

1. Azhar Ahmad. "Gwadar: Potential and Prospects", Islamabad: Pak Institute for Conflict and Security Studies, 2015, p. 3.
2. Ibid., p. 4.
3. Shoaib A. Rahim. "Afghanistan-Pakistan Transit Trade- Background, Legal Perspective and the Agonies of a Landlocked Country", VIF Occasional Paper, October 2017, pp. 11-12.

4. "Convention on Transit Trade of Land-locked States", United Nations Treaty Series, vol. 597, New York: United Nations, 1968, pp. 3-8.
5. Shoaib A. Rahim. op. cit., pp. 11-12.
6. Initially, Karachi was the only port available; however, after Port Qasim became operational, it was also included in the ATTA.
7. Shoaib A. Rahim. op. cit., p. 13.
8. In fact, none of the Central Asian Republics have access to the open oceans; however, Kazakhstan and Turkmenistan have access to the Caspian Sea.
9. Shoaib A. Rahim. op. cit., pp. 13-14.
10. Gilgit-Baltistan, a part of Pakistan occupied Jammu and Kashmir, is claimed by India as part of the Union Territory of Ladakh, but is under Pakistan's occupation since 1948. After the reorganisation of Jammu and Kashmir State into two Union Territories, the region is considered a part of the Union Territory of Ladakh, which is under Pakistan's illegal occupation.
11. Shoaib A. Rahim. op. cit., p. 14.
12. Javed Mirza. "Transit trade with CARs under consideration", *The News*, 17 March 2020, p. 19.
13. Ibid.
14. Ibid.
15. Shoaib A. Rahim. op. cit., pp. 5-7.
16. Javed Mirza. op. cit.
17. Shoaib A. Rahim. op. cit., p. 7.
18. "Pak-Afghan trade slips to $720.4mln in July-January", *The News on Sunday*, 22 March 2020, pp. 17-18.
19. Ibid.
20. Ibid.
21. Javed Mirza. op. cit.
22. Ariba Shahid and Asif Shahzad. "Pakistan outlines process for barter trade with Afghanistan, Iran, Russia", *Reuters*, 2 June 2023, from https://www.reuters.com/world/pakistan-engage-barter-trade-with-afghanistan-iran-russia-2023-06-02/ (Accessed on 10 July 2023).
23. "Pakistan, Afghanistan agree to boost trade, lower border tensions", *Al Jazeera*, 8 February 2023 from https://www.aljazeera.com/news/2023/5/8/pakistan-afghanistan-agree-to-boost-trade-lower-border-tensions (Accessed on 10 July 2023).
24. Meena Singh Roy. "Iran: India's Gateway to Central Asia", *Strategic Analysis*, 36(6), November–December 2012, p. 958.
25. Murray Hughes. "Opening up Afghan trade route to Iran" *Railway Gazette*, 29 January 2008, from https://www.railwaygazette.com/opening-up-afghan-trade-route-to-iran/33162.article (Accessed on 10 March 2020).
26. Ibid.
27. "Herat-Iran railway track 90% completed: Herat Officials" *Wasdam Afghan Business News Portal*, 17 September 2012, (Accessed on 11 March 2020).
28. Agha Iqrar Haroon. "Politics of Trade Corridors', *DND*, 5 November 2017.
29. Jayanth Jacob and Saubhadra Chatterji. "India's Track 3: Afghan-Iran rail link", *The Hindustan Times*, New Delhi, 1 November 2011.
30. "Chabahar Port vs Gwadar Port – Can Indian Chabahar Port Compete Against Chinese Funded Gwadar Port?" *The EurAsian Times*, 11 January 2019.

31. Roy. op. cit., 960-961.
32. Khurram Iqbal. "CPEC: A Corridor for Minimising Political Fault lines in South Asia" in Sarah Siddiq Aneel (ed.), *Changing Security Situation in South Asia and Development of CPEC*, Islamabad: Islamabad Policy Research Institute, p. 102.
33. Tariq-al-Shammari. "Dubai and Gwadar: the silent economic war in the Gulf of Oman' from https://www.opendemocracy.net/en/north-africa-west-asia/dubai-and-gwadar-silent-economic-war-in-gulf-of-oman/ (Accessed 12 December 2019).
34. Ibid.
35. Mary Sophia. "Dubai Ranks Fifth Among Top Global Destinations For Travellers", *Gulf Business*, 10 July 2014.
36. Tariq al-Shammari. op. cit.
37. Ibid.
38. Ibid.
39. Hussain Haqqani, Former Ambassador of Pakistan to the United States, Director, South & Central Asia, Hudson Institute, in reply to a question by the author in September 2020.
40. Ibid.
41 Alex Edwards. *"Dual Containment" Policy in the Persian Gulf: The USA, Iran, and Iraq, 1991–2000.* New York: Palgrave Macmillan, 2014, pp. 17-18.
42. Shibley Telhami. "The Persian Gulf: Understanding the American Oil Strategy", from Brookings Website https://www.brookings.edu/articles/the-persian-gulf-understanding-the-american-oil-strategy/ (Accessed on 21 March 2020).
43. Ibid.
44. GCC countries include Bahrain, Kuwait, Oman, Qatar, Saudi Arabia, and the United Arab Emirates. The access to most of them is through ports in the Persian Gulf.
45. "Crown Prince of Bahrain Visits NAVCENT', from US Naval Forces Central Command website, https://www.cusnc.navy.mil/Media/News/Display/Article/2101160/crown-prince-of-bahrain-visits-navcent/ (Accessed on 19 March 2020).
46. Khurram Minhas, "Expulsion of US from the Persian Gulf?", *The Nation*, 17 January 2020.
47. Nafiseh Kohnavard. "Iraq military bases: US pulling out of three key sites" *BBC*, 16 March 2020, from https://www.bbc.com/news/world-middle-east-51914600 (Accessed on 21 March 2020).
48. Michael E. O'Hanlon and Sara Allawi. "The relationship between Iraq and the US is in danger of collapse. That can't happen." From Brookings website https://www.brookings.edu/blog/order-from-chaos/2020/03/20/the-relationship-between-iraq-and-the-us-is-in-danger-of-collapse-that-cant-happen/ (Accessed on 21 March 2020).
49. "Pentagon chief, on surprise trip, says US troops to stay in Iraq", *Al Jazeera*, 7 March 2023, from https://www.aljazeera.com/news/2023/3/7/pentagon-chief-surprise-trip-says-us-troops-stay-iraq (Accessed on 10 July 2023).
50. Benjamin Roussey, "Is America Energy Self-Sufficient Yet?" from Energy Central website https://energycentral.com/c/gn/america-energy-self-sufficient-yet (Accessed on 1 March 2020).
51. "North America becomes Self-Sufficient in Oil", Rystad Energy Press Release, 7 March 2019 from https://www.rystadenergy.com/newsevents/news/press-releases/North-America-becomes-self-sufficient-in-oil/ (Accessed on 1 March 2020).
52. Maria Abi-Habib. "What China Gets for Building up Pakistan: A Military Toehold",

The New York Times, New York edition, 20 December 2018, Section A, p. 1.

53. Syed Fazl-e-Haider. "Shifting alliances in the Gulf a boon to China", from https://www.lowyinstitute.org/the-interpreter/shifting-alliances-gulf-boon-china (Accessed on 12 December 2019).
54. Hasan Yaser Malik, "Strategic Importance of Gwadar Port", *Journal of Political Studies*, vol. 19, issue 2, 2012, p. 62.
55. Frederic Grare, "Along the road: Gwadar and China's power projection" European Union Institute for Security Studies (EUISS), *Issue Brief*, July 2018, p. 3.
56. Hasan Yaser Malik. op. cit, p. 61.
57. Malik Siraj Akbar, former Editor of Baloch Haal, in reply to a question by the author in December 2020.
58. Syed Fazl-e-Haider. op. cit.
59. "Maritime coalition launched to protect Gulf shipping after Iran attacks", *Arab News*, 8 November 2019.
60. Khalid Mustafa and Muhammad Saleh Zafir. "Russia allowed use of Gwadar Port", *The News*, 26 November 2016.
61. Andrew Korybko. "This Five-Phase Strategy Can Strengthen Russian-Pakistani Trade Ties", Global Research, 28 January 2020 from https://www.globalresearch.ca/five-phase-strategy-strengthen-russian-pakistani-trade-ties/5702095 (Accessed on 1 March 2020).
62. "Pakistan, Russia to boost defence ties", *The Nation*, 8 August 2018.
63. "Pakistan, Russia cooperating to boost defence ties", *The News*, 2 December 2018.
64. Ayaz Gul. "Pakistan, Russia Sign Rare Military Cooperation Pact", from https://www.voanews.com/south-central-asia/pakistan-russia-sign-rare-military-cooperation-pact (Accessed on 1 March 2020).
65. Snehesh Alex Philip, "Russia rejects Pakistan request for 50,000 AK rifles, assures India of no deals in future", *The Print*, 17 July 2019, from https://theprint.in/defence/russia-rejects-pakistan-request-for-50000-ak-rifles-assures-india-of-no-deals-in-future/264004/ (Accessed on 1 March 2020).
66. Combined Task Force 150 (CTF-150) is a naval task force operating under the 33-nation coalition of Combined Maritime Forces and is based in Bahrain. It was established to monitor, board, inspect, and stop suspect shipping in pursuance of "Global War on Terrorism". It operates in the North Arabian Sea to support operations in the Indian Ocean. The Combined Task Force 152 or CTF-152 is a multinational naval task force, set up in 2004 to coordinate security operations in the Persian Gulf and is one of three task forces operated by Combined Maritime Forces (CMF). Amongst the European countries Belgium, the UK, France, Germany, Spain, Portugal, the Netherlands, Italy, Greece, Norway and Denmark are part of Combined Maritime Forces.
67. Frederic Grare. op. cit., p. 4.
68. "The Chinese-African relationship is important to both sides, but also unbalanced", *The Economist*, May 20, 2022.
69. Eleanor Albert. "China in Africa", Council on Foreign Relations 12 July 2017, from https://www.cfr.org/backgrounder/china-africa (Accessed on 10 July 2023).
70. Thomas P. Sheehy. "10 Things to Know about the U.S.-China Rivalry in Africa", United States Institute of Peace, 7 December 2022, from https://www.usip.org/publications/2022/12/10-things-know-about-us-china-rivalry-africa (Accessed on 10 July 2023).

6

Implications for India

The Gwadar deep sea port poses a long-term threat to India's strategic and security interests in many ways. Firstly, it creates problems for India's maritime security by embedding a major external power, namely, China, in the Northern Arabian Sea, which is an area of immense geo-economic significance. In the process, it could also erode the maritime edge that India enjoys over China in the Indian Ocean Region and eliminate Beijing's maritime vulnerabilities. More significantly, the port provides both China and Pakistan with the capability to directly threaten India's energy security and disrupt its thriving economy. In the realm of geopolitics, the presence of an external power in India's immediate vicinity has the potential to disrupt the existing power structure in South Asia, which could have long-term repercussions for India. These issues have been analysed in the succeeding paragraphs.

Erosion of India's Maritime Leverage over China

The Gwadar port project could provide China, a permanent presence in the Indian Ocean and would therefore erode the maritime edge that India enjoys over China in the Indian Ocean. At the moment, the Indian Navy has an edge over China in the Indian Ocean and this allows it to interdict Chinese shipping transiting through the Ocean, in case of any conflict. China is dependent on trade passing through the Ocean to market products coming from its huge industrial complexes. At the same time, it needs raw materials for these industries, a substantive part of which also transits through the Indian Ocean. More significantly, China is the largest importer of crude and the second largest importer of Liquefied Natural Gas (LNG) today. Most of its energy imports, whether from the Persian Gulf or Africa, traverse the Indian Ocean and pass through the Malacca Strait and other narrow straits of South East Asia. This makes its cargo extremely susceptible to interception by the Indian Navy, which can also carry out an effective blockade of these channels.[1]

Gwadar will eliminate this huge vulnerability of China and resolve its 'Malacca Dilemma', as in the case of a crisis it can transport its cargo from Gwadar and more significantly, its energy needs could be met by transporting hydrocarbons through pipelines from Gwadar to China, which are being proposed as part of the CPEC,[2] or to a limited extent by the existing road infrastructure or proposed rail link. Even more significantly, the Chinese presence at Gwadar provides it with an opportunity to interdict Indian shipping transiting to and from the Persian Gulf, should it want to do so. The bulk of India's energy imports originate in the Persian Gulf region and their non-availability could seriously jeopardize India's energy security.

On the other hand, the United Arab Emirates (UAE) is one of India's largest trading partners and a major destination for Indian exports.[3] Any maritime power, which has its presence at Gwadar, can easily interfere with these exports which are headed for the UAE. In addition, Gwadar is seen as part of China's 'String of Pearls' strategy, which includes setting up a number of military bases in the Indian Ocean Region. Once established, this would completely eradicate the locational advantage that the Indian Navy enjoys over the PLA Navy in the Indian Ocean region.

Adverse Economic Impact

Most of the Persian Gulf states have a large Indian Diaspora. A vast majority of them are businessmen and employees, who work there and remit large sums of money in foreign exchange to their families back home in India year after year. These remittances are a major source of foreign exchange for India. The Gulf Cooperation Council (GCC) countries are amongst the top sources for outward global remittances. In 2017, with $ 44 billion of outflow, the UAE was the second largest source of global remittances after the USA and was followed by Saudi Arabia with $ 36 billion in the third place. Kuwait with

$ 13.8 billion and Qatar with $ 12.8 billion were also amongst the top ten sources for global outward remittances.[4]

According to the World Bank, in 2022, India remained the largest recipient of global remittances, with inflows of $ 111 billion, posting a historic growth of 24.4 per cent over the previous year.[5] This was $ 11 billion more than forecasted by the World Bank and accounted for 3.3 per cent of the GDP. Not only for India, but for the entire South Asia, remittances were at least two to three times the FDI,[6] which reflects the significance of remittances for the region. In 2017, the Persian Gulf countries contributed $ 38.4 billion out of approximately $ 69 billion received as remittances by India.[7] Although, in 2020-21, the USA with 23 per cent share, overtook the UAE as the top source of remittances and the overall share of GCC countries in remittances received by India has come down from 54 per cent in 2016-17 to 28 per cent in 2020-21;[8] however, at over $ 31 billion, they are still a substantial amount.

As a result, any turbulence in the region could disturb this inflow into India and a perennial source of foreign exchange with it. With its presence in Gwadar just at the mouth of the Persian Gulf, China should be able to enhance its influence in the countries of the region, which are mostly ruled by autocratic rulers, who may be popular, but lack mass-based support. The growing Chinese influence and resulting tension with the USA could create massive turbulence in this region, affecting the economic activities in these countries. This in turn could lead to massive migration of Indian workers, as was seen during the two Gulf wars. Even otherwise, with its enhanced influence stemming from its presence in Gwadar, China could be in a position to influence the Gulf States to reduce the employment of Indian workers in the region. This could be a huge economic blow to the Indian economy.

In 2017, India received $ 13.823 billion as remittances from the UAE, which made it the largest source of remittances to India in the entire world.[9] Most of the Indians in the UAE live and work in Dubai, which has emerged as the business hub of the region and is also the biggest city in the Persian Gulf. As mentioned earlier, Dubai's advent as a business centre is primarily due to its emergence as a transhipment hub on account of its ports. These ports are major transportation centres of the region and virtually all the global cargo meant for the region is first unloaded here. However, as brought out earlier, if the Gwadar deep sea port emerges as a busy harbour, it has enormous locational advantages over Dubai to replace it as the transhipment hub of the region. This may result in major shipping lines calling at Gwadar and dropping Dubai from their regular liner services. This could have a catastrophic impact on Dubai's economy, as the Emirate does not have large oil reserves like Abu Dhabi. Any reduction in shipping traffic could see the hot money invested in Dubai vanish from there. This may result in the bursting of the real estate bubble and could lead Dubai in to serious economic crisis. This will force a large number of Indian expatriates earning their livelihood there to return to India, thereby drying up this perennial source of foreign exchange.

Investment in Chabahar

Considering the huge adverse impact that Gwadar could cast on Indian strategic interests, India has been collaborating with Iran to establish Chabahar port as the gateway for Central Asia. In May 2016, India signed a trilateral agreement with Afghanistan and Iran to facilitate transit to Afghanistan through Chabahar port. The agreement envisages opening of new routes, which connect Chabahar to Afghanistan and Central Asia, and making Chabahar port a regional transit hub. The strategic location of the port on the Gulf of Oman just outside the Strait of Hormuz could provide Indian cargo direct access to West Asia, Afghanistan, and the Central Asian Republics and even Russia and Mongolia, without any need of transiting though the territory of Pakistan. Like Gwadar, ships calling at Chabahar would not have to pass through the narrow and congested Strait of Hormuz, which could make it an ideal transhipment port.[10]

The port allows India to gain access to Central Asia, the trans-Caucasus region and West Asia, thereby allowing it to counter China's strategy of developing Gwadar as a strategic outpost. India is trying to augment the port facilities and has also taken over the operations of the port, so as to enhance its influence in the region. It has already committed $ 400 million worth of steel for the construction of the railway line connecting Chabahar and Zahidan near Iran's border with Afghanistan. The port and the transport linkages accrue enormous economic benefits to India as it would allow New Delhi to access huge mineral deposits in Afghanistan and Central Asia, as well as trade with the Eurasian heartland on account of its proximity to the International North-South Transport Corridor (INSTC). The port therefore allows India to reduce Pakistan's economic and political influence in Afghanistan and the Central Asian Republics.[11]

However, all these expectations from Chabahar and investments therein will be futile if Gwadar starts functioning optimally and emerges as a major transhipment port. The huge Indian investment in the Chabahar port and in establishing road and rail links from there to and from Afghanistan will become completely useless, because the international trade would invariably shift to the port that finally emerges as the ideal 'gateway' to Afghanistan and Central Asia.[12]

Making Pakistan's Maritime Blockade Difficult

Till the emergence of Gwadar port, India had an extremely significant trump card against Pakistan that the Indian Navy could easily blockade Pakistan's two main ports, namely, Karachi and Port Qasim, which were both located close to each other. In fact, the Indian Navy had clearly demonstrated its reach during the 1971 war between the two countries. During the war, it not only attacked Karachi port successfully on two different occasions, but also ensured that the Pakistan Navy, with the exception of its submarines, which were already deployed; remained completely bottled up inside the port.[13] Since then, the Indian Navy has effectively used the threat of blockade and has successfully brought Pakistan to the negotiating table. The relative dissimilarities in the size and capabilities of the two navies had further aggravated the sense of insecurity in Islamabad.

During the Kargil conflict in which Pakistani troops occupied dominating heights, it was the fear of a maritime blockade that sent Nawaz Sharif rushing to Washington DC, to seek intervention of the US President to end hostilities. During the conflict, the Indian Navy had launched Operation Talwar to blockade Pakistan's ports. The operation resulted in the largest ever deployment of warships in the North Arabian Sea. The Western Fleet, which had adequate platforms and fire power to deal with the Pakistan Navy, was further bolstered by reinforcing it with the ships from the Eastern Fleet.[14] This threatened Pakistan's economic survival and set the alarm bells ringing both in Islamabad as well as in Rawalpindi, where Pakistan's General Headquarters are located. According to Nawaz Sharif, who was the prime minister of Pakistan during the Kargil conflict, the fuel stock in Pakistan had come down to such an abysmally low level that it could barely last for six days in case of a full-fledged war.[15]

However, with a functioning Gwadar port, any blockade by the Indian Navy will be extremely difficult. Firstly, it will require two different forces to blockade Karachi and Port Bin Qasim as well as Gwadar and Ormara. Secondly, on account of Gwadar being quite far from the Indian coast, it will be much more difficult to blockade the port, as it would be extremely difficult to provide continuous shore-based air support to any naval force blockading the port. Thirdly, Gwadar's proximity to major global shipping lanes of the world will make identification of targets fairly difficult and could bring international pressure to lift the blockade. More significantly, with the Chinese presence at the port, the authorities in Islamabad as well as its military hierarchy perceive that India would not be in a position to blockade the port, as it would make China a stakeholder in the functioning of the port and could bring the PLA Navy of China into the game. As a result Pakistan is now far more confident about withstanding any threat of blockade by India and consequently, far more belligerent.

Gwadar is perceived as part of China's 'String of Pearls' strategy, which includes building of seaports in Bangladesh, Myanmar, Malaysia, and Sri Lanka. These sea ports are seen as part of China's strategy to surround India.[16] Many Indian military analysts perceive these ports as China's southern and eastern pincers, while developments in Pakistan and Central Asia are viewed as its western and northern pincers, which are all aimed at strategic encirclement of India. Pakistan on the other hand perceives Indian investments in Afghanistan, Tajikistan, and Iran, as an Indian attempt at Pakistan's encirclement.[17] Consequently, it perceives the Chinese military presence in Gwadar as some sort of security insurance for itself. According to a Pakistani military officer, the Chinese naval presence at Gwadar will immensely bolster Pakistan's coastal defence.[18]

Consequently, as and when Gwadar starts functioning as a thriving port, with a significant Chinese presence, the threat of a maritime blockade that could throttle its economy would virtually vanish for Pakistan. Thus, the Gwadar deep sea port will result in India losing a big leverage against Pakistan.

India's Energy Security

India is the fastest growing large economy in the world and its GDP having grown by 7.2 per cent in 2022 is expected to grow by 6.3 per cent in 2023.[19]

This growing economy requires energy for economic growth and sustainable development. Energy plays a significant role in the economic and social development of any country and its role has got further enhanced in view of the changing climate patterns. In India's case, several factors, like growing population and technological developments, could further enhance the energy demand in the foreseeable future.[20]Although India has been trying to diversify its energy mix, many sectors of its economy, especially the transport sector, is mostly dependent on hydrocarbons. Unfortunately, India is the most populous country of the world, with 17 per cent of the global population but barely has 0.8 per cent of the proven oil and natural gas reserves of the globe. Consequently, India's petroleum sector depends overwhelmingly on import of crude, as India has adequate refining capacity to meet local demand of refined products. India is today the world's third-largest importer and consumer of petroleum and consumes approximately 3.9 million barrels per day. According to the Petroleum Planning and Analysis Cell, 198 million tonnes of crude oil worth $ 62.7 billion was imported in 2020–21, a yearly increase of 22 per cent.[21]

The problem has been further aggravated on account of the Russia-Ukraine war and attempts by the OPEC-plus to increase the cost of crude by production cuts. According to Hardeep Singh Puri, Minister of Petroleum and Natural Gas, India has tried to tide over the problem by diversification of energy supplies; increasing India's exploration and production footprint; alternate energy sources and meeting energy transition through gas-based economy, green hydrogen and EVs. India increased the number of its crude oil suppliers from 27 countries in 2006-07 to 39 in 2021-22, adding countries like Colombia, Russia, Libya, Gabon, Equatorial Guinea, etc., to the list of existing suppliers, besides strengthening relationship with countries like the USA and Russia. India has also been trying to cut its crude imports by blending petrol with ethanol and has achieved over 10 per cent blending and hopes to achieve the target of 20 per cent by 2025-26.[22] However, in spite of all these efforts, the share of imported crude in India increased to a record 87.3 per cent of domestic consumption in 2022-23, from 85.5 per cent in 2021-22.[23]

Despite the diversification and large-scale import of Russian crude at discounted rates, Iraq and Saudi Arabia remained the largest source of Indian crude imports. The UAE, Kuwait, Oman, and Qatar also figure in the top

15 import destinations of crude for India. As a result, in 2022, over 57 per cent of India's crude imports originated in the Persian Gulf region.[24] Besides crude oil, India also imports almost half of its requirements of liquefied natural gas (LNG). In 2021, 42 per cent of it was sourced from Qatar, 13 per cent from the UAE and 5 per cent from Oman, making a total of 60 per cent from just three countries of the Persian Gulf region.[25] This share is bound to increase as and when the US sanctions on Iran are lifted and the conflict in Ukraine comes to an end.

As brought out earlier, most of India's energy imports originate in various ports of the Persian Gulf and the bulk of these imports are offloaded at the single point mooring (SPM) at Vadinar in the Gulf of Kutch from where it is transferred to various refineries through pipelines. The sea line of communication (SLOC) connecting the Persian Gulf with the Gulf of Kutch passes less than 40 nm from Gwadar and consequently, tankers travelling along the SLOC would be extremely vulnerable to interception from Gwadar, in case of any conflict with Pakistan. The surveillance facilities at the port and naval assets positioned there would also enable the Pakistan Navy to monitor Indian ships leaving and entering the Persian Gulf and interdict them, if and when the need arises. This could give Islamabad, a strong leverage to pressurise India to accommodate Pakistan on contentious issues.

Impact on South Asian Balance of Power

South Asia has acquired greater salience in the post-Cold War era on account of its unique characteristics, which span the complete gamut of human activities varying from cultural, economic and social affairs to political and strategic matters. The presence of major global powers, multinational corporations (MNCs) and various international and regional institutions, have drawn global attention towards South Asia, where diplomacy, economy, and security blend together to create a complex scenario.[26] The security situation in the region is continuously transforming; consequently, the security threat which primarily emanated from external actors during the Cold War era has been confined to that emanating primarily from internal actors. Although, the rivalry between India and Pakistan continues unabated, internal disorders remain a major security threat to most South Asian states. Ethnic tensions tend to exacerbate when there are no threats from abroad, or external threats have diminished.[27]

India has been the dominant power of the region, which has acquired some sort of security equilibrium and there has been no major inter-state clash for decades; however, new developments could disturb the existing equilibrium and status quo.

South Asia has been a volatile region, where the security situation has been in a flux. The Afghanistan-Pakistan border continues to be the epicentre of global terror. Terrorism and radicalisation have become endemic to the region. The region is also home to lingering territorial disputes.[28] The region has within its confines two nuclear powers, which have been engaged in armed conflicts and border skirmishes for the last seven decades. In the recent past, China has increased its interaction with the region through different components of the Belt and Road Initiative (BRI) and has been trying to promote its own version of global integration.[29]

India has a dominant position in the power structure of South Asia. It shares either a land or maritime boundary with all the states in the region, whereas most other states do not share boundaries with other states of the region. This unique geography of India coupled with its size, population, economy, and military power give it tremendous influence over most countries of South Asia, with the sole exception of Pakistan, with which it has had an adversarial relationship. Its dominant position has also been recognised by the USA, which sees it as a net security provider in the region and has assigned it the status of a de facto nuclear power, by signing the Indo-US Nuclear Deal.[30] Pakistan perceives its ties with China as a 'strategic hedge' against a rapidly growing India.[31] It assesses that the Gwadar deep sea port and the Chinese presence there, coupled with the China Pakistan Economic Corridor (CPEC) will inextricably tie China's security interests with those of Pakistan. It also feels that the Chinese presence in Gwadar will make it a permanent stake holder in South Asia, which will break the Indian hegemony over the region.

Apart from Pakistan, other South Asian states have generally had good relations with India and look up to India as a 'net security provider'. They could be considered to be under India's sphere of influence. Among South Asian countries, apart from Pakistan, Afghanistan, Bhutan, and Nepal share borders with China. Except for Bhutan, all South Asian countries, including India have a thriving economic relationship with Beijing. Similarly, not only Pakistan, but also Afghanistan, Bangladesh, the Maldives, Nepal, and Sri Lanka have joined the BRI, leaving only India and Bhutan out of it. These countries have huge Chinese investments and some of them have also been burdened with huge Chinese debts. Despite China's huge economic impact in the region, most of the countries by and large support India as far as security and international relations are concerned. This has been on account of India's proximity, historical linkages, cultural similarities, and the overwhelming superiority of the Indian security infrastructure.

As brought out earlier, remittances from the Gulf region are extremely important for most of the South Asian countries and are significantly higher than the FDI. The Chinese presence at Gwadar will enable China and Pakistan to have greater influence on the Gulf States, which could impact the flow of remittances from the region. This coupled with their ability to interrupt the trade of these states with the Gulf region, could prevent other South Asian states from sticking to their pro-India stance.

Similarly, Gwadar port could provide the countries of the Trans-Caucasus region an avenue to trade with the littorals of the Indian Ocean Region (IOR). Presently, the trade of the Trans-Caucasus region with South Asia or Africa is quite insignificant and this could change with Gwadar emerging as a vibrant commercial hub. More significantly, this would give other countries of South Asia an opportunity to boost their negligible trade with countries of the Trans-Caucasus region and Central Asia. The increased trade through Gwadar could make them dependent on Pakistan, which could result in their assuming a more neutral stance in any disputes between India and Pakistan.[32]

Gwadar provides China a permanent presence in South Asia and makes it a de facto South Asian power. According to Hussain Haqqani, the former Pakistani Ambassador to the USA, the Chinese control over Gwadar implies the PLA's presence there, especially the naval and air arm of the PLA. According to him, Chinese submarines have already visited the port.[33] According to Baloch journalist Malik Siraj Akbar, it provides China the space "to impress the Pakistanis with its capabilities and remind its rivals, mainly India and the USA, of its presence at a port of immense geostrategic significance".[34]

According to Ayesha Siddiqa, Gwadar is a security base for China in the Arabian Sea, which could be used in times of crisis.[35] This presence, coupled with China's enormous economic muscle, could result in shifting of loyalties within South Asia. With the massive infusion of funds, China has successfully created a pro-China lobby in most South Asian states. Consequently, a Chinese presence in Gwadar could exacerbate fault lines between India and its other South Asian neighbours and move them away from New Delhi, thereby disturbing the carefully cultivated influence by India in its neighbourhood.

Impact on Approach of Extra-Regional Powers

There are many extra-regional powers, which have a permanent/semi-permanent presence in South Asia's vicinity and have historically influenced developments in the region. In the recent past, they have generally looked at the region through New Delhi's prism, as India has been unquestionably, the dominant power. However, not only these extra-regional powers and their influence will be affected by varying degrees by the Gwadar deep sea port project, but their approach also towards India and other countries of South Asia might undergo a significant change. This could in turn impact India's relationship with its neighbours and consequently, its security.

The USA continues to be the strongest extra-regional power in the IOR, of which South Asia is an integral part. The USA has a large military presence in the Indo-Pacific region and its military bases in the Persian Gulf and Diego Garcia are in the vicinity of South Asia. The Gwadar port provides China a listening post to monitor US naval activities in the Persian Gulf.[36] According to a Pakistani defence analyst, the presence of the PLA Navy at this critical choke point not only prevents Indo-US domination of the Indian Ocean, but also makes China a credible naval power of the region.[37] According to Malik Siraj Akbar, China's growing presence in the region threatens American interests. However, the USA and other Western countries have not offered much resistance to China as far as the port project is concerned, possibly due to their lack of interest or as they have not yet understood the full impact of the project.[38]

From the viewpoint of the USA, Gwadar, as part of the BRI, has clearly indicated China's strategic interests in the Indo-Pacific Region. The port's development and operation gives Chinese naval power a strong foothold in the Indian Ocean and threatens the US supremacy and brings it closer to India.[39] India's proximity to the global superpower influences other South Asian states to a great extent, as far as their relations with India are concerned. However, if China manages to challenge American supremacy and consequently erodes its influence in the region, it could create problems for India's dominance in South Asia.

Another extra-regional power, which is likely to be affected, is Russia, which had historically very good relations with India and some other countries of the region. It also had a long military presence in Afghanistan. The radical Islamist ideology emanating from Afghanistan-Pakistan impacts Russia's soft underbelly. More significantly, at this moment, the countries of Central Asia and the Trans-Caucasus region are overwhelmingly dependent on Russia for their economic sustenance as well as external trade. However, once Gwadar starts functioning as a major transhipment hub, these countries will find newer avenues of trading with Asia and Africa, and this could reduce their dependence on Moscow and reduce its influence on them.

More significantly, Russia, which has been promoting the International North–South Transport Corridor (INSTC), in conjunction with India and Iran, to access the warm water ports on the Iranian coast for its trade with Asia and Africa, will also look at Gwadar to access these regions. It has been reported that Russia has sought permission from Pakistan to use Gwadar port for its exports to the region. According to the Pakistani media, Islamabad has approved the usage of the Gwadar port by Russia for trade allowing Russia round-the-year access to the warm waters of the Arabian Sea. More significantly, Russia has apparently shown a desire to join the CPEC, "to reap the maximum dividends." This could lead to greater strategic ties between Russia and Pakistan,[40] which could impact Russia's relations with India.

Russia has already agreed to help Pakistan construct a railway line from Quetta to Taftan on its border with Iran and is reportedly investing $ 14 billion in Pakistan's energy sector. It is also financing a north-south pipeline with an investment of $ 2.5 billion. The two countries have started coordinating their policies on Afghanistan and have already commenced joint anti-terrorism drills.[41] Russia and its predecessor, the USSR, have traditionally backed India in South Asia and it has been the largest supplier of defence hardware to India. Russia is generally perceived to be a time-tested ally of India, but all that seems to be changing and India could lose its long-term strategic partnership with Russia. A Russia-Pakistan Joint Military Consultative Committee (JMCC) was established in 2018 to boost defence ties and strengthen, expand and diversify mutual cooperation.[42]

The Russian Navy and the Pakistan Navy are already carrying out joint exercises, called Arabian Monsoon, since 2014. The ships of the two navies have been visiting ports in each other's country.[43] Russia has already supplied Pakistan four Mi-35M combat helicopters and has agreed to train Pakistan's army officers.[44] According to Russian authorities, Pakistan had also sought 50,000 AK 47 rifles from Russia, which apparently was rejected by Russia, due to Indian sensitivities. Pakistan has also shown interest in acquiring T90 tanks and new air defence systems from Russia.[45] Gwadar's emergence as a 'gateway' to Central Asia could bring the two countries closer at the cost of India.

The European powers had a strong presence in South Asia during the colonial period and enjoy tremendous influence on account of their colonial legacy, not only in South Asia, but in the entire IOR. France still has a significant presence in the Indian Ocean both in terms of territory as well as forces. Similarly, the UK has territory in the Indian Ocean. Both these countries have a significant presence in South Asia's vicinity in West Asia and the Indian Ocean. Many European countries import oil from the Persian Gulf and have huge commercial as well as strategic interests in this region. As colonial powers, many of them have strong people-to-people connect with the region. Many citizens of these countries reside in the region and many European companies have their establishments in the region. Consequently, the security of this region is important for them and as a result many of them have sent their naval forces to patrol the North Arabian Sea and the Persian Gulf as part of Combined Task Force 150 and/or Combined Task Force 152.[46]

The presence of China in Gwadar presents the European nations with a new regional dynamic that will in all probability affect the power equation in the region. If Gwadar emerges as a fully developed vibrant port, with Chinese presence along with their anti-access and area denial capabilities, then it would definitely enhance China's leverage in the region. This would simultaneously reduce the influence of other traditional powers including the European countries. In case of any conflict with Iran, Gwadar could easily threaten the sea lanes passing through the Strait of Hormuz, thereby affecting vital European interests. A fully developed Gwadar deep sea port, with a Chinese presence, therefore poses direct as well as indirect conventional and non-conventional threats to European interests.[47] This could push European powers, especially erstwhile colonial powers like the UK and France to see closer cooperation with India.

To sum up, the Gwadar deep sea port could transform the geo-strategic environment in India's vicinity in a manner that could be highly detrimental to India's interests. It could pose a direct threat to India's energy security, while reducing India's capability to deal with China and Pakistan in the maritime domain. It could greatly diminish India's influence in the Indian Ocean Region in general and India's vicinity in particular. It also has the potential to adversely impact India's economy.

NOTES

1. H.I. Sutton. "Could The Indian Navy Strangle China's Lifeline In The Malacca Strait?", Forbes, 8 July 2020, from https://www.forbes.com/sites/hisutton/2020/07/08/could-the-indian-navy-strangle-chinas-lifeline-in-the-malacca-strait/?sh=2d40cbb478e8 (Accessed on 15 May 2021).
2. Frederic Grare. "Along the road: Gwadar and China's power projection", European Union Institute for Security Studies, Issue Brief 7/2018, July 2018, p. 3.
3. The UAE is India's second largest export destination and third largest source of imports.
4. "Migration and Remittances: Recent Developments and outlook", *Migration and Development Brief 31*, April 2019, Washington DC, KNOMAD-World Bank, p. 4.
5. Dilip Ratha et al. "Remittances Remain Resilient but Are Slowing", *Migration and Development Brief 38*, June 2023, Washington DC, KNOMAD-World Bank, p. 4.
6. Ibid., pp. 27-28.
7. "Remittance flows worldwide in 2017", Pew Research Centre, Global Attitudes and Trends, 3 April 2019.
8. Dilip Ratha et al. "Remittances Brave Global Headwinds. Special Focus: Climate Migration", *Migration and Development Brief 37*, November 2022, Washington DC, KNOMAD-World Bank, p. 47.
9. "Remittance flows worldwide in 2017", Pew Research Centre, Global Attitudes and Trends, 3 April 2019.
10. Syed Fazl-e-Haider. "Shifting alliances in the Gulf a boon to China", from https://www.lowyinstitute.org/the-interpreter/shifting-alliances-gulf-boon-china (Accessed on 12 December 2019).
11. "India's Chabahar port plan is to counter China's plan to develop Gwadar port: Media", *The Economic Times*, 12 July 2018.
12. Alok Bansal. "Gwadar Port: A South Asian Gateway for Central Asia?" in K. Warikoo (ed.), *Central Asia and South Asia: Energy Cooperation and Transport Linkages*. New Delhi: Pentagon Press, 2011, p. 265.
13. Arun Prakash. "From Karachi To Bay of Bengal, How the Indian Navy Played a Stellar Role in the 1971 War", *The Wire*, 5 April 2021, from https://thewire.in/security/1971-series-indian-navy-bangladesh-war-stellar-role-arun-prakash (Accessed 19 May 2021).
14. Srikant Kesnur and Digvijay Sinh Sodha. "Operation Talwar: How the Navy silently

contributed to Kargil win", *The Asian Age*, Mumbai, 4 December 2019.

15. Siddhi Gaharwar. "Did you know Indian Navy too played a rather unsung role during Kargil War? Know all about Operation Talwar", from https://www.timesnownews.com/india/article/did-you-know-indian-navy-too-played-a-rather-unsung-role-during-kargil-war-all-about-operation-talwar/459303 (Accessed on 1 March 2020).
16. Sulman Ali. "Pakistan-China Gwadar Port Agreement: Balance of Power Game in South Asia", *South Asian Voices*, 20 May 2015 from https://southasianvoices.org/pakistan-china-gwadar-port-agreement-balance-of-power-game-in-south-asia/ (Accessed on 18 February 2021).
17. Rory Daniels. "Strategic Competition in South Asia: Gwadar, Chabahar and the Risks of Infrastructure Development", *American Foreign Policy Interests*: The Journal of the National Committee on American Foreign Policy, 35 (2), 25 March 2013, p. 94.
18. Hasan Yaser Malik. "Strategic Importance of Gwadar Port", *Journal of Political Studies*, vol. 19, issue 2, 2012, p. 62.
19. "ADB lowers India GDP growth outlook for this fiscal to 6.3%", *The Hindu*, Delhi, 21 September 2023, p. 20.
20. Sourabh Kumar. "Evaluation and analysis of India's energy security: A policy perspective", *Energy*, vol. 278, part B, article 127993, 1 September 2023.
21. Ibid.
22. "India's 4-plank energy security strategy is based on diversifying supplies, increasing E&P, alternate energy sources and energy transition through a gas-based economy, Green Hydrogen, etc." Ministry of Petroleum & Natural Gas press release posted by PIB on 10 January 2023 from https://www.pib.gov.in/PressReleasePage.aspx?PRID=1889967#:~:text=India%20has%20been%20able%20 to,sources%20and%20meeting%20energy%20transition (Accessed on 6 September 2023).
23. Sukalp Sharma. "India reliance on imported crude oil at record high of 87.3% in FY23", *Indian Express*, 25 April 2023.
24. Daniel Workman. "Crude Oil Imports by Country", World's Top Exports, from https://www.worldstopexports.com/crude-oil-imports-by-country/#google_vignette (Accessed on 21 September 2023).
25. "Distribution of liquefied natural gas imported into India in 2021, by country of origin", from https://www.statista.com/statistics/1237488/lng-import-share-india-by-country/ (Accessed on 21 September 2023).
26. Irfan Mahar. "Changing Security Dynamics of South Asia: Implication for the Security of the region", *Eurasia Review News & Analysis*, 16 April 2020, from https://www.eurasiareview.com/16042020-changing-security-dynamics-of-south-asia-implication-for-the-security-of-region-oped/ (Accessed on 31 August 2020).
27. Aakriti Tandon and Michael O. Slobodchikoff. "Security in South Asia", *The Round Table*, vol. 108, issue 2 (2019), p. 117.
28. Abdul Basit et al. "Introduction" in Sarah Siddiq Aneel (ed.) *Changing Security Situation in South Asia and Development of CPEC*, Islamabad: Islamabad Policy Research Institute, 2018, p. vi.
29. Zahid Khan et al. "CPEC: A Game Changer in the Balance of Power in South Asia" *China Quarterly of International Strategic Studies*, vol. 4, issue 4, April 2019, p. 598.
30. Syed Rifaat Hussain, (2018), "South Asian Security and CPEC: A Pakistani Perspective" in Sarah Siddiq Aneel (ed.), *Changing Security Situation in South Asia and Development*

of CPEC, Islamabad: Islamabad Policy Research Institute, 2018, pp. 45-46.

31. Ibid., p. 51.
32. At the moment most South Asian countries tend to side with India, in various disputes between India and Pakistan. This phenomenon has been more pronounced since 2014.
33. Hussain Haqqani on 4 September 2020 by personal email, in reply to a questionnaire sent by the author.
34. Malik Siraj Akbar on 20 December 2020 by personal email, in reply to a questionnaire sent by the author.
35. Ayesha Siddiqa on 13 September 2020 by personal email, in reply to a questionnaire sent by the author.
36. Hasan Yaser Malik. op. cit.
37. Ibid., p. 61.
38. Malik Siraj Akbar. op. cit.
39. Zahid Khan et al. op. cit., p. 611.
40. Khalid Mustafa and Muhammad Saleh Zafir. "Russia allowed use of Gwadar Port", *The News*, Karachi, 26 November 2016.
41. Andrew Korybko, "This Five-Phase Strategy Can Strengthen Russian-Pakistani Trade Ties", *Global Research*, 28 January 2020, from https://www.globalresearch.ca/five-phase-strategy-strengthen-russian-pakistani-trade-ties/5702095 (Accessed on 1 March 2020).
42. "Pakistan, Russia to boost defence ties", *The Nation*, Lahore, 8 August 2018.
43. "Pakistan, Russia cooperating to boost defence ties", *The News*, Karachi, 2 December 2018.
44. Ayaz Gul. "Pakistan, Russia Sign Rare Military Cooperation Pact", *Voice of America*, 8 August 2018 from https://www.voanews.com/south-central-asia/pakistan-russia-sign-rare-military-cooperation-pact (Accessed on 1 March 2020).
45. Snehesh Alex Philip. "Russia rejects Pakistan request for 50,000 AK rifles, assures India of no deals in future", *The Print*, 17 July 2019, from https://theprint.in/defence/russia-rejects-pakistan-request-for-50000-ak-rifles-assures-india-of-no-deals-in-future/264004/ (Accessed on 1 March 2020).
46. Combined Task Force 150 (CTF-150) is a naval task force operating under the 33-nation coalition of Combined Maritime Forces and is based in Bahrain. It was established to monitor, board, inspect, and stop suspect shipping in pursuance of "Global War on Terrorism" It operates in the North Arabian Sea to support operations in the Indian Ocean. The Combined Task Force 152 or CTF-152 is a multinational naval task force, set up in 2004 to coordinate security operations in the Persian Gulf and is one of three task forces operated by Combined Maritime Forces (CMF). Amongst the European countries, Belgium, the UK, France, Germany, Spain, Portugal, the Netherlands, Italy, Greece, Norway and Denmark are part of Combined Maritime Force.
47. Frederic Grare. "Along the road: Gwadar and China's power projection", European Union Institute for Security Studies, Issue Brief //2018, July 2018, p. 4.

7

Conclusion

In July 2023, as China and Pakistan celebrated a decade of the CPEC, Beijing claimed that the CPEC has already attracted around $ 24.5 billion and has generated around 192,000 jobs, built over 500 km of highways and power transmission network of 886 km, besides adding 6,000 MW of power. Of the six economic corridors of the BRI, it has made phenomenal progress as energy, industrial and infrastructural projects worth $ 25 billion have been executed.[1] However, it has become quite clear that Gwadar is the lynchpin of this initiative, which in itself is a crucial artery of the BRI. Consequently, the success of Gwadar deep sea port is essential to the economic viability of the CPEC and thereby of the BRI.

The port is an ambitious project in a remote part of Pakistan, which aims to revive the economies of Pakistan and China's western region. Both China and Pakistan visualise it as a solution to the problems of underdevelopment and backwardness in their remote sparsely populated regions of Xinjiang and Balochistan, respectively. The two countries also hope that the project will trigger development in these two provinces and assuage the hurt feelings of the populations in these restive provinces. The CPEC is expected to make this remote port economically viable by generating trade at the port and triggering other economic activities. To further bolster Pakistan's economy and to prevent stoppage of work, Beijing has provided loans worth 30 million Yuan and has established a currency swap arrangement.

Pakistan strives to nurture its blue economy through the Gwadar Port, which it claims has undergone a remarkable metamorphosis and has emerged as a key component of this ambitious initiative. Policy makers in Islamabad keep projecting that Gwadar is emerging as a fully operational maritime hub that would link Pakistan to the world and bolster trade and commerce in the region.[2] However, local residents are not convinced and have been opposing it tooth and nail. The genesis of their opposition lies in the peculiar geography of Gwadar and the chequered history of its inhabitants – The Baloch.

Gwadar has been an isolated town and a fishing port in the remote and barren Makran coast, which is a part of Balochistan province. Its rugged geography makes access to the port extremely difficult. Consequently, it has had a chequered history. It was contested by the Greeks as well as the Mauryan Empire, subsequently annexed by the Sassanid Empire and finally by the Caliphate. In the recent past, Gwadar was a territory of Oman, a gift from the Khan of Kalat to a fleeing prince. Oman was pressurised by the British to hand over Gwadar to Pakistan for a monetary consideration. At that point of time, the British had de facto control over the Sultan and were responsible for Oman's defence. Consequently, the Sultan of Oman was in no position to resist and eventually handed over Gwadar to Pakistan in 1958 after ruling over it for 174 years. Despite a change in political control, Gwadar's linkages with Oman remain to this day and many people from Gwadar and its surrounding areas serve in the armed forces of the Sultanate.

The early history of the Baloch is fairly obscure. The Baloch emerged as a distinct political entity only in the twelfth century, further consolidated in the fifteenth century and finally emerged as a distinct political entity in the seventeenth century, when the Khanate (the princely state, whose ruler was called the Khan) of Kalat brought diverse tribes under one administration. It was Nasir Khan, the sixth ruler of Kalat, who succeeded in bringing various Baloch tribes and most of their land under his rule and thereby consolidated the Baloch national identity.

During the colonial period, the traditional Baloch land was divided amongst three different countries. The Goldsmid Line in 1871 gave away almost one fourth of Baloch land to Iran, while the Durand Line in 1893 gave away a part to Afghanistan. The Baloch in all the three countries consider themselves to be one and follow similar cultural traits, although, they speak two distinct languages Balochi and Brahui, which belong to different linguistic groups. According to geomorphologists, this huge land mass is a part of Central Asia. The region also exhibits enormous physical diversity from snow-capped mountains in the north to a rugged coast line in the South with lush green valleys and barren deserts in the middle.

The region is full of natural resources and its vast mineral wealth has not been exploited optimally. More significantly, the locals continue to live in abject poverty in this resource- rich but sparsely populated region. Pakistan wants to tap the vast resources of this region by developing and bringing it into the economic mainstream to revive its own sagging economy. The Makran coast, which encompasses Gwadar and the entire coast of Balochistan, is an extremely dry region, which does not support agriculture and, consequently, the main occupation is cattle rearing for most of the population. The region is also rich in marine life and fish is accordingly an important ingredient of the staple diet of the people.

Gwadar has always been a significant port on the Makran coast and was a battle ground between Iranian and Turanian kings. It has been mentioned by all famous travellers who traversed the region like Ibn Batuta, Marco Polo, and the Turkish admiral, Sidi Ali. All of them have talked about the inhospitable nature of the weather and the terrain in the vicinity of the port, which discouraged invaders from residing permanently in the area. Alexander's admiral, Nearchus, also described the region as extremely dry and mountainous.

Despite its extremely arid climate and inhospitable terrain, the British colonial masters realised the strategic significance of the Gwadar port and established a telegraph office there and ran regular steamer services to the port. Even, before Gwadar and its surrounding areas were transferred to the newly-created state of Pakistan by the Sultanate of Oman, the US Geological Survey, which surveyed the coast of Pakistan, identified Gwadar as the ideal location for the establishment of a deep sea port. Consequently, from the time, Gwadar was given to Pakistan, its rulers have wanted to set up a big port there. However, financial, technical, and institutional constraints prevented it from fructifying.

Gwadar was also eyed by the Soviet Union when its army was present in Afghanistan. Many believe that a warm water port at Gwadar was their ultimate objective. However, it was the very disintegration of the Soviet Union and emergence of the new Central Asian Republics that brought the focus back to Gwadar. A port at Gwadar was considered as the ideal gateway for tapping the markets of the Central Asian Republics as well as for harnessing their immense natural resources, including hydrocarbons. Consequently, the government of Pakistan decided to set up a deep sea port at Gwadar in 1991, the year the Soviet Union disintegrated. However, acute political and economic instability prevailing in Pakistan prevented the work from commencing till 2001. It was eventually China's interest in the port that led to the project seeing the light of the day. China's financial and technical support enabled an impoverished Pakistan to undertake such an ambitious and massive project.

Situated at the cusp of the Strait of Hormuz through which most of the world's oil flows, the Gwadar deep sea port project being completed with financial assistance from China is the largest developmental project being undertaken in Pakistan and has enormous economic potential. At a time when the energy demand in both South Asia and China is rising sharply and expected to double in the coming decade; the port along with the Trans-Karakoram pipeline creates a huge potential for business and opens up new opportunities for tapping the vast energy resources of the landlocked region that surrounds the Caspian Sea. Consequently, the port has the potential to become a big business hub like Dubai and change the landscape of Balochistan. Various economic activities associated with the port and the CPEC have the potential to take the Pakistani economy to great heights.

Despite Gwadar's enormous potential, there is no dearth of sceptics who doubt its ability to deliver. The underlying reason behind such apprehensions is that notwithstanding its huge potential, the port cannot attain economic viability till it is connected to Quetta by road or rail for it to emerge as a bridgehead to Central Asia. Similarly as far as China or even access to Central Asia through China is concerned its viability depends on the timely completion of the Gwadar-Ratodero motorway. The use of the Makran coastal highway to transport goods does not make commercial sense because it almost amounts to taking goods to Karachi by road which could be done much more economically by sea.

Gwadar's prospects of emerging as the future hub of trade and energy transportation for the vibrant economies of East, South and West Asia as well as landlocked Central Asia, therefore depends wholly on cutting down transportation costs and time taken to reach the port. However, it is not feasible to achieve it as long as the restive population of Balochistan does not feel enthusiastic about the potential of Gwadar port. As long as violence continues, Pakistan cannot emerge as an energy corridor to China nor can a direct road link to Central Asia be established. Not only does violence affect investor confidence, it also affects the implementation of infrastructural projects, especially the pipelines, roads and rail links, which cannot be perpetually defended in their entirety.

Gwadar is the first major port outside the Karachi-Port Bin Qasim complex and removes a critical vulnerability as it will provide Pakistan with another option to disembark vital supplies in case of non-availability of the Karachi-Bin Qasim complex either due to natural disasters, accidents or naval blockade. The port is connected by the newly-constructed Makran coastal highway (653 km) from Sheikh Raj, approximately 105 km north of Karachi to Gabd near the Pak-Iran border. This highway links the ports at Ormara, Pasni, Gwadar, and Jiwani with Karachi and has the potential to boost trade between Pakistan and Iran. Another road link in the pipeline is the Gwadar-Ratodero motorway which would join the Indus highway through Turbat, Awaran, and Khuzdar.

A rail link is also being planned to connect the Gwadar Port to Quetta and Zahidan. The port along with the communication links is expected to boost economic development in a region that has remained most backward in Pakistan. The Asian Development Bank (ADB)'s Ports Master Plan studies considered Gwadar to be the best alternative to the Persian Gulf ports in terms of location, which could handle mother ships and large oil tankers, to capture the transit trade of the Central Asian Republics as well as the trans-shipment trade of the region.

The port, due to its location at the entrance of the Persian Gulf, has immense geo-strategic significance. It provides the shortest and cost-effective access to the landlocked Afghanistan and Central Asian Republics. The continued unstable regional environment in the Persian Gulf after the Gulf war and the emergence of the new Central Asian States has added to the importance of this port. Pakistan has been interested in the project to seek strategic depth further to the southwest from its major naval base in Karachi that has always been vulnerable to the Indian Navy on account of its proximity to the Indian coast. To diversify the site of its naval and commercial assets,

Pakistan has already built a naval base at Ormara, the Jinnah Naval Base, which has been in operation since June 2000. It can berth about a dozen ships, submarines and similar harbour craft. The Gwadar port project, however, is billed to crown the Pakistan Navy and make it a force that can rival regional navies. The government of Pakistan has accordingly designated the port area as a 'sensitive defence zone.'

Apart from its enormous geostrategic importance, the project is the cornerstone of economic development in Pakistan and specifically in Balochistan. It has the potential to change the landscape of this backward region and the fortunes of its people. The major economic benefits that the authorities perceive from the project are opportunities for trade with China, the Central Asian States, and Afghanistan, promotion of trade and transport with the Gulf states and evolution of the port as a trans-shipment hub for computerised cargo. The port is planned to be linked with the hinterland in Pakistan, as well as with Xinjiang in China, the Central Asian Republics and Afghanistan through a network of roads and railways. The development of townships and other civic facilities at Gwadar has already been started by the Gwadar Development Authority under a master plan. The Pakistani government, with the aim of attracting foreign investment in the region, has permitted China and South Korea to set up tax-free special industrial development zones near Gwadar port.

China's keen interest in the port and associated infrastructure, as well as its involvement in the construction and subsequent operations has raised numerous questions about its motives. China has always tried to portray the CPEC of which the Gwadar deep sea port is the most important component, as purely an economic venture, devoid of any security underpinnings. However, the strategic location of Gwadar makes it impossible to ignore other geo-strategic and geo-political advantages that China could reap from the fulfilment of this project.

The CPEC constitutes one of the six corridors that comprise the ambitious Belt and Road Initiative (BRI) of China. The primary objective of the CPEC is to link the trading town of Kashgar in the Xinjiang Uyghur Autonomous Region in Western China to the Gwadar deep sea port on the Arabian Sea in the Balochistan province of Pakistan. This is to be achieved through parallel networks of infrastructure, energy projects, and gas and oil pipelines, which originate at Gwadar and converge at Khunjerab Pass in the Karakoram Mountain Range, on China's border with Gilgit-Baltistan, which is presently under the occupation of Pakistan.

The Gwadar deep sea port project is the lynchpin of the CPEC and, consequently, the very success of the CPEC depends on its successful completion and optimal operation. On account of its strategic location near the Persian Gulf, at the cross-section of South, West, and Central Asia, Gwadar holds immense strategic, security and economic significance for China. More significantly, Gwadar offers a link between the Silk Road Economic Belt and the 21st century Maritime Silk Road, and can be regarded as the very fulcrum of the BRI.

China's economic interests in Gwadar are threefold. Firstly, it aims to completely integrate Pakistan's tottering economy into its own. It hopes to do so by outsourcing low-end, labour intensive, resource-intensive and polluting industrial production to Islamabad. The policy makers in Beijing hope to convert Gwadar and the various SEZs, being set up along the CPEC into giant factory floors to produce goods for China and Chinese companies. Secondly, it expects to gain access to the vast untapped markets of Central Asia for Chinese exports as well as their energy resources by developing transportation linkages from Gwadar through Pakistan and Afghanistan into Central Asia. Thirdly, China hopes to appease its restive Uyghur population in the Muslim-majority Xinjiang Uyghur Autonomous Region. Beijing hopes that trade through Gwadar will lead to the development of this remote and isolated region, through a massive infusion of developmental funds and enhanced economic linkages with the predominantly Islamic Central Asian states as well as Pakistan and Afghanistan.

The port, on account of its location, does provide China a strategic foothold in the Arabian Sea and the Indian Ocean. This could provide it an opportunity to further enhance its strategic influence on major South Asian nations, especially Bangladesh, Nepal, Pakistan, and Sri Lanka, which would be to the detriment of India, the regional power. The Gwadar port is next to the Strait of Hormuz, the key oil route in and out of the Persian Gulf through which 20 per cent of global and 80 per cent of China's oil imports pass.

China faces significant strategic challenges in the Indian Ocean region as its sea lines of communications (SLOCs) across the Indian Ocean, are critical for its economic well-being especially for the transportation of much-needed energy resources. The SLOC originating in the Persian Gulf, transiting through the Strait of Hormuz, going around the Indian subcontinent to the Malacca Strait and the Pacific Ocean is the most important for China's energy security. Other important Chinese SLOCs in the Indian Ocean pass from the Suez Canal to Malacca and from the Cape of Good Hope to Malacca. This makes China extremely vulnerable in the Malacca Strait, through which 82 per cent of its oil imports transit.

This is what has been described by analysts as China's Malacca Dilemma. The Chinese SLOCs, however, are vulnerable throughout the Indian Ocean from state as well as non-state actors. China's sense of vulnerability is further accentuated by the fact that it does not have a clear overland route between China and the Indian Ocean. Formidable geographical barriers block China's overland access to the Indian Ocean through which almost all of its trade with Europe, Africa, and West Asia passes.

According to the US Director of Net Assessment, China is attempting to work on a strategy of robust engagement with the countries all along its SLOCs from the Middle East to the South China Sea by setting up bases in their territory and strengthening diplomatic relations with them. This strategy has often been called as the 'string of pearls'. At the moment, the USA dominates the Persian Gulf with its overwhelming military presence and is able to ensure freedom of navigation through the Hormuz. However, the Chinese presence in Gwadar and rising tensions between Iran and the USA could give China a major stake in the region.

More significantly, from India's point of view, the Gwadar deep sea port is perceived to be a component of China's 'String of Pearls' strategy, which includes setting up a number of military bases in the Indian Ocean Region. Once established, this would eradicate to a great extent, the locational advantage that the Indian Navy presently enjoys over the PLA Navy. The Chinese presence at Gwadar also gives China a significant capability to interdict India's energy supplies.

Most of India's crude imports come from ports in the Persian Gulf and are disembarked in the Gulf of Kutch, as most of India's refining capacity is located in its vicinity. More significantly, almost all the refineries in North and Central India are supplied from there by pipelines. The SLOC from the

Persian Gulf to the Gulf of Kutch, which is extremely crucial for India's energy security, passes just 40 nautical miles from Gwadar. This allows any surveillance facility at Gwadar to monitor the movement of tankers to and from the Gulf of Kutch. Even a gunboat based at Gwadar can interdict a tanker moving along this SLOC. This capability could help China create a 'Hormuz Dilemma' for India, posing a grave threat to India's core security interests and challenging India in its own maritime backyard. It would considerably enhance China's capacity to support Pakistan in case of any future conflicts with India. China could also leverage this capability against India to ensure a 'quid pro quo' freedom of its own shipping in the Indian Ocean.

It can, therefore, be concluded that Gwadar is a huge geopolitical constituency for China. The development of infrastructure and transport facilities in the region, allows China to address two of its core concerns, namely, ensuring its energy security and ensuring economic development of its relatively undeveloped western regions. At the strategic level, a port facility at Gwadar allows China a strategic foothold in the Indian Ocean Region, and allows it to emerge as a counter balance against India, in India's neighbourhood.

The Gwadar deep sea port project thus has a huge impact on India and its neighbourhood. It could influence almost all the regional powers as well as extra-regional powers and the way they look at India and its neighbourhood. Chinese presence at Gwadar could change their perception and disturb the existing regional equilibrium.

The shortest possible exit to the open oceans for Afghanistan and the countries of Central Asia continues to be through the warm water ports in the North Arabian Sea. Unfortunately, despite geographical proximity, almost negligible trade to and from the Central Asian states, transits through these ports but this could change with the emergence of the Gwadar deep sea port. If the Gwadar port project fructifies and roads through the hinterland start functioning, it would lead to greater dependence of Afghanistan on Pakistan. Not only Afghanistan, even the dependence of Central Asian states on Pakistan would also increase significantly if Gwadar emerges as a major trading port for them. This could reduce their dependence on Russia to a great extent and even on China to some extent.

Within Afghanistan, the preferred border crossing would shift from Torkham to Chaman as the route from Gwadar to Chaman passes through relatively more peaceful parts of Pakistan and Afghanistan, rather than the route through Torkham. It could result in opening of new avenues of economic activities along the route through which cargo would pass. This could consequently result in greater economic development of Southern Afghanistan that could wean the population away from the Taliban and its radical ideology. However, if the Taliban were to profit from taxation on this trade it could aggravate the internal turmoil within Afghanistan.

In order to counter the locational advantage that Gwadar port and, to some extent, Karachi Port, enjoy over Bandar Abbas, the main Iranian port for embarking and disembarking Afghan and Central Asian trade; Iran has collaborated with India to conceptualise the Chabahar port, outside the Persian Gulf. The Chabahar port is being connected to Afghanistan and the Central Asian Republics by a network of roads and railways.

Considering the huge investments in both Gwadar and Chabahar, Gwadar's emergence as the preferred gateway to Central Asia, could make the huge investment in the Chabahar port an economic liability. Both Gwadar and Chabahar lie in territory dominated by the Baloch, who have been protesting against their respective governments. The Baloch will play a major role in determining which of these two ports emerges as the gateway to Afghanistan and Central Asia, as their cooperation or opposition will impact the security environment and, consequently, the pace of infrastructural development at the two ports.

If the Gwadar deep sea port emerges as a thriving and vibrant port, it would be a major rival for Dubai in the UAE. As Gwadar is closer to the Eurasian heartland, it could reduce transportation time for goods slated for Western China and Central Asia. It could also enhance trade between the Middle East and the central Eurasian landmass, as connectivity between these two energy and resource-rich regions has been extremely tenuous and long. More significantly, ships coming to Gwadar do not have to enter the Persian Gulf through the narrow Strait of Hormuz, a process, which considerably slows them down enhancing the financial burden for ships entering Dubai. A substantive portion of the transhipment cargo is bound for ports outside the Gulf, which results in cargo crossing the narrow Strait of Hormuz twice. This would be completely eliminated in the case of Gwadar Port. The UAE, especially Dubai, will be a big loser if Gwadar really establishes itself as a transhipment hub, as its revenue from transportation and tourism would drop drastically.

The USA at present is no longer dependent on energy supplies from the Persian Gulf; however, its allies in Europe and Japan are still overwhelmingly dependent on supplies from the region. As a result, the Persian Gulf will continue to remain important for the USA and it will have a stake in the free movement of goods in and out of the Gulf. However, the Chinese presence at Gwadar gives China a unique capacity to monitor every vessel leaving or entering the Persian Gulf. The Gwadar deep sea port provides China a strategic outpost, which it can use against the USA and its allies if tensions between the two aggravate to the extent of naval blockades, as the USA and China confront each other at sea.

The surveillance facilities being set up at the Gwadar port and the naval assets positioned there would also enable the Pakistan Navy to monitor Indian ships leaving and entering the Persian Gulf and interdict them, if and when the need arises. This could give Islamabad a strong leverage to pressurise India to accommodate Pakistan on contentious issues.

With its presence in Gwadar just at the mouth of the Persian Gulf, China should also be able to enhance its influence on the countries of the region, which are mostly ruled by autocratic rulers without any support from the masses. The growing Chinese influence and resulting tension with the USA could create massive turbulence in this region, which could affect the economic activities in these countries. This, in turn, could lead to massive migration of Indian workers. Even otherwise, with its enhanced influence stemming from its presence in Gwadar, China would be in a position to adversely affect the employment of Indian workers in the region. This could be a huge economic blow to the Indian economy.

Any reduction in shipping traffic to Dubai could result in the vanishing of the 'hot money'[3] invested there. This could lead to the bursting of the real estate bubble and Dubai could be in a serious economic crisis. This will force a large number of Indian expatriates earning their livelihood there to return to India, thereby drying up this perennial source of foreign exchange.

In the past, one of the powerful tools that Indian policy makers could employ against Pakistan was the threat of a blockade. The blockading of the

Karachi-Port Bin Qasim complex was virtually child's play for the Indian Navy, as the two ports are extremely close to each other and not quite far from the Indian coast. Consequently, any naval force involved in enforcing the blockade could be supported by shore-based aircraft. However, with a functioning Gwadar port, any blockade by the Indian Navy will be extremely difficult. Firstly, it will require two different forces to blockade Karachi and Port Bin Qasim as well as Gwadar and Ormara. More significantly, it will be much more difficult to blockade Gwadar as it quite far from the Indian coast and it would be extremely difficult to provide continuous shore-based air support to any naval force blockading the port. More significantly, with the Chinese presence at the port, the authorities in Pakistan feel that India would not be in a position to blockade the port, as it could bring the PLA Navy into the game. Consequently, as and when Gwadar starts functioning as a thriving port, the threat of maritime blockade that could throttle Pakistan's economy would virtually vanish. This would result in India losing a big leverage against Pakistan.

The economic success of the project, even at this moment, is an uncertainty, but if it succeeds, it has the potential to provide an ideal all-weather gateway for the former Soviet republics of Central Asia as well as Afghanistan, whose progress has been thwarted to a great extent on account of their landlocked status. It could be hugely beneficial to Pakistan. However, eventually it is going to be Islamabad's handling of unrest in its province of Balochistan and to a much lesser extent in Gilgit-Baltistan through which the China Pakistan Economic Corridor passes, which will ultimately decide the financial viability of the Gwadar port project. As far as access to Central Asia is concerned, it needs to get off the block fast, because Chabahar is already operational and can give Gwadar a run for its money.

Recommendations

As the Gwadar deep sea port would be a geopolitical game changer with a potentially adverse impact on India's security interests, the following policy recommendations are made for the consideration of the Indian authorities:

- Indian agencies should carefully monitor the progress of infrastructural developments in the Gwadar deep sea port and around it. They should also monitor the traffic and the cargo that is being handled by the port.

- The commercial success of Gwadar port depends on the successful implementation of projects associated with the CPEC, especially the road and rail links being built to connect Gwadar to the hinterland. It is therefore essential for Indian authorities to constantly monitor various projects being implemented as part of the CPEC and their financial viability.
- There is significant opposition to CPEC within Pakistan, as many economists perceive that the whole project is not economically viable and will lead Pakistan into a Chinese debt trap. It would therefore be appropriate for the government of India to encourage such opposition and prop up protests against CPEC projects, which could lead to time and cost over-runs.
- The Baloch hold the key to the successful implementation of the CPEC as well as the ports of Gwadar and Chabahar. It is therefore essential for India to engage with various Baloch nationalist groups to ensure that Chabahar emerges as the preferred gateway to Central Asia, much before the CPEC is fully operational. It needs to be impressed upon the Baloch that the Gwadar port is being developed on their land without in any way allowing them to reap any benefits from it.
- India has invested large resources in developing Chabahar port and building infrastructure there. It has taken lot of efforts and spent resources to connect it to Afghanistan, while avoiding its southern part, where the Taliban has much greater influence. India Global Ports Limited (IGPL) is operating two berths at the port. However, all these investments in Chabahar would result in complete loss if Gwadar attains commercial success and emerges as the preferred gateway to the Eurasian heartland. It is therefore essential for India to maintain synergy with authorities in Tehran so as to expedite all works that are essential to make Chabahar commercially viable.
- One of the biggest impediments to making Chabahar a thriving port is the US sanctions on Iran, although, Chabahar has specifically been exempted from sanctions on account of its importance to Afghanistan. In reality, no shipping company is even willing to disembark heavy machinery there. Similarly, most of the European companies are even unwilling to even supply essential equipment like heavy cranes. It is therefore absolutely essential for Indian authorities to discuss this issue

with the USA to find a way out, so as to enhance the traffic to the port.

- India needs to establish good relations with the Arab states of the Persian Gulf, especially the tiny sheikhdoms in the region. India's principal focus should be on the United Arab Emirates, which need to be apprised of the serious economic threat that Gwadar could pose to the well-being of the Emirates. The Gulf states must be persuaded to continue trading through Dubai port and retain it as the regional transhipment hub.
- India may need to counter China at various international fora and impress upon the global community that the CPEC passes through Indian territory. To that extent, India must raise issues of restoration of sovereignty and territorial integrity at all such fora and bilateral talks.
- India needs to engage with various nationalist groups in Gilgit-Baltistan and provide them all facilities entitled to Indian citizens. The nascent opposition to the CPEC in the region must be encouraged and provided full support in this 'de jure' Indian territory, so as to delay various projects associated with the CPEC.
- India needs to maintain and further build on its good relations with the littoral states of the Indian Ocean, so as to emerge as the 'net security provider' in the Indian Ocean Region (IOR), thereby increasing India's clout and credibility.
- India would need to collaborate with the USA, especially its naval forces. in the Persian Gulf, to ensure safe transit of Indian shipping through the Strait of Hormuz.
- India would need to further enhance its cooperation and influence among its South Asian neighbours so as to prevent them from aligning with China and Pakistan.
- India would need to further augment its maritime forces, so as to be in a position to counter any threat emanating from the presence of Chinese forces in Gwadar.

NOTES

1. Murad Ali. "A decade of CPEC", *The News*, Karachi, 11 July 2023, p. 7.
2. Imran Khalid, "CPEC: a decade of transformation", *The News*, Karachi, 22 July 2023, p. 6.
3. 'Hot money' is generally referred to portfolio investment, in which foreign investors make their investments through stocks and bonds, which can be liquidated very quickly, if required.

Bibliography

Books

Akbar, Malik Siraj (2011). *The Redefined Dimensions of Baloch Nationalist Movement.* Bloomington, IN: Xlibris Books.

Ali, Tariq (1983). *Can Pakistan Survive? The Death of a State.* Suffolk: Penguin Books.

Amin, Tahir (1988). *Ethno National Movements of Pakistan.* Islamabad: Institute of Policy Studies.

Anwar, Muhammad (1999). *Role of smaller navies: a focus on Pakistan's maritime interests.* Islamabad: Directorate of Naval Educational Services, Naval Headquarters.

Baloch, Inayatullah (1987). *The Problem of Greater Baluchistan: A Study of Baluch Nationalism.* Stuttgart: Steiner Verlag Wiesbaden GmbH.

Baluch, Mir Ahmed Yar Khan (1975). *Inside Baluchistan.* Karachi: Royal Book Company.

Bansal, Alok (2009). *Balochistan in Turmoil: Pakistan at Crossroads.* New Delhi: Manas Publications.

Bray, Denys (1977). *The Life History of A Brahui.* Karachi: Royal Book Company.

Breseeg, Taj Mohammad (2004). *Baloch Nationalism: Its Origin and Development,* Karachi: Royal Book Company.

Buzan, B. (2007). *People, states and fear,* Colchester: European Consortium for Political Research Press, Reprinted 2009.

Buzan, B. and L. Hansen (2009). *The evolution of international security studies,* Cambridge: Cambridge University Press.

Cohen, Stephen P. (2005). *The Idea of Pakistan.* New Delhi: Oxford University Press.

Devasher, Tilak (2019). *Pakistan: The Balochistan Conundrum*. New Delhi: HarperCollins Publishers India Pvt. Ltd.

Dutt, Sagarika and Alok Bansal (2013). *South Asian Security: 21st Century Discourses*, London and New York: Routledge.

Edwards, Alex (2014). *'Dual Containment' Policy in the Persian Gulf: The USA, Iran, and Iraq, 1991–2000*. New York: Palgrave Macmillan, 2014, pp. 17-18.

Haqqani, Husain (2018). *Reimagining Pakistan: Transforming A Dysfunctional Nuclear State*. New Delhi: HarperCollins Publishers India.

Harrison, Selig S. (1981). *In Afghanistan's Shadow: Baloch Nationalism and Soviet Temptations*, New York: Carnegie Endowment for International Peace.

Hilali, A. Z, (2005). *US-Pakistan Relationship: Soviet Invasion of Afghanistan*, London: Ashgate Publishing Limited.

Hussain, Sajid (2015). *Politico-Strategic and Economic Importance of Gwadar Port, Pakistan*, LAP Lambert Academic Publishing.

Iyer, Mani Shankar (1994). *Pakistan Papers*, New Delhi: UBS Publishers Distributors Ltd.

Jafferlot, Christophe (2002). *Pakistan Nationalism without a Nation?*, New Delhi: Manohar Publishers & Distributors.

Jones, Owen Bennett (2002). *Pakistan: Eye of the Storm*, New Delhi: Penguin Books India (P) Ltd.

Khan, Adeel (2005). *Politics of Identity: Ethnic Nationalism and the State in Pakistan*, New Delhi: Sage Publications.

Kondapalli, Srikanth and Hu Xiaowen (eds.) (2017). *One Belt One Road: China's Global Outreach*. New Delhi: Pentagon Press.

Kukreja, Veena (2003). *Contemporary Pakistan: Political Processes, Conflicts and Crises*. New Delhi: Sage Publications.

Kutty, B. M. (ed.) (2009). *In Search of Solutions: An Autobiography of Mir Ghaus Bakhsh Bizenjo*. Karachi: Pakistan Study Centre, University of Karachi and Pakistan Labour Trust.

——— (2011). *Sixty Years in Self Exile: No Regrets - A Political Autobiography*. Karachi: Pakistan Study Centre, University of Karachi and Pakistan Labour Trust.

Matheson, Sylvia (1998). *The Tigers of Balochistan*. Karachi: Oxford University Press.

Miller, Frederic, P; Agnes F. Vandome and John McBrewster (2010). *Gwadar*, Talinn: Alphascript Publishing.

Pechilis, Karen and Selva J. Raj (2013). *South Asian Religions: Tradition and Today*, New York: Routledge.

Rizvi, Hasan-Askari (2000). *Military, State and Society in Pakistan*. London: Macmillan Press Limited.

Sabahi, Farian and Daniel Warne, (2004). *The OSCE and the Multiple Challenges of Transition: The Caucasus and Central Asia*. London: Ashgate Publishing Limited.

Sahadevan, P. (2000). *Coping with Disorder – Strategies to End Internal Wars in South Asia*, RCSS Policy Studies 17, Colombo: Regional Centre for Strategic Studies.

Weaver, Mary Anne (2002). *Pakistan in the Shadow of Jihad and Afghanistan*. New York: Farrar, Straus and Giroux.

Wikipedians (2008). *Countries and Territories of the World Volume II – the Middle East & the Caucasus*.

Ziring, Lawrence (1999). *Pakistan in the Twentieth Century: A Political History*. Karachi: Oxford University Press.

Articles or other Work in Journals

Bansal, Alok (2005a) "The Revival of Insurgency in Balochistan", *Strategic Analysis*, 29 (2), Apr-Jun 2005: 250-268.

——— (2008). "Factors leading to insurgency in Balochistan", *Small Wars & Insurgencies*, 19 (2), June 2008: 182-200.

Berlin, Donald L. (2004). "The 'great base race' in the Indian Ocean littoral: conflict prevention or stimulation?" *Contemporary South Asia*, 13 (3): 239-255.

Blanchard, Jean-Marc F. and Colin Flint (2017). "The Geopolitics of China's Maritime Silk Road Initiative", *Geopolitics*, 22 (2): 223-245.

Brewster, David (2014). "Beyond the String of Pearls: Is there really a Sino-Indian Security Dilemma in the Indian Ocean?", *Journal of the Indian Ocean Region*, 10(2): 133-149.

Chawla, Muhammad Iqbal (2018). "Belt and Road Initiative: Regional and Global Dimensions", *Journal of Political Studies*, 25 (1): 81-94.

Chang, Yen-Chiang and Mehran Idris Khan (2019). "China–Pakistan economic corridor and maritime security collaboration: A growing Bilateral Interests", *Maritime Business Review*, 4(2): 217-235.

Cohen, Stephen P. (1975). "Security Issues in South Asia", *Asian Survey*, 15 (3): 202-214.

Daniels, Rory (2013). "Strategic Competition in South Asia: Gwadar, Chabahar and the Risks of Infrastructure Development", *American Foreign Policy Interests: The Journal of the National Committee on American Foreign Policy*, 35 (2), 25 March 2013, 93-100.

Djamarani, M. (2002). "Getting the oil and gas out of the Caspian region", *Petroleum Review* 56 (661), 20 February 2002: 16-18.

Fayyaz, Shabana and Salma Malik (2019). "China-Pakistan Economic Corridor (CPEC): Security Concerns", *Global Regional Review* (GRR) 4 (4), Fall 2019: 432-440.

Garver, John W. (2006). "Development of China's Overland Transportation Links with Central, South-west and South Asia", *The China Quarterly*, no. 185, March 2006: 1-22.

Grare, Fredric (2006). "Pakistan: The Resurgence of Baloch Nationalism", *Carnegie Endowment Paper*, no. 65, January 2006: 1-22.

Haider, Ziad (2005). "Baluchis, Beijing, and Pakistan's Gwadar Port", *George Town Journal of International Affairs*, 6 (1), Spring/Winter 2005: 95-103.

Hussain, Fakhar and Mezhar Hussain (2017). "China-Pak Economic Corridor (CPEC) and its Geopolitical Paradigms", *IJSSHE-International Journal of Social Sciences, Humanities and Education*, 1 (2), January 2017: 79-95.

Husseinbor, Mohammed Hassan. (2016). "Chabahar and Gwadar Agreements and Rivalry among Competitors in Baluchistan Region", *Journal for Iranian Studies*, 1 (1): 82-99.

Ibrar, Muhammad et al. (2017). "The China-Pakistan Economic Corridor: Security Challenges", *DEStech Transactions on Social Science, Education and Human Science*, April 2017.

Khan, Shabir Ahmad (2013). "Geo-Economic Imperatives of Gwadar Sea Port and Kashgar Economic Zone for Pakistan and China", *IPRI Journal* 13(2): 87-100.

Khan, Zahid et al. (2018). "CPEC: A Game Changer in the Balance of Power in South Asia" *China Quarterly of International Strategic Studies*, vol. 4, no, 4 (April 2019): 595-611.

Khetran, Mir Sherbaz (2014). "The Potential and Prospects of Gwadar Port", *Strategic Studies*, Islamabad: Institute of Strategic Studies, 34(4)/35(1), Winter 2014 and Spring 2015: 70-89.

Kumar, Sourabh (2023). "Evaluation and analysis of India's energy security: A policy perspective", *Energy*, vol. 278, part B, article 127993, 1 September 2023.

Malik, Hasan Yaser (2012). "Strategic Importance of Gwadar Port", *Journal of Political Studies*, 19(2): 57-69.

Malik, Hasan Yaser (2013). "Strategic Carnage of Balochistan", *IOSR Journal of Humanities and Social Sciences*, 8(4), Mar-Apr 2013: 01-10.

Mushtaq, Faisal et al. "Coal Fired Power Generation Potential of Balochistan", *Petroleum and Coal*, 54 (2), June 2012: 132-142.

Niazi, Tarique (2006) "The Ecology of Strategic Interests: China's Quest for Energy Security from the Indian Ocean and the South China Sea to Caspian Sea Basin", *China and Eurasia Forum Quarterly*, 4(4): 97-116.

Nicolini, B. (2002). "Historical and Political Links between Gwadar and Muscat from Nineteenth-Century Testimonies," in Proceedings of the Seminar for Arabian Studies, vol. 32, London: Brepols, 2002, 281-286.

Rehman, Iskander (2009). "Keeping the Dragon at Bay: India's Counter-Containment of China in Asia", *Asian Security* 5 (2): 114-143.

Roy, Meena Singh (2012). "Iran: India's Gateway to Central Asia', *Strategic Analysis*, 36(6), November–December 2012, 957–975.

Tandon, Aakriti and Michael O. Slobodchikoff (2019). "Security in South Asia", *The Round Table*, 108(2), 117-119.

Tull, Denis M. (2006). "China's engagement in Africa: scope, significance and consequences', *The Journal of Modern African Studies*, 44(30, September 2006: 459-479.

Zeb, Rizwan, (2003). "Gwadar and Chabahar: Competition or Complementarity?", *Central Asia-Caucasus Institute Analyst,* 22 October 2003.

Article, Chapter, or Work in an Edited Volume

Bansal, Alok (2011). "Gwadar Port: A South Asian Gateway for Central Asia" in K. Warikoo (ed.) *Central Asia and South Asia: Energy Cooperation and Transport Linkages*. New Delhi: Pentagon Press.

Basit, Abdul et al. (2018). "Introduction" in Sarah Siddiq Aneel (ed.) *Changing Security Situation in South Asia and Development of CPEC*, Islamabad: Islamabad Policy Research Institute.

Brewster, David (2014). "The Changing Balance of Power in the Indian Ocean: Prospects for a Significant Chinese Naval Presence" in David Michel and Ricky Passarelli (eds.), *Sea Change: Evolving Maritime Geopolitics in the Indo-Pacific Region*, Washington DC: Stimson Centre.

Hussain, Syed Rifaat (2018). "South Asian Security and CPEC: A Pakistani

Perspective" in Sarah Siddiq Aneel (ed.), *Changing Security Situation in South Asia and Development of CPEC*, Islamabad: Islamabad Policy Research Institute.

Iqbal, Khuram (2018). "CPEC: A Corridor for Minimising Political Fault lines in South Asia" in Sarah Siddiq Aneel (ed.), *Changing Security Situation in South Asia and Development of CPEC*, Islamabad: Islamabad Policy Research Institute.

Phadnis, Urmila (1984). "Ethnic Movements in Pakistan" in Pandav Nayak (ed.), *Pakistan: Society and Politics* – South Asian Studies Series, 6. New Delhi: South Asian Publishers Pvt. Ltd.

Pratibha, M. S. (2017). "China-Pakistan Economic Corridor", in Srikanth Kondapalli and Hu Xiaowen (eds.), *One Belt One Road: China's Global Outreach*. New Delhi: Pentagon Press.

Rourke, Ronald (2007). "China Naval Modernization: Implications for U.S. Navy Capabilities—Background and Issues for Congress', in Jerald D. Finn (ed.), *China-US Economic and Geopolitical Relations*. New York: Nova Science Publishers Inc.

Article in a Newspaper or Magazine

"12 MW approved for New Gwadar International Airport", *Daily Times*, 7 June 2023.

Abi-Habib, Maria (2018). "What China Gets for Building Up Pakistan: A Military Toehold", *The New York Times*, New York edition, 20 December 2018.

Abrar, Mian (2016). "Jinnah Naval Base – Navy expands strategic outreach to West Coast, Persian Gulf", *Pakistan Today*, Lahore, 13 January 2016.

Abubakar, Syed Muhammad (2018). "Welcome to thirsty Gwadar", *The News on Sunday*, Karachi, 1 July 2018.

ADB lowers India GDP growth outlook for this fiscal to 6.3%", *The Hindu*, Delhi, 21 September 2023.

Ahmad, Azhar (2013). "Unraveling Gwadar Town", *The Frontier Post*, Peshawar, 4 May 2013.

Ahmed, Ashfaq (2019). "Pakistan's Gwadar International Airport will be the largest in the country", *Gulf News*, Dubai, 31 March 2019.

Akbar, Malik Siraj (2004). "Who leads the Baloch", *The Nation*, Lahore, 29 December 2004.

——— (2018). " Beijing to Balochistan", *The News on Sunday*, Karachi, 4 March 2018.

Ali, Murad (2023). "A decade of CPEC", *The News*, Karachi, 11 July 2023.

Ali, Sabahat (2016). "Gwadar - the Gateway of CPEC" *Centreline*, Islamabad, 13 December 2016.

Azmie, Sohail (2017). "Maritime security: Pakistan's perspective', *Pakistan Today*, Lahore, 24 September 2017.

——— (2019). "Pakistan Navy's evolving maritime security concept", *The Nation*, Lahore, 28 June 2019.

Bakhtiar, Idrees (2004). "Mega-projects are a Conspiracy to turn the Balochis into a Minority in their Homeland", an interview with Sardar Ataullah Mengal, *The Herald*, Karachi, August 2004.

Baloch, Behram (2019). "Senate panel resents slow pace of work on Gwadar port", *Dawn*, Karachi, 17 January 2019.

Baloch, Bahram (2022). "Gwadar Port to be utilised for Afghan transit trade", *Dawn*, Karachi, 19 March 2022.

Baloch, Behramand Muhammad Akbar Notezai. "Gwadar's Haq Do Tehreek – genuine movement or political ambition", *Dawn*, Karachi, 26 December 2022.

"Balochistan's Grievances", Editorial, *Dawn*, Karachi, 9 November 2004.

Baluch, Abdul Hakim (2004). "Bringing development to Balochistan', *Dawn*, Karachi, 13 December 2004.

Bansal, Alok (2006a). "Gwadar - A Chinese Gibraltar", *India Strategic*, New Delhi, vol. 1, February 2006.

Bhutta, Zafar (2022). "Riyadh renews $10b refinery project", *The Express Tribune*, 25 October 2022.

Bokhari, Farhan and Kiran Stacey (2018). "China woos Pakistan militants to secure Belt and Road projects", *Financial Times*, London, 19 February 2018.

"Border projects: Pakistan, Iran inaugurate Polan-Gabd electricity transmission line", *Business Recorder*, 18 May 2023.

Butt, Naveed (2015). "Economic corridor: China to extend assistance at 1.6 percent interest rate", *Business Recorder*, 3 September 2015.

Chaudhury, Dipanjan Roy (2019a). "China-Pakistan Gwadar Port runs into rough weather", *The Economic Times*, Mumbai, 10 September 2019.

——— (2019b). "PoK projects suffer as China focuses on Gwadar", *The Economic Times*, Mumbai, 12 November 2019.

"China could project military power from Pakistan's Gwadar port", *The Economic Times*, 28 March 2023.

"China may be looking at setting up a military base in Pakistan", *The Times of India*, New Delhi, 12 May 2023.

"China picks UAE as regional production hub for Sinopharm Covid-19 vaccine", *The Strait Times*, Singapore, 28 March 2021.

"China sees Pakistan as energy corridor", *The News*, Karachi, 17 June 2006.

"China tables railway project linking to Pakistan" *Dawn*, Karachi, 30 June 2014.

"China to build $2.5 billion worth LNG terminal, gas pipeline in Pakistan", *Deccan Chronicle*, 1 October 2015.

"Confrontation No Solution to Balochistan Imbroglio", Editorial, *The News*, Karachi, 16 January 2005.

Daud, Hassan (2018). "Gwadar: the economic gateway", *The News*, Karachi, 21 November 2018.

"Desalination plant in Gwadar to be inaugurated on June 30", *Pakistan Today*, 4 June 2023.

"Eastbay Expressway Gwadar expected to complete in October, says Asim Bajwa", *The Nation*, Lahore, 3 May 2021.

"Expectations from Gwadar", Editorial, *The News,* Karachi, 7 October 2004.

Fassihi, Farnaz and Steven Lee Myers (2021). "Big Iran Deal Gives Beijing an Oil Supply and Influence", *The New York Times*, New York, 28 March 2021.

Fazl-e-Haider, Syed (2005). "Gwadar Project in second phase", *Dawn*, Karachi, 27 June 2005.

——— (2019a). "Emerging Hub Port in the Asian region", *Pakistan & Gulf Economist*, Karachi, 23 June 2019.

"First phase of Gwadar port completed", *Dawn*, Karachi, 4 December 2004.

Gishkori, Zahid (2015). "Army assigned security of Chinese engineers", *The Express Tribune*, Karachi, 22 April 2015.

"Gwadar-KKH link", Editorial, *Dawn*, Karachi, 6 July 2006.

"Gwadar rail track would be completed soon", *The Frontier Post,* Peshawar, 19 November 2004.

"Gwadar port: 'history-making milestones'," *Dawn*, Karachi, 14 April 2008.

"Gwadar port as trade, energy corridor", *The News*, Karachi, 20 June 2006.

"Gwadar to be linked with Quetta through railway: minister" *Dawn*, Karachi, 23 October 2018.

"Gwadar's rich potential", Editorial, *Dawn*, Karachi, 13 June 2006.

Hamid, Mohsin (2007). "Waiting for the Boom", *Time,* New York, 26 July 5 August 2007.

Hanif, Haseeb (2019). "Gwadar port operationalised for exports", *The Express Tribune*, Karachi, 15 December 2019.

Haq, Noorul (2005). "Balochistan: its past and present", *The Kashmir Times,* Jammu, 8 February 2005.

Haque, Ihtashamul (2005). "Tax-free zones in Gwadar planned: Wooing foreign investment", *Dawn*, Karachi, 17 June 2005.

Huang, Kristin (2020). "Iranian relations built on trade, energy and arms', *South China Morning Post*, Hong Kong, 9 January 2020.

"India's import of US oil jumps 10-fold to 2,50,000 bpd", *The Economic Times*, Mumbai, 25 February 2020.

"India's Chabahar port plan is to counter China's plan to develop Gwadar port: Media", *The Economic Times*, Mumbai, 12 July 2018.

Iqbal, Nasir (2019). "CPEC: phases and challenges', *The News*, Karachi, 3 January 2019.

Jabri, Parvez (2018). "Gwadar, a challenge to develop a new economic city", *Business Recorder*, Karachi, 15 August 2018.

Jacob, Jayanth and Saubhadra Chatterji (2011). "India's Track 3: Afghan-Iran rail link", *The Hindustan Times*, New Delhi, 1 November 2011.

Jalal, Umair (2023). "China-Pakistan Ties Steam Ahead With Proposed Rail Project", *The Diplomat*, 3 May 2023.

Kaplan, Robert D. (2009). "Pakistan's Fatal Shore", *The Atlantic*, Washington DC, May 2009.

Kesnur, Srikant Kesnur and Digvijay Sinh Sodha (2019). "Operation Talwar: How the Navy silently contributed to Kargil win", *The Asian Age*, Mumbai, 4 December 2019.

Khalid, Imran. "CPEC: a decade of transformation", *The News*, Karachi, 22 July 2023.

Khan, M. Ismail (2006). "The Trans-Karakoram Oil Pipeline", *The News*, Karachi, 31 October 2006.

Khan, Safdar (2006). "Karakoram Highway's Gwadar link likely", *Dawn*, Karachi, 5 July 2006.

Lintner, Bertil (2020). "China eyes a Covid-19 edge in the Indian Ocean", *Asia Times*, Hong Kong, 23 April 2020.

Mahmood, Nazir (2019). "As Balochistan bleeds", *The News*, Karachi, 20 April 2019.

"Maritime coalition launched to protect Gulf shipping after Iran attacks", *Arab News*, Riyadh, 8 November 2019.

Memon, Naseer (2007). "Disaster unleashed by Mirani Dam", *Dawn*, Karachi, 20 August 2007.

Minhas, Khurram (2020). "Expulsion of US from the Persian Gulf?", *The Nation*, Lahore, 17 January 2020.

Mir, Shabbir (2016). "First Chinese shipment rolls into Sost dry port in Gilgit-Baltistan", *The Express Tribune*, Karachi, 1 November 2016.

Mirza, Javed (2020). "Transit trade with CARs under consideration", *The News*, Karachi, 17 March 2020.

Mustafa, Khalid and Muhammad Saleh Zafir (2016). "Russia allowed use of Gwadar Port", *The News*, Karachi, 26 November 2016.

Noack, Rick (2018). "China's new train line to Iran sends message to Trump: We'll keep trading anyway', *The Washington Post*, Washington DC, 12 May 2018.

"Pak-China Dosti Zindabad (Long live China-Pakistan friendship)", *Daily Times*, Lahore, 19 April 2015.

"Pak-Afghan trade slips to $720.4mln in July-January", *The News on Sunday*, Karachi, 22 March 2020.

"Pakistan hands over 2000 acres to China in Gwadar port city", *Indian Express*, 12 November 2015

"Pakistan hands over Gwadar Port operation to China", *The Nation*, Lahore, 25 February 2013.

"Pakistan, Russia to boost defence ties", *The Nation*, Lahore, 8 August 2018.

"Pakistan, Russia cooperating to boost defence ties", *The News*, Karachi, 2 December 2018.

Perlz, Jane (2016). "Chinese Leader Is All Business in Middle East", *The New York Times*, New York edition, 31 January 2016.

"President for completing Gwadar port by June 2006", *The News*, Karachi, 11 June 2005.

Rahim, Nasir (2006). "The Deep End", *The Herald*, Karachi, June 2006.

Rana, Shahbaz (2016). "Pakistan approves massive tax exemptions for Gwadar port operators", *The Express Tribune*, Karachi, 24 May 2016.

——— (2019). "Chinese vow to make Gwadar more valuable than Karachi", *The Express Tribune*, Karachi, 9 October 2019.

Rathore, Tahir (2004). "Pak, Chinese presidents to open Gwadar Port", *The News*, Karachi, 27 November 2004.

Raza, Syed Irfan (2013). "China given contract to operate Gwadar port", *Dawn*, Karachi, 19 February 2013.

Said, Summer and Ahmed Al Omran (2016). "Saudi Aramco Set for Chinese Energy Deals", *Wall Street Journal*, New York, 20 January 2016.

Shah, Sabir (2019). "Pakistan among nations that depend substantially on foreign remittances", *The News*, Karachi, 25 December 2019.

Sharma, Sukalp (2023). "India reliance on imported crude oil at record high of 87.3% in FY23", *Indian Express*, New Delhi, 25 April 2023.

Sophia, Mary (2014). "Dubai Ranks Fifth Among Top Global Destinations For Travellers", *Gulf Business*, Dubai, 10 July 2014.

"Terrorism in Balochistan", Editorial, *Dawn,* Karachi, 18 December 2004.

"The Chinese-African relationship is important to both sides, but also unbalanced", *The Economist*, London, 20 May 2022.

"The tribes arise", *The Economist,* London, 7 May 2005.

"Pak Navy takes over CTF-150 command', *The Nation*, Lahore, 12 April 2019.

"Under CPEC: First container vessel anchors at Gwadar", *The Express Tribune*, Karachi, 8 March 2018.

Zhen, Summer (2015). "Chinese firm takes control of Gwadar Port free-trade zone in Pakistan", *South China Morning Post*, Hong Kong, 11 November 2015.

Zulfiqar, Shahzada (2004). "Port of Terror", *Newsline*, Karachi, June 2004.

Unpublished Dissertation or Paper

Ahmed, Soomro Shabbir (2016). *Strategical Importance and Potential of Gwadar for the Regional Countries*, Master's Thesis, Jinan: Jinan University.

Hassan, Ammad (2005). *Pakistan's Gwadar Port – Prospects of Economic Revival.* Master's Thesis, Monterey, California: Naval Post Graduate School.

Shah, Abid Hussain (2007). *The volatile situation of Balochistan - options to bring it into streamline*, Master's Thesis, Monterey, California: Naval Post Graduate School.

Translated Book

Nicolini, Beatrice (2004). Makran, Oman and Zanzibar: Three Terminal Cultural Corridor in the Western Indian Ocean (1799-1856), Translated by Penelope-Jane Watson, Leiden and Boston: Brill.

Government, International Organisations and NGO Publications

European Union Institute for Security Studies, (2018). "Along the Road: Gwadar and China's power projection", by Fredric Grare, Issue Brief 7/2018, July 2018.

Govt. of Pakistan White Paper on Balochistan published on 1974.

European Union Institute for Security Studies (2018) "Along the road: Gwadar and China's power projection", by Fredric Gare, Issue Brief 7/2018, July 2018.

India Office Records "File 22/16 I (A 41) GWADUR, Oil, Proposed Cession and Ownership", London: British Library, IOR/R/15/1/378.

African Development Bank Group (2019). "China's Presence in Africa: A Boon or a Bust?', by Joseph Ingram, Africa Economic Brief 10 (1).

International Crisis Group (2006). "Pakistan: The Worsening Conflict in Balochistan", Asia Report no. 119, 14 September 2006.

——— (2018). "China-Pakistan Economic Corridor: Opportunities and Risks", Asia Report no. 297, 29 June 2018.

The Lowy Institute (2020). "China's pipeline dream in Pakistan", by Rahul Jaybhay, 30 June 2020.

Federation of Indian Chambers of Commerce & Industry, New Delhi (2018). *The Belt Road Initiative aka One Belt One Road Scheme*, 24 January 2018.

Observer Research Foundation (2020). "China's Belt and Road Initiative: Implications in Africa", by Venkateswaran Lokanathan, Issue Brief 395, August 2020.

The Jamestown Foundation (2005). "Gwadar: China's Naval Outpost on the Indian Ocean", by Tarique Niazi, *China Brief* 5 (4), 15 February 2005.

Pew Research Centre (2019). "Remittance flows worldwide in 2017", Global Attitudes and Trends, 3 April 2019.

Vivekanand International Foundation (2017). *Afghanistan-Pakistan Transit Trade-Background, Legal Perspective and the Agonies of a Landlocked Country*, by Shoaib A. Rahim, Occasional Paper, October 2017

The Jamestown Foundation (2015). "China-Pakistan Economic Corridor: Road to Riches?", by Sudha Ramachandran, *China Brief* 15(15), 31 July 2015.

Ratha, Dilip et al. (2022). "Remittances Brave Global Headwinds - Special Focus: Climate Migration", *Migration and Development Brief 37*, November 2022, Washington DC, KNOMAD-World Bank.

Ratha, Dilip et al. (2023). "Remittances Remain Resilient but Are Slowing", *Migration and Development Brief* 38, June 2023, Washington DC, KNOMAD-World bank.

Renaud, Karnie M. (2018). "The Mineral Industry of Pakistan" in *2015 Mineral Year Book*, US Department of the Interior, US Geological Survey, November 2018 (Advance Release).

The Imperial Gazetteer of India (1908). Volume XII, "EINME to GWALIOR", The Clarendon Press: Oxford.

United Nations Treaty Series, vol. 597 (1968), "Convention on Transit Trade of Land-locked States", New York: United Nations.

Wolf, Siegfried O. (2020). "The Growing Security Dimension of the China-

Pakistan Economic Corridor", Italian Institute for International Political Studies, 10 March 2020.

World Bank Group (2019). "Migration and Remittances: Recent Developments and Outlook" Migration and Development Brief 31, Published 30 April 2019.

Ministry of Petroleum & Natural Gas (2023). "India's 4-plank energy security strategy is based on diversifying supplies, increasing E&P, alternate energy sources and energy transition through a gas-based economy, Green Hydrogen, etc.", Press release posted by PIB Delhi on 10 January 2023.

Internet Sources

Aamir, Adnan (2019). "Is it wise for China to build Pakistan's largest airport at Gwadar?" *Asia Dialogue*, 21 May 2019, [Online: web] Accessed 28 December 2019, URL: https://theasiadialogue.com/2019/05/21/is-it-wise-for-china-to-build-pakistans-largest-airport-at-gwadar/

Abbasi, Zaheer (2018). "Gwadar Port Terminal Expansion Plan', *Business Recorder*, 19 March 2018, [Online: web] Accessed on 19 February 2020, URL: https://epaper.brecorder.com/2018/03/19/20-page/705796-news.html

Ahmad, Azhar (2012). "Gwadar: Hope alive", *Opinion Maker*, 5 August 2012, [Online: web] Accessed 3 November 2012, URL: http://www.opinion-maker.org/2012/08/gwadar-hope-alive/

Ahmed, Ashfaq (2019). "Pakistan's Gwadar International Airport will be the largest in the country", *Gulf News*, 31 March 2019 [Online: web] Accessed 28 December 2019 URLhttps://gulfnews.com/world/asia/pakistan/pakistans-gwadar-international-airport-will-be-the-largest-in-the-country-1.63033953

Alam, Omar (2015). "China-Pakistan Economic Corridor: Towards a New 'Heartland'?", CSS Website [Online: web] Accessed on 1 April 2020, URL: https://isnblog.ethz.ch/international-relations/china-pakistan-economic-corridor-towards-a-new-heartland

Albert, Eleanor (2017). "China in Africa", Council on Foreign Relations 12 July 2017, [Online: web] Accessed on 10 July 2023, URL: https://www.cfr.org/backgrounder/china-africa

Al Jazeera (2023a). "Pakistan, Afghanistan agree to boost trade, lower border tensions", *Al Jazeera*, 8 February 2023 [Online: web] Accessed on 10 July 2023, URL: https://www.aljazeera.com/news/2023/5/8/pakistan-afghanistan-agree-to-boost-trade-lower-border-tensions

Al Jazeera (2023b). "Pentagon chief, on surprise trip, says US troops to stay in Iraq", *Al Jazeera*, 7 March 2023, [Online: web] Accessed on 10 July 2023,

URL: https://www.aljazeera.com/news/2023/3/7/pentagon-chief-surprise-trip-says-us-troops-stay-iraq

Al-Shammari, Tariq (2017). "Dubai and Gwadar: the silent economic war in the Gulf of Oman', *Open Democracy*, 14 August 2017 [Online: web] Accessed 12 December 2019, URL: https://www.opendemocracy.net/en/north-africa-west-asia/dubai-and-gwadar-silent-economic-war-in-gulf-of-oman/

Ali, Sulman (2015). "Pakistan-China Gwadar Port Agreement: Balance of Power Game in South Asia", *South Asian Voices*, 20 May 2015 [Online: web] Accessed 18 February 2021, URL: https://southasianvoices.org/pakistan-china-gwadar-port-agreement-balance-of-power-game-in-south-asia/

Aneez, Shihar (2017). "China's 'Silk Road' push stirs resentment and protest in Sri Lanka", *Reuters*, 2 February 2017, [Online: web] Accessed 18 February 2021, URL: https://www.reuters.com/article/us-sri-lanka-china-insight-idUSKBN15G5UT.

Arab News (2020). "US warns vessels transiting Gulf amid tensions with Iran", *Arab News*, 14 January 2020, [Online: web] Accessed 1 November 2021, URL: https://www.arabnews.com/node/1612766/middle-east?page=4

Asia News (2018). "The opening of Gwadar Free Trade Zone on China's new Silk Road disappoints New Delhi", *Asia News*, 30 January 2018, [Online: web] Accessed 24 Nov 2019, URL: http://www.asianews.it/news-en/The-opening-of-Gwadar-Free-Trade-Zone-on-China%E2%80%99s-new-Silk-Road-disappoints-New-Delhi-42969.html

Balachandran, P. K. (2018). "Challenges to South Asian security", *Daily Mirror* Online, 18 December 2018, [Online: web] Accessed 31 August 2021, URL: https://www.dailymirror.lk/Opinion/Challenges-to-South-Asian-security/172-159907

Bansal, Alok (2005b). "Gwadar - Port of Hope or Despair?", IPCS Website 8 July 2005, [Online: web] Accessed on 1 October 2021, URL: http://www.ipcs.org/article/pakistan/gwadar-port-of-hope-or-despair-1783.html

—— (2006b). "Gwadar Port: Economic Panacea or A Red Herring", IPCS Website 8 August 2006, [Online: web] Accessed on 24 November 2021, URL: http://www.ipcs.org/comm_select.php?articleNo=2089

Bowen, Jeremy (2021). "China sets sights on Middle East with Iran co-operation deal", *BBC News*, 31 March 2021, [Online: web] Accessed 14 May 2021, URL: https://www.bbc.com/news/world-middle-east-56574336

Broadman, Harry G. (2021). "Africa's debt dance with China in creating the Belt Road Initiative", *The Africa Report*, 21 April 2021 [Online: web] Accessed 15

May 2021, URL: https://www.theafricareport.com/81857/africas-debt-dance-with-china-in-creating-the-belt-road-initiative/

Business World (2020). "Middle East Share Of India's Oil Imports Falls To Four-Year-Low In 2019: Trade", *Business World*, 20 January 2020 [Online: web] Accessed 1 April 2020, URL: http://www.businessworld.in/article/Middle-East-Share-Of-India-s-Oil-Imports-Falls-To-Four-Year-Low-In-2019-Trade-/20-01-2020-182346/

Chatzky, Andrew and James McBride (2020). "China's Massive Belt and Road Initiative", Council on Foreign Relations, 28 January 2020, [Online: web] Accessed on 24 November, 2021 URL: https://www.cfr.org/backgrounder/chinas-massive-belt-and-road-initiative

Chowdhary, Mahwish (2015). "China's Billion-Dollar Gateway to the Subcontinent: Pakistan May be Opening a Door It Cannot Close" *Forbes*, 25 August 2015, [Online: web] Accessed 1 April 2020, URL: https://www.forbes.com/sites/realspin/2015/08/25/china-looks-to-pakistan-to-expand-its-influence-in-asia/#3eeda9093de9

CPEC (2019a). "New Gwadar International Airport" China Pakistan Economic Corridor [Online: web] Accessed 27 December 2019, URL: http://cpec.gov.pk/project-details/33

——— (2019b). "Gwadar Port City Projects", CPEC [Online: web] Accessed 28 December 2019, URL: https://obortunity.org/cpec-news/gwadar-port-city/

——— (2021). "Gwadar will become a gateway to Central Asia: PM Khan", CPEC, 16 March 2021, [Online: web] Accessed 10 July 2021, URL :http://cpecinfo.com/gwadar-will-become-a-gateway-to-central-asia-pm-khan/

Daily Times (2005). "Aziz directs acceleration of Gwadar work", *Daily Times*, 5 June 2005, [Online: web] Accessed 8 June 2005, URL: http://www.dailytimes.com.pk/default.asp?page=story_5-6-2005_pg7_28

Deccan Herald (2013). "Pakistan hands over Gwadar port to Chinese company", *Deccan Herald*, 18 February 2013, [Online: web] Accessed 28 December 2019, URL: https://www.deccanherald.com/international/pakistan-hands-over-gwadar-port-to-chinese-company-304229.html

Dunya News (2023). "China starts Oil Refinery Construction in Gwadar", *Dunya News* 17 January 2023 from https://dunyanews.tv/en/Business/690634-(Accessed on 30 June 2023).

Embassy of the Peoples Republic of China in the Islamic Republic of Pakistan (2018). "Development of Gwadar Free Zone" Special Report on CPEC Projects (Transportation Infrastructure: Part 4), 1 October 2018, [Online: web]

Accessed 29 December 2019, URL: http://pk.chineseembassy.org/eng/zbgx/t1627112.htm

Erickson, Andrew and Kevin Bond (2015). "Essay: China's Island Building Campaign Could Hint Toward Further Expansions in Indian Ocean", *USNI News*, 17 September 2015, [Online: web] Accessed 10 July 2020. URL: https://news.usni.org/2015/09/17/essay-chinas-island-building-campaign-could-hint-toward-further-expansions-in-indian-ocean

Esfandiary, Dina (2021). "Iran's 'New' Partnership with China is just Business as Usual", *World Politics* review, 22 April 2021 [Online: web] Accessed 14 May 2021, URL: https://www.worldpoliticsreview.com/articles/29593/the-iran-china-deal-isn-t-all-that

Faizan, M. (2019). "Gwadar Port generates Rs 358.151m revenue during last three years: Ali Haider Zaidi", 20 March 2019 [Online:web] Accessed on 10 July 2023. URL: https://customstoday.media/gwadar-port-generates-rs358-151m-revenue-during-last-three-years-ali-haider-zaidi/

Fazl-e-Haider, Syed (2019). "Shifting alliances in the Gulf a boon to China", *The Interpreter*, 18 November 2019 [Online:web] Accessed on 12 December 2019. URL: https://www.lowyinstitute.org/the-interpreter/shifting-alliances-gulf-boon-china

Fordham University (2012). "Medieval Sourcebook: Sidi Ali Reis (16th Century CE): Miratul Memalik (The Mirror of Countries), 1557 CE" [Online: web] Accessed on 10 December 2012. URL: https://sourcebooks.fordham.edu/source/16csidi1.asp

Gaharwar, Siddhi (2019). "Did you know Indian Navy too played a rather unsung role during Kargil War? Know all about Operation Talwar", *Times Now* News.Com 26 July2019. [Online: web] URL: https://www.timesnownews.com/india/article/did-you-know-indian-navy-too-played-a-rather-unsung-role-during-kargil-war-all-about-operation-talwar/459303

Ghosh, Iman (2020). "Mapped: The Ins and Outs of Remittance Flows", *Visual Capitalist* 12 February 2020. [Online: web] Accessed 10 March 2020 URL https://www.visualcapitalist.com/global-remittance-flows/

Govt. of Pakistan Board of Investment (2005). "Gawadar", [Online: web] Accessed 22 June 2005, URL: http://www.pakboi.gov.pk/News_Event/Gawadar.html

Gul, Ayaz (2018). "Pakistan, Russia Sign Rare Military Cooperation Pact", *Voice of America* 8 August 2018. [Online: web] Accessed 1 March 2020, URL: https://www.voanews.com/south-central-asia/pakistan-russia-sign-rare-military-cooperation-pact

Gwadar City (2012). "History of Gwadar" [Online: web] Accessed on 3 November 2012, URL: http://gwadarcity.info/history-of-gwadar/

Gwadar Port home page (2005). [Online: web] Accessed 5 May 2012, URL: http://www.gwadarport.gov.pk/Home.aspx

Gwadar Port Authority (2019). [Online: web] Accessed 31 December 2019, URL: http://www.gwadarport.gov.pk/portprofile.aspx

Haroon, Agha Iqrar (2017). "Politics of Trade Corridors', *DND*, 5 November 2017, [Online: web] Accessed 11 March 2020, URL: https://dnd.com.pk/politics-of-trade-corridors/135121

Hashim, Asad (2019). "Gunmen kill 14 bus passengers in Pakistan's Balochistan" *Al Jazeera* Website, 18 April 2019. [Online: web] Accessed 22 April 2019, URL: https://www.aljazeera.com/news/2019/04/gunmen-kill-bus-passengers-pakistan-balochistan-official-190418045138814.html

Hughes, Murray (2008). "Opening up Afghan trade route to Iran', *Railway Gazette*, 29 January 2008, [Online: web] Accessed 10 March 2020, URL: https://www.railwaygazette.com/opening-up-afghan-trade-route-to-iran/33162.article

Hussain, Rafaqat (2016). "Gwadar in Historical Perspective" Muslim Institute, [Online: web] Accessed 10 March 2020. URL: https://www.muslim-institute.org/newsletter-op-gwadar.pdf

Iftikhar, Mohid (2015). "Challenges to Pakistan's maritime security", Centre for Security Governance, 3 June 2015, [Online: web] Accessed 28 December 2019, URL: https://secgovcentre.org/2015/06/maritime-security-in-the-indian-ocean-challenges-for-pakistan/

Khaleej Times (2006) "Pakistan to decide operator for Gwadar Port next Week", *Khaleej Times*, 13 August 2006, [Online: web] Accessed 21 July 2020, URL: http://www.khaleejtimes.com/DisplayArticleNew.asp?xfile=data/business/2006/August/business_August318.xml§ion=business

Khan, M. Ilyas (2015). "Is China-Pakistan 'silk road' a game-changer?", *BBC News*, 22 April 2015, [Online: web] Accessed 9 July 2018, URL: https://www.bbc.com/news/world-asia-32400091

Khan, Mushtaq and Danish Hyder (2017). "CPEC: The devil is not in the details" *Herald*, 11 January 2017, [Online: web] Accessed 10 July 2020, URL: https://herald.dawn.com/news/1153597

Kohnavard, Nafiseh (2020). "Iraq military bases: US pulling out of three key sites", *BBC*, 16 March 2020, [Online: web] Accessed 21 March 2020, URL: https://www.bbc.com/news/world-middle-east-51914600

Korybko, Andrew (2020). "This Five-Phase Strategy Can Strengthen Russian-

Pakistani Trade Ties", *Global Research*, 28 January 2020, [Online: web] Accessed 1 March 2020, URL: https://www.globalresearch.ca/five-phase-strategy-strengthen-russian-pakistani-trade-ties/5702095

Lu, Christina (2023). "China's Belt and Road to Nowhere", *Foreign Policy*, 13 February 2023, [Online: web] Accessed 7 July 2023, URL:https://foreignpolicy.com/2023/02/13/china-belt-and-road-initiative-infrastructure-development-geopolitics/

McBride, James; Noah Berman and Andrew Chatzky (2023). "China's Massive Belt and Road Initiative", Council on Foreign Relations, 2 February 2023, [Online: web] Accessed 7 July 2023, URL: https://www.cfr.org/backgrounder/chinas-massive-belt-and-road-initiative

Mahar, Irfan (2020). "Changing Security Dynamics of South Asia: Implication for the Security of the region", *Eurasia Review News & Analysis*, 16 April 2020, [Online: web] Accessed 31 August 2020, URL: https://www.eurasiareview.com/16042020-changing-security-dynamics-of-south-asia-implication-for-the-security-of-region-oped/

O'Hanlon, Michael E. and Sara Allawi (2020). "The relationship between Iraq and the US is in danger of collapse. That can't happen." Brookings Website, 20 March 2020, [Online: web] Accessed 21 March 2020, URL: https://www.brookings.edu/blog/order-from-chaos/2020/03/20/the-relationship-between-iraq-and-the-us-is-in-danger-of-collapse-that-cant-happen/

Pakistan Today Profit (2018). "Gwadar, a challenge for stakeholders to develop as successful economic city", *Pakistan Today* profit, 16 August 2018, [Online: web] Accessed 1 April 2020, URL: https://profit.pakistantoday.com.pk/2018/08/16/gwadar-a-challenge-for-stakeholders-to-develop-as-successful-economic-city/

Pakistan Today (2019). "14 people, including nine navy men, shot dead in Balochistan", *Pakistan Today*, 18 April 2019, [Online: web] Accessed 22 April 2019, URL: https://www.pakistantoday.com.pk/2019/04/18/navy-personnel-among-14-shot-dead-after-being-offloaded-from-bus-on-makran-coastal-highway/

Philip, Snehesh Alex (2019). "Russia rejects Pakistan request for 50,000 AK rifles, assures India of no deals in future", *The Print*, 17 July 2019, [Online: web] Accessed 1 March 2020, URL: https://theprint.in/defence/russia-rejects-pakistan-request-for-50000-ak-rifles-assures-india-of-no-deals-in-future/264004/

Prakash, Arun (2021). "From Karachi to Bay of Bengal, How the Indian Navy

Played a Stellar Role in the 1971 War", *The Wire*, 5 April 2021, [Online: web] Accessed 19 May 2021, URL: https://thewire.in/security/1971-series-indian-navy-bangladesh-war-stellar-role-arun-prakash

Rahman, Asad (2005). "Focus on Balochistan Part III – After Independence" *Baloch Voice*, [Online: web] Accessed 19 May 2005, URL: http://www.balochvoice.com/asad_rahman.html#Part%20III

Raman, B. (2005). "The Baloch Cause", *Outlook*.com, 18 April 2005, [Online: web] Accessed 19 May 2021, URL: https://www.outlookindia.com/website/story/the-baloch-cause/227109

——— (2006). "Let Down by India", *Outlook*.com, 16 June 2006, [Online: web] Accessed 4 July 2006, URL: https://www.outlookindia.com/website/story/let-down-by-india/231577/?next

Rana, Arif (2008). "'Defence Complex' at Gwadar" *Gwadar News*.com, [Online: web] Accessed 19 April 2008, URL: http://www.gwadarnews.com/newsdetail.asp?newsID=1052

Roussey, Benjamin (2019). "Is America Energy Self-Sufficient Yet?", Energy Central Website, 11 March 2019, [Online: web] Accessed 1 March 2020, URL: https://energycentral.com/c/gn/america-energy-self-sufficient-yet

Rystad Energy (2019). "North America becomes Self-Sufficient in Oil", Rystad Energy Website, 7 March 2019, [Online: web] Accessed 1 March 2020, URL: https://www.rystadenergy.com/newsevents/news/press-releases/North-America-becomes-self-sufficient-in-oil/

SAARC (2008). "South Asia Regional Overview", [Online: web] SAARC Website, Accessed 21 July 2020, URL: https://web.archive.org/web/20081121043924/http://www.sardeg.org/marketana.asp

Saran, Shyam (2015). "What China's One Belt and One Road Strategy Means for India, Asia and the World", *The Wire*, 9 October 2015, [Online: web] Accessed 15 December 2020, URL: https://thewire.in/external-affairs/what-chinas-one-belt-and-one-road-strategy-means-for-india-asia-and-the-world

Shahid, Ariba and Asif Shahzad. "Pakistan outlines process for barter trade with Afghanistan, Iran, Russia", *Reuters* 2 June 2023, [Online: web] Accessed on 10 July 2023, URL: https://www.reuters.com/world/pakistan-engage-barter-trade-with-afghanistan-iran-russia-2023-06-02/

Sheehy, Thomas P. (2022). "10 Things to Know about the U.S.-China Rivalry in Africa", United States Institute of Peace, 7 December 2022, [Online: web] Accessed on 10 July 2023, URL: https://www.usip.org/publications/2022/12/10-things-know-about-us-china-rivalry-africa

Shepard, Wade (2019) "What China is Really up to in Africa", *Forbes*, 3 October 2019, [Online: web] Accessed 15 May 2021, URL: https://www.forbes.com/sites/wadeshepard/2019/10/03/what-china-is-really-up-to-in-africa/?sh=6fc9362a5930

Statista (2023). "Distribution of liquefied natural gas imported into India in 2021, by country of origin", [Online: web] Accessed 21 September 2023 URL:https://www.statista.com/statistics/1237488/lng-import-share-india-by-country/

Sutton, H.I. (2020). "Could The Indian Navy Strangle China's Lifeline In The Malacca Strait?", *Forbes*, 8 July 2020 [Online: web] Accessed 15 May 2021, URL: https://www.forbes.com/sites/hisutton/2020/07/08/could-the-indian-navy-strangle-chinas-lifeline-in-the-malacca-strait/?sh=2d40cbb478e8

Taneja, Kabir and Kalpit Mankikar (2021). "$400 bn deal an eye-catcher. But Iran is just a square in China's geopolitical chessboard', *The Print*, 2 April 2021 [Online: web] Accessed 14 May 2021, URL: https://theprint.in/opinion/400-bn-deal-an-eye-catcher-but-iran-is-just-a-square-in-chinas-geopolitical-chessboard/632683/

Telhami, Shibley (2002). "The Persian Gulf: Understanding the American Oil Strategy", from Brookings Website 1 March 2002 [Online:web] Accessed on 21 March 2020, URL: https://www.brookings.edu/articles/the-persian-gulf-understanding-the-american-oil-strategy/

The EurAsian Times (2019). "Chabahar Port vs Gwadar Port – Can Indian Chabahar Port Compete Against Chinese Funded Gwadar Port?", *The EurAsian Times*, 11 January 2019, [Online: web] Accessed 15 May 2021, URL: https://eurasiantimes.com/chabahar port vs gwadar-port-can-indian-chabahar-port-compete-against-chinese-funded-gwadar port/

Times of Islamabad (2018). "Gwadar Port Expansion Plan 2018 - 19 unveiled", *Times of Islamabad*, 19 March 2018, [Online: web] Accessed 15 December 2021, URL: https://timesofislamabad.com/19-Mar-2018/gwadar-port-expansion-plan-2018-19-unveiled

U.S. Naval Forces Central Command (2020). "Crown Prince of Bahrain Visits NAVCENT', US Naval Forces Central Command Website, 4 March 2020, [Online: web] Accessed 19 March 2020, URL: https://www.cusnc.navy.mil/Media/News/Display/Article/2101160/crown-prince-of-bahrain-visits-navcent/

Vatanka, Alex (2019). "China's Great Game in Iran", *Foreign Policy*, 5 September

2019, [Online: web] Accessed 28 February 2020, URL: https://foreignpolicy.com/2019/09/05/chinas-great-game-in-iran/

Venkataraman, M. (2020). "Regional security dynamics of south Asia" [Online: web] Accessed 15 September 2020, URL: https://www.springeropen.com/collections/securitysouthasia

Wasdam (2012). "Herat-Iran railway track 90% completed: Herat Officials" *Wasdam Afghan Business News* Portal, 17 September 2012, [Online: web] Accessed 11 March 2020, URL: https://wadsam.com/afghan-business-news/herat-iran-railway-track-90-completed-herat-officials-4853/

Woodward, Martin (2017). "Gwadar: the Sultan's Possession", Qatar Digital Library, 18 May 2017, [Online: web] Accessed 10 December 2019, URL: https://www.qdl.qa/en/gwadar-sultan%E2%80%99s-possession

Wordpress (2005). "President at Ground Breaking Ceremony of Gwadar Deep-Sea Port", 24 January 2005, [Online: web] Accessed 10 July 2023, URL: https://presidentmusharraf.wordpress.com/2005/01/24/musharraf-ground-breaking-gwadar/

Workman, Daniel (2023). "Crude Oil Imports by Country", World's Top Exports, [Online: web] Accessed 21 September 2023, URL: https://www.worldstopexports.com/crude-oil-imports-by-country/#google_vignette

Xinhuanet (2019). "Projects inaugurated in Gwadar to help implement China-Pakistan Economic Corridor" *XinhuaNet*, 5 November 2019, [Online: web] Accessed 29 December 2019, URL: http://www.xinhuanet.com/english/2019-11/05/c_138530508.htm

Yazdanshenas, Zakiyeh and Alam Saleh. "Iranian-Saudi détente and 'Asianisation' of the Persian Gulf: China fills the gap", Middle East Institute, 5 April 2023 [Online: web] Accessed on 1 July 2023, URL:https://www.mei.edu/publications/iranian-saudi-detente-and-asianization-persian-gulf-china-fills-gap

Yusufzai, Amin (2019). "Rail Connectivity of Gwadar with Other Parts of Pakistan Not a Priority: Officials", [Online: web] Accessed 10 December 2019, URL: https://propakistani.pk/2019/04/06/rail-connectivity-of-gwadar-with-other-parts-of-pakistan-not-a-priority-officials/

Class Lecture, Conference Paper, Speech, or Performance

Ahmad, Azhar (2015). "Gwadar: Potential and Prospects", Research Paper presented on 29 January 2015 at one-day seminar on Gwadar by PICSS and FPCCI at Serena Hotel Islamabad.

Cohen, Stephen P. (1998). "Security Challenges in South Asia", Keynote lecture delivered at the summer workshop of the Regional Centre for Strategic Studies, Colombo, URL: https://www.brookings.edu/opinions/security-challenge-in-south-asia/

Durrani, Mahmud Ali (2008). "Gwadar Deep Sea Port - A New Transportation Hub for Central Asia" A Perspective by Pakistan Ambassador in USA at John Hopkins University on 13 February 2008.

Ministry of Ports & Shipping, Gwadar Port Authority (2015), "Gwadar Port & CPEC" presentation to Parliamentary Committee on CPEC at Gwadar on 28 November 2015.

Musharraf, Pervez (2002). Address at the Ground-Breaking Ceremony of Gwadar Deep Sea Port on 22 March 2002.

Karpaviciute, Leva (2007). "Security Dynamics and Power Division within the South Asian Region", Paper presented for ECPR Joint Session of Workshops at Workshop No. 9, *The Rise of (New) Regional Powers in Asia, Africa, Latin America - contribution to regional and world peace or protracted conflicts?* at Helsinki from 7-12 May 2007.

Personal or Phone Interview, Letter or e-mail

Akbar, Malik Siraj (2020). Reply to author's questionnaire sent by email on 20 December 2020.

Haqqani, Hussain (2020). Reply to author's questionnaire sent by e-mail on 4 September 2020.

Nawaz, Shuja (2020). Reply to author's questionnaire sent by e-mail on 15 July 2020.

Siddiqa, Ayesha (2020). Reply to author's questionnaire sent by e-mail on 13 September 2020.

Index